# CROSSBILL GUIDES

# Rhodope Mountains
BULGARIA

Crossbill Guide: Rhodope Mountains – Bulgaria
First print: 2013 (under the title Eastern Rhodopes)
Second Print: 2023

Text and research first print: Dirk Hilbers, Alex Tabak, Albert Vliegenthart, Herman Dierickx
Additional text and research second print: Dirk Hilbers
Editing: Dirk Hilbers, John Cantelo, Stefan Avramov, Polihron Karapachov, Desislava Kostadinova, Kim Lotterman, Gino Smeulders, Albert Vliengenthart
Illustrations: Horst Wolter
Maps: Alex Tabak, Dirk Hilbers
Type and image setting: Oscar Lourens
Print: ORO grafic projectmanagement / PNB Letland

ISBN 978-94-91648-24-3

This book is made with FSC-certified paper. The printing process is CO2-neutral through carbon-offsetting. To compensate for the CO2-emissions of the printing processes, we've invested in the project 'Sustainable farming for the future'. For more information, see www.southpole.com under the listed project. You can find the certificate of the carbon-offset on our website under 'downloads' on the Rhodope Mountains Guidebook page.

© 2023 Crossbill Guides Foundation, Arnhem, The Netherlands

All rights reserved. No part of this book may be reproduced in any form by print, photocopy, microfilm or any other means without the written permission of the Crossbill Guides Foundation.
The Crossbill Guides Foundation and its authors have done their utmost to provide accurate and current information and describe only routes, trails and tracks that are safe to explore. However, neither the Crossbill Guides Foundation nor its authors or publishers can accept responsibillity for any loss, injury or inconveniences sustained by readers as a result of the information provided in this guide.

This book is published in association with KNNV Publishing and with the generous support and information from Rewilding Rhodopes.

www.crossbillguides.org
www.knnvpublishing.nl
www.rewilding-rhodopes.com

KNNV Publishing

# CROSSBILL GUIDES FOUNDATION

This guidebook is a product of the non-profit foundation Crossbill Guides. By publishing these books we want to introduce more people to the joys of our beautiful natural heritage and to increase the understanding of the ecological values that underlie conservation efforts. Most of this heritage is protected for ecological reasons and we want to provide insight into these reasons to the public at large. By doing so we hope that more people support the ideas behind nature conservation.
For more information about us and our guides you can visit our website at:

WWW.CROSSBILLGUIDES.ORG

## About this guide

This guide is meant for all those who enjoy being in and learning about nature, whether you already know all about it or not. It is set up a little differently from most guides. We focus on explaining the natural and ecological features of an area rather than merely describing the site. We choose this approach because the nature of an area is more interesting, enjoyable and valuable when seen in the context of its complex relationships. The interplay of different species with each other and with their environment is astonishing. The clever tricks and gimmicks that are put to use to beat life's challenges are as fascinating as they are countless.

Take our namesake the Crossbill: at first glance it's just a big finch with an awkward bill. But there is more to the Crossbill than meets the eye. This bill is beautifully adapted for life in coniferous forests. It is used like scissors to cut open pinecones and eat the seeds that are unobtainable for other birds. In the Scandinavian countries where Pine and Spruce take up the greater part of the forests, several Crossbill species have each managed to answer two of life's most pressing questions: how to get food and avoid direct competition. By evolving crossed bills, each differing subtly, they have secured a monopoly of the seeds produced by cones of varying sizes. So complex is this relationship that scientists are still debating exactly how many different species of Crossbill actually exist. Now this should heighten the appreciation of what at first glance was merely a plump bird with a beak that doesn't close properly. Once its interrelationships are seen, nature comes alive, wherever you are.

To some, impressed by the virtual familiarity that television has granted to the wilderness of the Amazon, the vastness of the Serengeti or the sublimity of Yellowstone, our nature may seem a puny surrogate, good merely for the casual stroll. In short, the argument seems to be that if you haven't seen a Jaguar, Lion or Grizzly Bear, then you haven't seen the "real thing". Nonsense, of course.

But where to go? And how? What is there to see? That is where this guide comes in. We describe the how, the why, the when, the where and the howcome of Europe's most beautiful areas. In clear and accessible language, we explain the nature of the Rhodope Mountains and refer extensively to routes where the area's features can be observed best. We try to make the Rhodope Mountains come alive. We hope that we succeed.

# How to use this guide

This guidebook contains a descriptive and a practical section. The descriptive part comes first and gives you insight into the most striking and interesting natural features of the area. It provides an understanding of what you will see when you go out exploring. The descriptive part consists of a landscape section (marked with a red bar), describing the habitats, the history and the landscape in general, and of a flora and fauna section (marked with a green bar), which discusses the plants and animals that occur in the region.

The second part offers the practical information (marked with a purple bar). A series of sites and routes (walks and car drives) are carefully selected to give you a good flavour of all the habitats, flora and fauna that the Rhodope Mountains have to offer. At the start of each route description, a number of icons give a quick overview of the characteristics of each route. These icons are explained in the margin of this page. The final part of the book (marked with blue squares) provides some basic tourist information and some tips on finding plants, birds and other animals.

There is no need to read the book from cover to cover. Instead, each small chapter stands on its own and refers to the routes most suitable for viewing the particular features described in it. Conversely, descriptions of each route refer to the chapters that explain more in depth the most typical features that can be seen along the way.

In the back of the guide we have included a list of all the mentioned plant and animal species, with their scientific names and translations into German and Dutch. Some species names have an asterix (*) following them. This indicates that there is no official English name for this species and that we have taken the liberty of coining one. We realise this will meet with some reservations by those who are familiar with scientific names. For the sake of readability however, we have decided to translate the scientific name, or, when this made no sense, we gave a name that best describes the species' appearance or distribution. Please note that we do not want to claim these as the official names. We merely want to make the text easier to follow for those not familiar with scientific names. An overview of the area described in this book is given on the map on page 11. For your convenience we have also turned the inner side of the back flap into a map of the area indicating all the described routes. Descriptions in the explanatory text refer to these routes.

 car route

 walking route

 beautiful scenery

 interesting history

 interesting geology

 interesting flora

 interesting invertebrate life

 interesting reptile and amphibian life

 interesting mammals

 interesting birdlife

 visualising the ecological contexts described in this guide

# Table of contents

## Landscape 9
Geographical overview 10
Geology 12
Climate 17
Habitats 18
Coniferous forests and Subalpine meadows 20
Beech, Pine and Oak woods of the Western Rhodopes 25
Forest-scrub-pasture mosaic of the Eastern Rhodopes 29
Steppes and arable land 35
Rivers and wetlands 39
Crags and cliffs 47
History 49
Nature conservation 60

## Flora and Fauna 65
Flora 68
Mammals 86
Birds 90
Reptiles and amphibians 112
Insects and other invertebrates 121

## Practical Part 133
Routes around Madzharovo 133
Route 1: Kovan Kaya and the Arda river 134
Route 2: The horseshoe bend in the Arda river 139
Route 3: Momina Skala 141
Route 4: Hisarya 145
Routes around Kardzhali and Momchilgrad 147
Route 5: Around Kardzhali 149
Route 6: The Borovitsa river 154
Route 7: Doirantsi 158
Route 8: The confluence of the Arda and Krumovitsa 161
Route 9: To the abandoned village of Boynik 166
Route 10: The ridge near Nanovitsa 170
Route 11: Krumovitsa river near Dolna Kula 173
Route 12: The border trail – Gyumyurdzhinski Snezhnik 176
Additional sites in the Kardzhali-Krumovgrad region 181
Routes in the Ivaylovgrad region 185

**TABLE OF CONTENTS**

| | |
|---|---|
| Route 13: The Armira Valley | 186 |
| Route 14: To the Byala Reka meanders | 189 |
| Other sites in Ivaylovgrad region | 193 |
| Routes in the Western Rhodopes | 196 |
| Route 15: Dobrostan – some highlights | 198 |
| Route 16: Two short walks in the Dobrostan mountains | 203 |
| Route 17: The Wonderful Bridges of Zabardo | 207 |
| Route 18: The plateau between Trigrad and Yagodina | 212 |
| Route 19: Walk to the Chairski lakes | 215 |
| Route 20: The Waterfall walk near Smolyan | 219 |
| Additional sites in the Western Rhodopes | 222 |
| Routes in the Thracian Plain and Sakar | 226 |
| Route 21: The Besaparski Hills | 228 |
| Route 22: Zlato Pole | 231 |
| Route 23: Sakar round trip | 235 |
| Route 24: Around Topolovgrad | 243 |
| Additional sites in the Thracian Plain and Sakar | 248 |
| **Tourist information and observation tips** | 253 |
| **Birdwatching list** | 264 |
| **Acknowledgements** | 270 |
| **Picture and illustration credits** | 271 |
| **Species list and translation** | 272 |

**List of text boxes**

| | |
|---|---|
| Unique rock forms | 15 |
| A mix of peoples | 54 |
| Madzharovo – a communist mining town | 59 |
| Rewilding Rhodopes | 63 |
| Special plant species of the Rhodope Mountains | 70 |
| The eagle and the tortoise | 95 |
| Amphibians and reptiles of the Rhodope Mountains | 119 |
| Special butterflies of the Rhodope Mountains | 123 |
| Special dragonflies of the Rhodope Mountains | 128 |

# LANDSCAPE

The Rhodope mountains, especially its eastern part, is the new kid on the block as a wildlife holiday destination. The mountains form the border between of Greece and Bulgaria, and for many centuries, therefore between 'the east' and 'the west'. During this time, the region was something of a backwater and has accordingly retained its original and unspoilt character and an impressive flora and fauna. As a birdwatching destination, this region rivals the most famous birding regions of the continent. Masked Shrike, Western Rock Nuthatch, Olive-tree Warbler, Eastern Imperial Eagle and Sombre Tit are just a few of the birds that justify such a claim.

But simply presenting the Rhodopes as a birdwatching destination would sell it short. There is so much more, as you'll quickly discover when you hear the Jackals and the Wolves howl on a starry night, when you stumble upon a Nose-horned Viper or Sand Boa on a walk through the woodlands, or when you're resting on a stone and enjoying your lunch while watching a tortoise stoically drag its bony burden through an orchid-strewn grassland. These are just some memories that come to mind from our preparatory trips.

But simply presenting the Rhodopes as a wildlife destination would sell it short too! The rural culture, the historic cities in the Thracian Plain, the mix of Bulgarian Orthodox, Islamic Pomak and Turkish cultures and the many Thracian archaeological sites – all situated in a breathtaking landscape. This is just as much part of the Rhodope experience. One of the wonderful aspects of this region is the almost unlimited access to these mountains. There are a few exceptions to protect specific vulnerable breeding birds, but overall, you can go where you please. And wherever you please to go, there is bound to be something of interest.

So perhaps a little focus would come in handy. That is where this book comes in. It covers the Rhodope mountains, both west and east, plus lowlands to the north (with their attractive wetlands) and the Sakar Mountains (great for steppe wildlife). This guide introduces you to the landscape, flora, fauna and ecology of a fascinating region, plus a range of detailed route descriptions and practical suggestions for its exploration. We intend not only to provide you with the information you need but also to convey that rush of anticipation that we always feel when embarking on a day's trip in the field. Enjoy!

The lovely landscape of the Eastern Rhodopes – a mixture of dry grasslands, scrub, woodlands and small streams (see page 29).

GEOGRAPHICAL OVERVIEW

## Geographical overview

The Rhodope Mountains rise up from the Thracian plain, a broad lowland area through which Bulgaria's southern large river, the Maritsa, flows. The Maritsa springs forth in the high Alp-like Rila Mountains in the western part of Bulgaria. From here, the river takes an eastern course, flowing through fertile agricultural land, passing the important towns of Plovdiv, Haskovo and Svilengrad. All along its course, the Rhodopes are a continuous presence as you look south. However, they gradually decrease in altitude as you proceed eastwards until they peter out near the small town of Ivaylovgrad. Here, the Maritsa swings south, leaves Bulgaria and continues to form the border between Turkey and Greece (where it is called the Evros) before plunging in the Aegean Sea.

Small-scale agricultural land in the higher part of the Eastern Rhodopes.

As already noted, the Rhodopes consist of a high western part and a lower eastern half. The western section reaches a height of 2191 m at Perilik mountain – a respectable altitude but still much lower than the two Alpine ranges of Pirin and Rila further west. As the winds mainly come from the west, the Rhodopes are effectively in the rain shadow of those mountains. With decreasing height as you travel from west to east, you go from thickly forested cool mountains in the Western Rhodopes to the less densely vegetated, warmer and drier mountains in the Eastern. This effectively creates a mountain range with two distinct facets – the green and damp Western Rhodopes and the more sparsely vegetated and drier Eastern Rhodopes. With a very different climate comes different wildlife. In this book, we cover both as separate regions whose border is a little west of the town of Kardzhali.

In the Western Rhodopes, most of the major valleys are oriented north to south, which means that you can get into these mountains from the Plain fairly easily, but there are only a few roads connecting the different valleys. The larger part of the Western Rhodopes consist of acidic bedrock, but for the naturalist and birdwatcher, the pockets of limestone are of greatest interest. This naturally narrows the focus down to two major areas – that of Trigrad (quite deep down in the mountains) and the area of Dobrostan and Zabardo which are closer to the plain.

# GEOGRAPHICAL OVERVIEW

Similarly, the Eastern Rhodopes have their hotspots. The most famous is the scenically stunning region of Madzharovo which has a large concentration of attractive sites. The lively capital of Kardzhali is another good entrance point. In many respects, the Eastern Rhodopes are the key attraction for naturalists in this region, as it is here that most birds, reptiles, insects and wildflowers are found.

North-east of the point where the Maritsa bends towards the south, higher ground is reduced to an area of low hills, just north of the Turkish border. These are officially outside the Rhodopes and are known as Sakar. Sakar is a small, little visited and isolated range of hills and low mountains. Its highest peak (856 m) is wooded, but the gentle slopes that fan out in all directions are covered in dry scrub and steppe-like grasslands. It is this latter habitat that makes Sakar a draw for visitors.

Finally, the Thracian Plain has its own attractions and, for naturalists, the main ones are the wetlands. The Maritsa River, with its many oxbows, river channels, sand banks and riparian forests, is beautiful. There are marshes with waterfowl dotted amongst fields harbouring birds you may also find in the steppe.

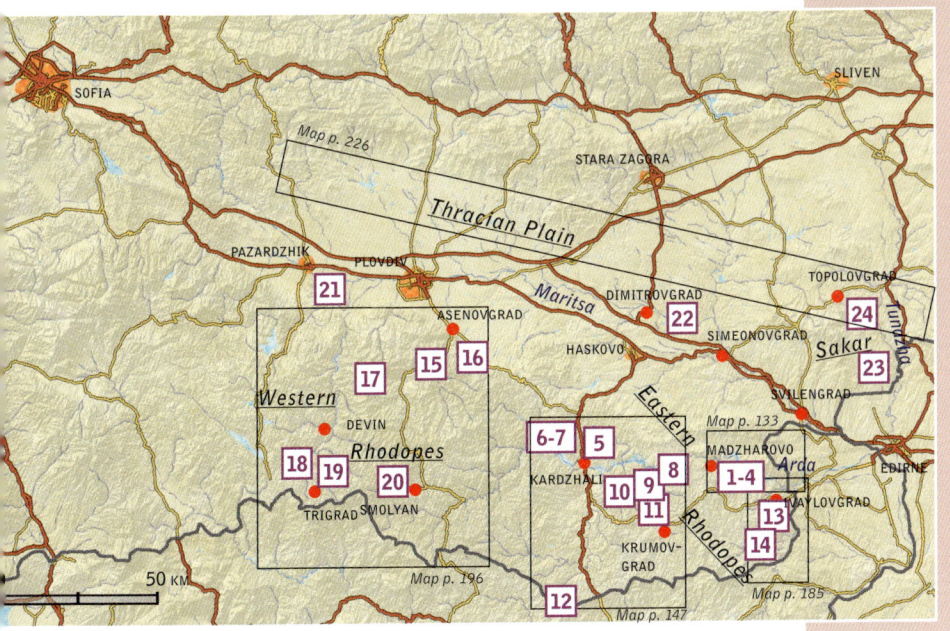

Overview of the Rhodope Mountains

**LANDSCAPE**

# Geology

In geological terms, the Rhodopes are part of the Rilo-Rhodopes massif: a kidney-shaped range that lies for the larger part in Bulgaria with important branches in North Macedonia and northern Greece. This is one of Europe's geologically more complex ranges as they are the result of confusing and still not entirely understood tectonics.

There are some odd geological features in the Rhodopes, such as these odd rock shapes, known as hoodoos or stone mushrooms (site B on page 184). They form where harder volcanic rock overlies and shields softer material of compressed volcanic ash.

The tectonic plate theory famously describes the formation of mountains through the collision of large sections of the earth crust. The Alps for example, formed through the crash of the African and the Eurasian plates. Less well known is that on the edges of these large plates, there are smaller segments, known as micro-plates or terranes. They move somewhat differently and form distinct mountains in the pressure zones. It is in the light of these micro-plate tectonics that the formation of the Rhodopes should be understood.

The collision of plates and terranes pushed up sedimentary rocks, but also led to volcanic eruptions that resulted in a hodgepodge of different rock types. In the Rhodopes, igneous rocks (which derive from volcanic eruptions) are found side by side with sandstones and limestones that were deposited when the region was covered by the sea. There are also large areas with metamorphic rocks, which derive from other rock types that chemically and physically transformed under the extreme pressures and elevated temperatures created by the tectonic movements. And finally, of course, there are the young sediments, deposited by the rivers and seas in recent times.

This variety of bedrocks mirrors, at least to an extent, the soils and the flora and fauna you can find in the various parts of the mountains. Some of the rock formations themselves are quite spectacular and have become attractions in their own right.

## A brief geological history

Research has shown that the rocks that surface in the Rhodopes vary greatly in age. Young rocks date 'only' back to the Oligocene (25 million

## GEOLOGY

years ago), but the oldest are a tenfold that age, stemming from the Paleozoic era (250 million years and older!). The latter are known as Variscan Massifs. They include not only part of the Rhodopes, but a wide variety of mountain chains all over Europe: the south German mountain ranges, the French Massif Central, Wales in the UK, central Iberia and several more. These Variscan mountains (also called Hercynian mountains) formed when two ancient continental plates (*Laurussia* or *Euramerica* on the one hand and *Gondwana* on the other) collided to form the super continent of Pangea, around 380-280 million years ago. Most of this ancient bedrock lies deep underneath the current mountains, which were formed at later stages.

Between 230 and 55 million years ago, Pangea broke up into the forerunners of our current continents. Present-day Africa was on one continental plate. At first it was merged with the American and Eurasian plates, but as it broke loose, it tilted and closed the wedge-shaped ocean known as the Tethys, that separated the African and European plates.

**The formation of the Rhodopes**
**A:** the African Plate (AP) and Eurasian Plate (EP) move towards each other, closing the Tethys ocean.
**B:** The AP moves underneath the EP.
**C:** the immense pressure of this subduction changes the bedrock. This metamorphosed rock is pushed up. Locally, the old, marine limestones are lifted up as well. In the meantime, the same forces stretch the Eurasian plate, which becomes thinner and lower.
**D:** Part of the subducted plate starts to melt deep in the earth's crust and is pushed up as magma, creating volcanic domes between the metamorphic bedrock and limestone pockets. The extended Thracian Plain is washed over by the sea, leaving the young marine sediments we see here today.

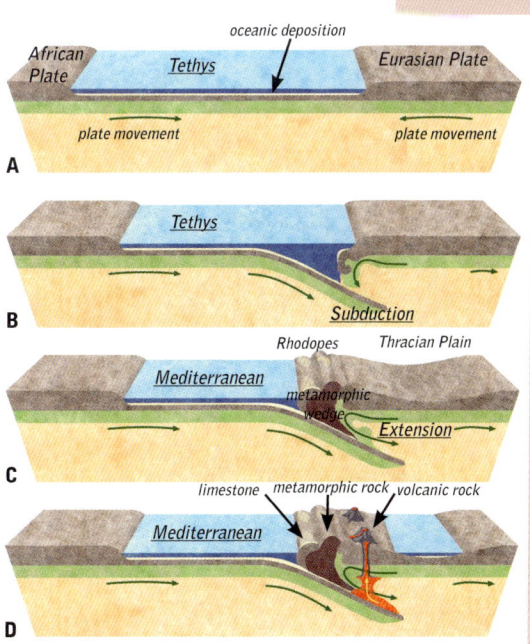

**LANDSCAPE**

## GEOLOGY

Geological map of the Rhodope with in brown the position of metamorphic bedrock.

What remains of this ocean today is the Mediterranean Sea.

The closing of the ocean coincided with massive volcanic activity. The first element of what would become the Rhodopes were seamounts created by underwater eruptions. Most of this ancient hard bedrock now lies buried deep underneath the current mountains. Only locally do these earliest volcanic rocks still surface.

As the African plate moved towards the Eurasian one, the region saw a confusing amount of subductions (one tectonic micro-plate shifting underneath the other), collisions (two plates smashing into one another, pushing the land up into mountains), thrusting (a compressing of tectonic plates) and extension (enlargement of the plate, thinning the crusts which results in volcanic eruptions). Much of this happened beneath the Tethys Ocean. As the Tethys contracted still further, between 170 million and 60 million years ago, the largely submarine Rhodopes increased in size and altitude. In southern Europe and the Balkans, several of these micro-plates were squeezed onto one another, which explains the large number of mountain ranges, separated by plains. In the case of the Rhodopes and the Rila mountains, it was the Apulian subplate (that consisted of parts of Italy, the Balkan states, Greece, and Turkey) that collided with the Eurasian plate. It pushed up the earlier Variscan mountains together with younger marine sediments (sandstones and limestones mainly) to give rise to the current day Rilo-Rhodopean mountain chain. A second chain, the Stara Planina, lies further north, in the middle of Bulgaria. What is now the Thracian Plain had long been a sea, but with the continued rising of the land (as the African plate pushed against the Eurasian) it dried out, first forming saline lakes, then freshwater lakes and subsequently marshes. Travelling the plain today, you can still find remnants of all of these: low hills of marine limestone (e.g. the Besaparski Hills), saline steppes where marine salts surface and wetlands, now mostly converted to rice paddies.

### Rhodope geology

Specific to the Eastern Rhodopes was formation of a number of geological domes between 70 and 65 million years ago. Ancient sediments that

# GEOLOGY

## Unique rock forms

The Eastern Rhodopes' interesting geology is underlined by some unique rock formations in the area around Kardzhali, called *Rock Mushrooms* and *Rock Wedding*. Their initial formation started as a result of intense underwater volcanic activity about 35 million years ago. After the sea withdrew as the seabed rose, the soft volcanic rock (tuffs) were sculpted over the millennia by the sun, the wind and the rain. The rocks consist of layers of zeolite stained in different colours by iron, manganese and other oxides. The bizarre shapes of the rocks (sometimes called *Hoodoos*) have long ago provoked the imagination of the local people.

The stone mushrooms (page 182) most definitely have the appearance of the real thing — their stalks are pink, and the hoods are green. The 'stalks' are up to 2.5 metres high and the diameter of the 'hoods' is roughly the same — truly giant mushrooms in other words. Consisting mainly of hard volcanic glass, the upper green layer resists erosion so is left perched on columns of the more rapidly eroding pink rock.

The 'stone wedding' is a zeolite formation near Kardzhali (route 5).

had formed below the Tethys Ocean were compressed by movements of the tectonic plates. The immense pressures changed (metamorphosed) the nature of the bedrock, forming 'metamorphic' rocks (like gneiss). This metamorphic rock was pushed up to form much of the Rhodope Mountains we see today (see map).

For geologists, these regions are highly interesting because of the presence of ophiolites. These are rocks from oceanic crusts that were uplifted onto the continental crust. Ophiolites played an important role in the formation of the plate tectonics theory. To botanists these areas are of interest, because of the special chemical make-up of the rock. Chemically, ophiolites create very alkaline conditions (high sodium and pH). These put particular constraints on plants and only specific species have adapted to growing here, called serpentine flora (serpentine minerals form when the ophiolite metamorphoses due to tectonic pressure).

**LANDSCAPE**

## GEOLOGY

The tectonic collisions are usually accompanied by abundant volcanism. Eruptions took place both below and above the sea surface, creating different types of rock. Several major eruptions occurred at the end of the Eocene (36-34 million years ago) and the Oligocene (29-25 million years ago). The volcanic activity was confined to several regions within the Eastern Rhodopes at the edges of the massif, where they have shaped the landscape and left some of the most curious geological formations visible today.

One such place is the area of Madzharovo. The town itself is built inside a large volcano crater, and its caldera can be seen in the shape of the surrounding mountains. Part of the crater wall is Kovan Kaya – the famous vulture rocks of the Eastern Rhodopes (route 1 and 2). Very impressive are the columnar basalts on the road near Studen Kladenets (route 8) and again on the flanks of Monyak (route 5).

Around Kardzhali, the bright white hillsides are made of zeolite. This dense volcanic ash reacted with water to something that superficially looks like chalk, but has a very different chemical structure and genesis. Unlike chalk, zeolite is almost impermeable to water. Zeolite can form some impressive formations (see box).

Although the Rhodopes formed as a massif, the ocean was never far away. In fact, in the early stages, what are now the mountains were below the sea level. As the mountains rose, the original seabed, consisting of limestone, was pushed up as well and in some areas, it remains on the surface. This explains the 'pockets' of limestone that are scattered throughout the area. In the Western Rhodopes, they form distinct plateau with karst and deep gorges, where rivers carved their course in the soft limestone.

Whereas the Rhodopes rose up as a result of the collision of the tectonic plates, the Thracian Plain originally sank. This is the result of the geological process of plate extension – as the Apulian Plate dived underneath the European one, it also pulled part of the Eurasian plate with it into to earth's interior, effectively stretching the Eurasian plate. Geologists call it the 'back arc', the area behind the mountains (in this case north, so the Thracian Plain), that is stretched and thus sinks down. And where the land sinks, the ocean washes over it.

The Thracian Plain was thus an ocean floor for much longer and became dry much more recently (in relative terms). Therefore, most of the marine limestones are found on the edge of the mountain range, such as around Ivaylovgrad, on the edge of Sakar and in the Besaparski Hills. These rocks are a bit younger and were deposited during the Palaeocene (roughly between 65 and 60 million years ago).

# CLIMATE

From the ridge of Momina Skala (route 3) you can recognise that the town of Madzharovo lies in the crater of an old volcano. The cliff in the background is the vulture rock of Kovan Kaya (route 1).

## Climate

Whichever chapter of this book you read, it won't take long before there is a reference to the special climate of this region. The Eastern Rhodopes lies at the crossroads of the Mediterranean, temperate and continental (steppic) climates. The climate is none of these, rather a mix of them.
This blend is optimal in the Eastern Rhodopes. When you head southeast (towards Ivaylovgrad), the balance leans towards the Mediterranean climate. Winters are not so extreme, but summers are very hot. This Mediterranean influence is also strong in the southern half of Sakar and in several places along the northern foothills of the Rhodopes, up to Besaparski, where the dry, limestone hills create a warm microclimate.
In all of these areas, though, the winters are too cold to be truly Mediterranean. The continental steppe influence is tangible, and greatest in the region of Sakar and the eastern Thracian lowlands.
Heading into the Western Rhodopes, the temperate climate quickly becomes more influential. It is cooler and damper overall. Though even here, the climate is not quite like the temperate regions in Western Europe. The winters are colder and the summers hotter in Bulgaria, and, above all, the shift from cold winter weather to hot summer conditions is very fast. In some years it seems as if you can pinpoint the date winter ended and summer began.
As you gain altitude, a montane climate starts to rule, with fairly cool summers and cold, snowy winters.

**LANDSCAPE**

# Habitats

The Rhodopes form one of these wonderful areas in which you can spend the morning in cool mountains and the afternoon on warm plains; where you can enjoy the wildlife of dry, rocky slopes at the one moment and watch the herons and pelicans on a lakeshore the next. In short, there is a great range of habitats.

Extensive forests dominate the scene in the Western Rhodopes – they come roughly in three belts – coniferous at higher elevations, a belt of Beech lower down (especially on a north face) and a mixed oak wood in the warmer foothills and valleys. In many places, there are meadows in between, and more locally, karst grasslands – very rocky, creviced limestone pavement with a thin scatter of shrubs and many wildflowers. In these limestone environments, steep valleys and cliffs drop down to thunderous rivers.

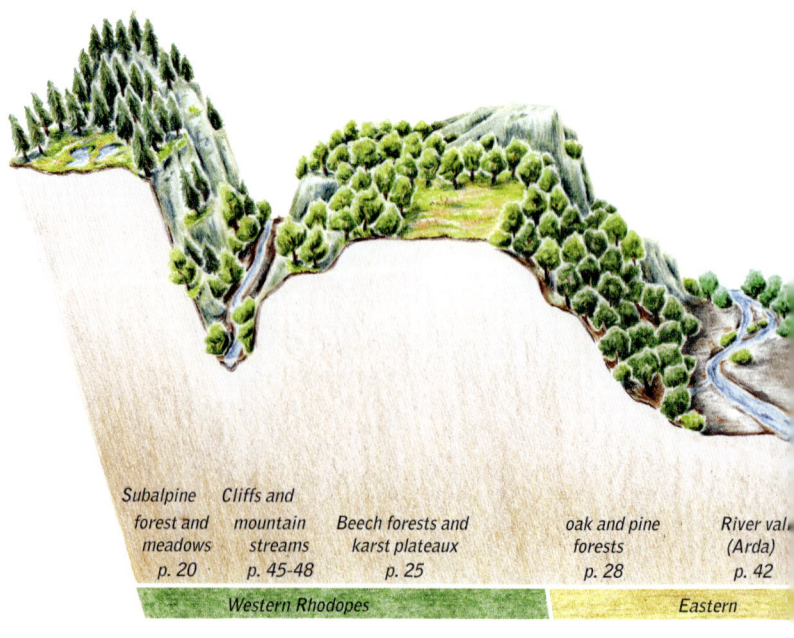

**HABITATS**

Further east in the Eastern Rhodopes, the mountains are lower, warmer and drier. This mosaic landscape is typical of the Eastern Rhodopes – stands of oak mix with open scrublands and areas of pastures and rock slopes to form a hybrid landscape (see for example, the photo on page 8). In places, woodlands dominate (particularly on north slopes), while grasslands are found mostly on the level areas and reflect both historic and current grazing pressure of cattle and wild animals. The hottest and rockiest parts are reserved for a scrubland with a high variety of species, amongst which Christ's-thorn, Wild Jasmin and Wild Lilac are the most eye-catching species.

The rivers in the Eastern Rhodopes are beautiful with pebble banks and islands, flanked by patches of woodland and set in wide valleys. They form a habitat of their own.

North of the Rhodopes (both east and west) are several dry, hilly areas. They are nearly treeless and steppe-like (the correct name for this grassland habitat is discussed on page 36) and boast a superb wildlife – one that is perhaps richest on the slopes of Sakar, east of the Maritsa River.

The Maritsa River valley with its fertile land and associated wetlands form the final habitat of the Rhodopes. These wetlands and riparian forests are rich in birds, but also butterflies, reptiles and amphibians.

| forest-scrub-pasture mosaic p. 29 | steppes and arable land p. 35 | River valley (Maritsa) p. 40 | steppes and scrub p. 29-35 |
| Rhodopes | Thracian Plain | | Sakar |

Cross section through the Western and Eastern Rhodope Mountains down to the Thracian Plain and Sakar.

**LANDSCAPE**

CONIFEROUS FORESTS AND SUBALPINE MEADOWS

## Coniferous forests and Subalpine meadows

> Subalpine Spruce forests are beautiful on routes 17 (small patch), 18, 19 and 20, plus site D on page 226. High mountain meadows are a feature of routes 18 and 19 and site C and D on page 225-226. High mountain bogs are uniquely present on route 19. Karst plateau an limestone slopes are part of route 15 (only the last part of the route), 16, 17 and 18, plus site E on page 226.

The highest parts of the western Rhodopes consist of a world that should be familiar to those who've travelled in the Alps, Pyrenees or any of the Central European mountains. Above 1200 metres approximately, spruce and fir dominate the slopes, interspersed with mountain heathlands and meadows. Locally, there are lakes and bogs to complete this Alpine image. The high zone of the Western Rhodopes corresponds with what is called the Sub-Alpine level in the Alps – the peaks don't reach quite high enough to exceed the tree limit, but the climate is too cold and rough for deciduous forest to survive. The open meadows are flowery and the result of pastoralism. There are relatively few meadows in the Western Rhodopes, because many of the local farmers that used to live in these mountains deserted them after the Balkan Wars and in the communist period (see page 58) at the end of the 20th century.

There are three coniferous trees that dominate this high zone. On the cool north slopes, it is the familiar Norway Spruce that is dominant. These spruce forests with a mix of Silver Fir and Balkan Fir* (*Abies borisii-regis*), are dense and dark, especially when compared to the more open pinewoods on the south slopes.

Typical of the Subalpine habitat are a short growing season and low temperatures. At the very base of the ecosystem, the soil itself, the low temperatures reduce the activity of bacteria and fungi and slows the turnover of nutrients in the soil. Nutrients needed for trees to grow are not as readily available as in the warmer forests further below, causing trees to grow more slowly and further apart. As a result, light is able to penetrate the forest floor, allowing a large variety of shrubs and herbs to grow. Many of them live in close relationship with other species, especially fungi. Both trees and all sorts of herbs have intimate relationship with mycorrhiza threads (the fungi) that provide them with nutrients, while the plant returns the favour by supplying sugars. The wintergreens and berries are good examples of this. Some plants went a step further and take all their nutrients from mycorrhiza or tree roots. They are easily

Facing page:
The classic image of the high zone of the Western Rhodopes, with subalpine meadows, coniferous forests and limestone cliffs.
The Silver Fir is a dominant tree here (inset photo).

recognisable as they lack green leaves and have pale, semi-transparent stems instead. Yellow Bird's-nest and Birds-nest Orchid are examples – their names referring to the nest-shaped roots that are optimally formed to connect with the mycorrhiza.

The Western Rhodopes has a relatively high proportion of old and old-growth forest.

What exactly constitutes old growth as opposed to just an old forest, remains a topic of debate. Ecologically, the presence of lots of standing and lying dead wood and a mix of living trees of various ages, is very important. Such woods are plentiful in the Western Rhodopes, even if many of them are not strictly old-growth in the sense of them being untouched by human activities. The oldest, most pristine forests are situated in the most inaccessible places, although there are also former hunting estates and (former) holy places where extremely old near-natural forests occur

The old-growth coniferous forests are home of a good number of rare and sought-after birds. There are Tengmalm's and Pygmy Owls, Three-toed Woodpecker, Hazel Grouse and Capercaillie. The latter two are not only dependant on old trees, but

## CONIFEROUS FORESTS AND SUBALPINE MEADOWS

also enjoy the cover and the twigs and needles of the young conifers. The dead wood offers plenty of insect prey for the birds as well as soft wood in which to make their nests.

Besides their rich ecology, the old-growth forests also simply form superb places, where the trees, snags and stumps are truly impressive natural monuments.

This ecosystem thrives in the cooler, damper parts of the continent, and the Western Rhodopes lies right at the south-eastern edge of where this ecosystem can develop. However, just west of it, outside the area covered in this book, lie the even higher mountains of Rila and Pirin, and here this Sub-alpine zone is even better developed. Combined with these regions, the Western Rhodopes forms a large area of Sub-alpine habitat, which is, aside from a few touristic areas, relatively extensive and quiet which encourages an abundance of wildlife. There are species here that need large areas and quietude: Brown Bear, Wolf, Balkan Chamois, Hazel Grouse and Capercaillie occur primarily in this high zone (although the Bear and Wolf also visit the lower parts of the mountains).

### Gorge forests

The qualities of the old growth reach their zenith in the gorges. Foresters could not easily reach these steep slopes, which is why the forest is here usually untouched. Furthermore, the natural dampness in the gorge and the accumulation of nutrients in the depths make for

Old-growth gorge forests, such as near Smolyan (right; route 20), are home to a range of northern-Alpine birds, such as the Pygmy Owl (top).

ideal growing conditions. At the same time, the lack of light triggers the trees to grow taller. All these factors combined make that the trees in gorge forests are a bit loftier and more impressive than in other areas.
At the bottom of these gorges, the atmosphere is permanently damp and relatively dark. Nutrients such as dead wood accumulate as does, in winter, snow. These conditions are ideal for willows and alders (both black and grey) and a large number of wildflowers. It is also a favoured habitat for Hazel Grouse, which feeds on the buds of the deciduous trees here.

## Meadows and karstic plateau

A key feature of the higher parts of the Rhodopes are the grasslands, which have a particularly rich flora and fauna. The most attractive ones are found in the limestone parts of the range and are one of the reasons that we concentrated our routes in these parts of the Western Rhodopes. Limestone is porous and rainwater easily seeps away through its cracks, which makes these places dry and rocky (relatively speaking, as much of the Eastern Rhodopes is much drier and rockier still). Underground, the water finds its way, through the cracks, where it dissolves the limestone, creating tunnels and caves through which the water runs. The interaction between water and limestone is well demonstrated in the Trigrad gorge, where the river suddenly disappears underground only to reappear several hundred metres further down in the valley (site A on page 224). Limestone bedrock that is fissured like this is known as karst and karst plateaux are found near Trigrad, Zabardo and Dobrostan. The plateaux have a spectacular flora and are rich butterfly haunts (see page 82 and 125 respectively), perhaps the best in the entire region. A score of ringlets, coppers, blues and fritillaries can be found here, and it is the favoured location of what is perhaps the most impressive of all the

Karst grasslands have a superb flora and rich insect life (Zabardo; route 17).

# CONIFEROUS FORESTS AND SUBALPINE MEADOWS

*Peatlands and mountain lakes are a northern habitat that reaches its southernmost distribution in the high parts of the Western Rhodopes (Chairski lakes; route 19).*

mountain butterflies, the Apollo. Among the wildflowers is a good range of orchids, although the climate of the area – too cold to be Mediterranean and too temperate to be Alpine – means that most orchids are widespread European species.

## Peatlands

The western Rhodopes are on the very south-eastern edge of where peatlands occur in Europe. These habitats form only where soils are waterlogged for most of the year. In such environments, the lack of oxygen prevents plant material to rot away so it becomes peat instead. There are only a few places where you can see this habitat, most obviously so at the Chairski lakes (route 19). Small, peaty patches may also be found close to trail edges or in small depressions on the plateau, but very rarely on limestone, as the water sinks away too quickly here.

A different kind of peaty soil is found where water trickles out of the limestone bedrock and feeds a mineral-rich version of a bog. There is one such place on the edge of the Dobrostan massif (route 15).

The peatlands support a rare flora and dragonfly fauna of ice age relicts – plants that are more familiar in central and northern Europe, like Bogbean, Marsh Cinquefoil and Giant Horsetail and a number of orchids, some of which are endemic to the Balkans (e.g. Heart-flowered Marshorchid and the Macedonian Marsh-orchid* (*Dactylorhiza kalopissii*).

# Beech, pine and oak woods of the Western Rhodopes

> Beech forests are encountered in many places in the Western Rhodopes, but only on route 12 and site B on page 224 are they a key feature. Pinewoods are present on routes 15, 16 and 17. Mature oak forests and other mixed deciduous forests form an important landscape component on route 15 and site E on page 226, and to lesser extent on route 16.

Whereas the coniferous forests described in the previous chapter are very much a feature of the Western Rhodopes, deciduous forests are found in both the western and eastern parts of the mountain range. The Beech, familiar to all central European mountain ranges and the lowlands of western Europe, covers large areas in the Western Rhodopes between an altitude of 1200 and 1700 metres. In contrast, the Eastern Rhodopes has only a few Beech forests, and they are restricted to the highest parts of the north-facing slopes, and sometimes considered to be of a distinct species, the Balkan or Moesian Beech (*Fagus moesiaca*, or according to some biologists, *Fagus orientalis*). The oak forest has the opposite distribution, being dominant in the Eastern Rhodopes and only locally present in the western part, where they occupy the warmest, lowest sections of the mountains.

The Western Rhodopes are densely forested.

**BEECH, PINE AND OAK WOODS OF THE WESTERN RHODOPES**

## Beech forests

The Beech is both a robust and a delicate tree. It is robust as, in the right conditions, it can dominate entire mountain slopes, outcompeting nearly all other tree species. It is also delicate, however, as it requires very specific conditions to thrive. Specifically, it should be neither very hot, nor very cold and the climate should be humid, without too much direct sunlight on the smooth, sensitive bark. Such conditions prevail in the mid-level slopes in the Western Rhodopes, particularly those that face north. Here you can find extensive and beautiful beech forests.

It is a fluke that some of the region's finest beech forests are found in the Eastern Rhodopes. At the edge of the protected site of Gyumyurdzhinski Snezhnik near the town of Kirkovo (route 12), the border with Greece runs over a high ridge. The slope to the north is steep, breezy and cool, and the strict border regulations during the Cold War spared the pristine beech forest of any disturbing activities. Currently, this is one of the last (nearly) untouched mountain beech forest left in Bulgaria.

Beech forests are naturally tall and shady. Its leaves are naturally acidic and inhibit the growth of other plants. There is hardly any herb or shrub layer, which is why well-developed Beech forests have such a wonderful, sacral atmosphere with the trunks as pillars supporting a vault of green leaves. If nature has a church, it must be a beech forest.

Old Beech trees are a specialty of the Western Rhodopes and can form dense forests on the north-facing parts of the mountain.

These soil conditions also imply that the interior of the forest has a limited flora, which consists of a combination of shade-adapted and parasitic plants. It is only as the trees come into bud in spring, but before the deep shade of summer develops, that there is a higher diversity of plants. Then plants like Wood Anemone, Primrose and Coralroot Bittercress appear. Even these plants, though, reach their optimum elsewhere, not in the pure beech forest, but where there's a mix of Hornbeam, Hop-hornbeam and Silver Linden (usually near streams or on the edge of the forest).

The beech forests in the Western

# BEECH, PINE AND OAK WOODS OF THE WESTERN RHODOPES

Rhodopes have an attractive birdlife. Besides all sorts of widespread forest birds, these are the haunts for a good number of woodpeckers, of which White-backed and Grey-headed are most typically tied to the Beech (although they will 'spill over' to other forest types). The small population of Semi-collared Flycatcher is also largely restricted to this forest type.

## Pine forest

At roughly the same altitude as the beech forests growing on the cooler north-facing mountain slopes, the warmer and drier south-facing slopes are clothed in pines. This is a radically different habitat from both the beech forests and the spruce woods at greater altitude. Pines have, like the beech forest, a canopy that spreads out like an umbrella over the forest floor, but it is one that allows much more light onto the ground. Furthermore, the annual autumnal bombardment of acidic leaves that is typical of the beech forest, is not present in the pinewoods (which shed their needles over a much longer period of time). Both factors make the forest floor brighter and drier. Add to this the temperature difference resulting from the southern aspect and it is clear that this is a very different habitat. Many of the plants that are found in the pastures also occur in the pine forest, only in lower numbers and joined by species that prefer half-shaded conditions.

Ants play an important role in these pinewoods as they are plentiful and make enormous nests. They are great predators, but perhaps are even more important as prey. Woodpeckers (Wryneck, Black, Green and Grey-headed particularly) love to feed on ants and their larvae. Wasp and bee nests are also numerous and much enjoyed by Honey Buzzard, while Brown Bears loves all of these.

The climatic conditions of the pine forests are perhaps most visible in winter and early spring. The lion's share of the snow load is caught by the canopy and what's on the ground melts away quicker due to the direct sunlight, making this the place with a very modest snow load, thus with the grasses, twigs and herbs within easy reach for

Dry Pine forest covers the south-facing slopes of the Western Rhodopes.

LANDSCAPE

grazing animals. Chamois, love these forests at this time of the year. Also Capercaillie seem to have a preference for the pine forests.

## Oak forests

Roughly between 250 to 600 metres in altitude (sometimes higher), light oak woodlands cover the slopes of the Western Rhodopes. Sessile Oaks (plus the closely related *Quercus dalechampii* and *Q. polycarpa*) dominate the higher parts within this zone with Turkish (*Quercus cerris*) and Hungarian Oaks (*Quercus frainetto*) joining the mix lower down. The first has rather small leaves with pointy lobes, while the second has large and deeply lobes leaves. They grow together with a large number of other trees – Manna Ash, various maples, Hornbeam, Oriental Hornbeam and more. One frequently encountered tree is the Silver Linden, a south-east European species that has a curious adaptation to drought – it turns its leaves by a 180 degrees to point the downy-white underside towards the sun so they act as a reflector. The silver-grey canopies are easily spotted on the hillsides.

Despite the large variety of Balkan trees, the oak forests in the Western Rhodopes look rather like the oak forests further north – fairly tall trees with full canopies. This appearance changes rather drastically when you travel to the Eastern Rhodopes.

The oak forests contain a large variety of different trees, besides various species of oak. These are century old Hornbeams.

# Forest-scrub-pasture mosaic of the Eastern Rhodopes

> Routes 1-11 and routes 23 and 24 all lead through extensive areas with a mosaic habitat of forest scrub and pasture. The best routes to experience this unique landscape are routes 3, 4, 9, 10 and 11, plus site A on page 183. The limestone version of this habitat, including its special flora, is the prime attraction of sites B and C on page 193-194, plus some locations on routes 23 and 24.

Large parts of the Eastern Rhodopes are covered with a mix of grasslands, rock, scrubland and woodland, which supports a very high biodiversity.

This smorgasbord of interlinked habitats covers large parts of the Eastern Rhodopes and more locally Sakar. Here the oak woods rarely form large, unbroken tracts. Instead, they grow within a mosaic of dry grasslands and pastures, scrub, solitary trees, rocky slopes and small arable plots. All these different components merge fluently into one another, creating a sort of 'meta-habitat' that is spectacular in its diversity and beauty. It is also very typical of a region in which the temperate biome of central Europe (where forests dominate) meets the Mediterranean (where scrubland is a key component) and the Eastern regions (where grasslands form the landscape). In the Eastern Rhodopes and Sakar, the landscape reflects this meeting point of biological realms (see also page 65). However, it would be misleading to say that the current landscape is entirely natural. In reality, grazing animals are the key to the formation and maintenance of this mosaic landscape. The Rhodopean Short-horn cattle, sheep and wild ungulates keep the landscape in this half-open state.

# FOREST-SCRUB-PASTURE MOSAIC OF THE EASTERN RHODOPES

Mature Oak grow on the cooler parts of the mountain (right). The large-leaved Hungarian Oak is locally common on such slopes.

## The forest

Various oaks dominate the woodlands, but they are seldom alone. Stands of Oriental Hornbeam, Manna Ash and Montpellier Maple are common, sometimes even outnumbering the oaks. In fact, these 'oak' forests in the Balkans have the greatest diversity of trees of any European forest type, with the oaks themselves forming a confusing bunch that have been the source of dispute amongst taxonomists and ecologists.

On the cooler, north-facing slopes, you'll find the pretty *Quercus frainetto*, generally called Hungarian Oak (since these vernacular names are not used consistently in other texts, we provide the scientific names as well). The Hungarian Oak is a beautiful tree with distinctive, large and deeply lobed leaves. It is about the only oak that is not difficult to recognise.

The Hungarian Oak shares its territory with the more widespread Turkey Oak (*Quercus cerris*) and *Quercus dalechampii*, the latter is sometimes considered a hybrid between Sessile (*Q. petraea*) and Downy Oak (*Q. pubescens*) and has intermediate characteristics.

On the warm slopes, there are 'pure' Downy Oaks, which are distinguished by the leathery leaves with pale, downy undersides. Downy Oak grow together with the aforementioned Turkey Oak and the Italian Oak (*Q. vergiliana*). The latter is a taller version of the Downy Oak, from which it is so hard to distinguish that botanists often consider them to be the same

## FOREST-SCRUB-PASTURE MOSAIC OF THE EASTERN RHODOPES

species. A large number of other oaks are listed for the region, but many of them seem to be hybrids or are simply synonyms for the aforementioned oaks. There is even one species, the Thracian Oak *Quercus thracica*, that is known from only a single specimen in the Eastern Rhodopes, near the village of Sarnak. It died in 2009 and the species is now considered extinct. In several places in the Eastern Rhodopes, you'll encounter pinewoods, mostly of Austrian Pine. None of these are native but were planted for the timber production. You don't need an expert eye to recognise that this project failed. The pines are all dead or dying, as this range is too hot and dry for the pines to thrive. Interestingly, the native range of the Turkish Pine lies just outside this region. The northernmost native stands of this east-Mediterranean tree are in Dadia Forest in Greece, barely 20 kms from the Bulgarian border.

The sub-Mediterranean oak forests form a splendid backdrop for long walks in spring and autumn (in summer it is too hot). Through the open canopy, the sun creates a shifting mosaic of light and shadow on the grassy undergrowth. Every now and then, little streams find their way through the woods, supporting the aquatic Grass and Dice Snakes, often to be found sunbathing in open patches. In many places, drifts of Peacock Anemones, Stars-of-Bethlehem and thousands and thousands of pretty little Grape-hyacinths colour the forest floor. This is also the place to look for orchids like Roman, Lady and Monkey Orchids, and for Pontic Fritillary.

This type of forest is excellent for reptiles. It is warm and sunny, and because of the mosaic structure of the forest, more open habitat is usually not far away. There is also sufficient shelter and shade to retreat into. Hence, most reptile species can be found in good numbers in the open oak woodlands. Three-lined and Green Lizards will frequently cross your path, while the delightful tortoises (both Hermann's and Spur-thighed) simply just sit there in the middle of the trail, mimicking a rock.

### The scrubland

In the drier or rockier parts, small trees and bushes replace the oaks –Wild Service Tree, Bladder Senna, Wild Lilac, Wild Jasmin, Cretan Cistus, Smoke-tree, Judas Tree, Wild Pistacio

The forest-scrub-pasture mosaic has one of the highest concentrations and diversity of reptiles in Europe. Both Spur-thighed and Hermann's Tortoises are common.

## FOREST-SCRUB-PASTURE MOSAIC OF THE EASTERN RHODOPES

Tree and many more. Several of these are species proper to the Mediterranean, such as Cretan Cistus and Wild Pistachio tree. They become more numerous as you get closer to the eastern edge of the mountain range where the climate is warmest. Perhaps the most eye-catching of these shrubs is the Wild Lilac, which grows in profusion on the rocky slopes. This is the ancestral species of the familiar Garden Lilac and is native to a small region in eastern Bulgaria and Turkey, and again in eastern Asia. This peculiar distribution range is the result of the ice ages that led to the extinction of the Wild Lilac in the centre of its once extensive range.

Traditionally, scrubland is considered to be a transitional stage. When an abandoned grassland gradually turns to woodland, it passes through the stage of scrubland. However, in the (sub)-Mediterranean regions, scrublands can persist over a long time in places where drought, poor or shallow soil are unfavourable for a further succession to forest. These natural scrublands are found in the hottest and driest places of the Eastern Rhodopes and in Sakar, usually on south-facing slopes or on thin, rocky soil.

The majority of scrubland areas, however, owe their existence to either the degradation of sub-Mediterranean oak forest or the abandonment of grazing. In the first case, development to forest is disrupted by cutting, grazing and the occasional fire. In the Rhodopes, many abandoned grasslands pass through a scrubland phase before reverting to young oak woodlands. However, since the climate is already tough on trees it takes a long time before trees replace the bushes, particularly on shallow ground. Throw in the natural grazing and an occasional bushfire and it is easy to understand that the scrubland is not just a phase but a permanent natural habitat in the lowland parts of the region.

Grazing keeps the grasslands open. You can recognise the areas with a high grazing pressure by the bitten-down bushes with small leaves.

# FOREST-SCRUB-PASTURE MOSAIC OF THE EASTERN RHODOPES

The scrublands of the Eastern Rhodopes and Sakar are not to be confused with the evergreen macchia (maquis) of the Mediterranean region. In our region, it is the deciduous Christ's-thorn shrub that plays a key role. This bush is easily recognized by its combination of parallel leaves, thorns and fruits that look like flying saucers. It is reputed to have been used as the thorny crown Christ had to wear on his way to the cross (hence its name *Paliurus spini-christi*). Christ's-thorn grows on the poorest and hottest soils, frequently together with Wild Jasmin. In places with a little more nutrients, Hawthorn and various fruit trees like Wild Pear may grow.

Another big difference with the Mediterranean scrublands is the patchy character of the Rhodopean scrublands. In most places, the bushes are scattered over dry grasslands. The ecology, flora and fauna of these scrublands is therefore very much connected to the open spaces in between.

The bushy grasslands (or are they grassy bushlands?) are one of the focal habitats for birdwatchers, as it is here that a large number of south-east European bird species are found – e.g. Black-headed Bunting, Barred, Eastern Subalpine and Eastern Orphean Warblers and a variety of shrikes. Most strongly linked to the Christ's-thorn scrub is the (therefore ill-named) Olive-tree Warbler. Additionally, one of the more attractive butterflies of the area, the boldly pattern Little Tiger Blue, is exclusively found around these shrubs.

The Christ's-thorn bushes with their typical appearance cover large parts of the driest and hottest slopes (top). This habitat has a rich birdlife. The Woodchat Shrike is one of the more conspicuous birds (bottom).

## Dry pastures

In the Eastern Rhodopes, the larger areas with dry grasslands are found on the gentle slopes and level land on the ridges. This pattern – woodland on the slopes and grassland on the ridges, is again the result of grazing – the level parts are more accessible for both sheep and people – the first to graze and the second to collect wood.

The dry pastures have a steppe-like appearance, especially towards the summer when the spring flowers have disappeared and the once green grass has turned to golden straw. The dry pastures of the Eastern Rhodopes are somewhat reminiscent of the karstic plateaux of the Western

## FOREST-SCRUB-PASTURE MOSAIC OF THE EASTERN RHODOPES

Rhodopes in the sense that they are dry and rocky, but they have a very different climate and bedrock. And so are the flora and fauna. It would be incorrect to say that the wildlife in the dry pastures of the Eastern Rhodopes is richer, but from a West-European perspective, it is certainly more exotic. The birdlife is radically different too and so are the wildflowers and insects. The latter group is quite spectacular. Besides the butterflies, there is a large variety of impressive critters, like tall ant-lions, owlflies (ascalaphids), praying mantises, grasshoppers and bush-crickets, which again form the prey of many birds and reptiles. No habitat is richer in lizards, snakes and tortoises than the dry pastures in the Eastern Rhodopes.

### A meta-ecosystem

As we stated at the start of this chapter, woodlands, scrublands and pastures naturally flow into one another. It is this matrix of different elements combined that is the great attraction. In this meta-ecosystem, the sum really is bigger than its parts. Here, most of the special wildlife of the region is found.

For Wolves, Jackals, Wild Boars and Roe Deer the woodlands are ideal places to retreat and rest, escape the summer heat and the winter cold. Yet these animals also need the open spaces to graze or to hunt. Likewise, reptiles need this combination of shelter and exposure as well, both for their thermo-regulation and for hunting and finding shelter. The highest diversity of reptiles is found in scrublands, especially where there are some small streams and woodland patches nearby. The high concentration of tortoises is testimony to the importance of this habitat to reptiles. Additionally, there is a large variety of lizards and snakes (see page 112). Many birds hunt on the grasslands, either for reptiles, small mammals or for insects. Solitary trees and bushes are ideal perches to scout the area, but most birds need the forest to nest in. Birds of prey, insofar as they don't use cliffs to build their nest, breed in the tall canopies of the oaks. In short, this wildlife would struggle to survive in a uniform grassland, pure scrubland or dense woodland, but thrive in the places where these habitats are combined. The mosaic ecosystem is the real strength of the Eastern Rhodopes.

The Pink Butterfly Orchid is among the most widespread orchids in the shrubby pastures of the Eastern Rhodopes.

# Steppes and arable land

> The best routes for both the rocky and the deep-soiled steppes are routes 5, 13, 21, 23 and 24, plus sites C and D on page 249-250. The latter site is also the only saline steppe site in this guide.

The steppes are the most oriental and perhaps most exotic habitat of the region. They form the wide vistas, have a splendid birdlife and an attractive mammalian fauna.

Loosely defined, steppes are naturally treeless grasslands with perhaps a thin scatter of bushes. They occur where the soil is either too dry or the growing season too short to support trees, but the conditions are still suitable for herbs and grasses. Fully natural steppe occurs on the Anatolian highlands and on the shores of the Black Sea. The latter stretches out east through Asia and into Mongolia. It has deep and fertile soils (the famous *chernozum* or black earth) and are by many considered the true steppe. At its edge lies the so-called forest steppe, where natural grasslands are mixed with woodlands in the places that are more favourable to tree growth (usually in sheltered river valleys).

The largest areas of steppe-like pastures are found in the foothills of Sakar (route 23).

**STEPPES AND ARABLE LAND**

The Thracian Plain and peripheral slopes of Sakar and the Eastern Rhodopes experience, with their cold winters and hot summers, conditions that are tough, but not impossible, for trees and shrubs. Where the soil is thin or saline, grasslands or scrublands form the natural vegetation. Elsewhere, shrubs and trees would, albeit slowly, colonise the land if nature had its way.

But nature doesn't have its way. Even low grazing pressure and the occasional bushfire keeps the vegetation open, creating a habitat that is close to the 'true' steppes and steppe woodlands. With the natural steppes so close by, the 'pseudo-steppes' of the region support a large number of plants and animals that have their core distribution areas on the natural grasslands further east. Often it is hard to tell whether a grassland is a natural (primary) steppe or one that formed under the grazing of domesticated animals. And most wildlife of the steppes doesn't care about the theoretical difference. In this book, we therefore use the term steppe for the larger expanses of grasslands, even though they are strictly speaking not the true steppe of the east.

### Different types of steppes

Within our region, there is an important ecological difference between the deep-soiled grasslands in the Thracian Plain and those on the stony slopes in the Eastern Rhodopes and Sakar that we described in the previous chapter. However, as everywhere in this region, habitat distinctions are vague and there are plenty of places where stony grasslands and deeper soils are mixed. You'll find these 'in-between habitats' a lot in Sakar and around Ivaylovgrad and Kardzhali.

The salt or saline steppe is the third type of natural grassland in the region. In places with mineral-rich clay, the intense summer heat forces ground water to rise through the soil's capillaries. At the surface the water evaporates, leaving the suspended salts and mineral behind. The salt is toxic to trees, so the natural vegetation at these sites consists of salt-tolerant plants forming a salt steppe.

Such saline soils are very local

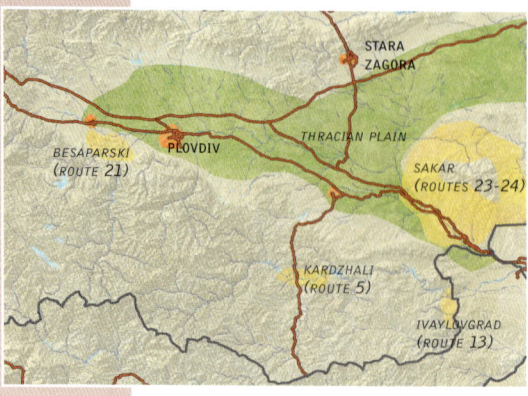

Location of the major areas of steppe-like pastures in the region. In green the agricultural land in which, locally, there are remnants of deep-soil steppes. The finest steppe-like pastures, both rocky and deep-soil, are indicated in yellow.

# STEPPES AND ARABLE LAND

and their occurrence is fully dependent on the geology. Since these patches are small, they have not developed as full-scale ecosystems as have the other two steppe types. Salt steppes do have a (limited) number of special plant species, related to the familiar coastal plants (e.g. sea-lavanders, plantago) that at these inland sites evolved into their own unique species.

## Deep-soil steppe

There are two reasons why the deep-soil steppe is so different from the grasslands on rocky slopes. First, is the high amount of nutrients in the soil and the second is that it is easy to dig holes in the ground. This is an ecosystem that extends underground, which becomes immediately evident when you meet the steppe animal *par excellence*: the Suslik. This handsome ground squirrel lives socially in burrows and needs the deep soils to dig its holes. Whenever it is too cold or too hot, the Suslik will be underground, but when the weather is nice, it will be out and about, collecting seeds to store in the chambers of the burrow. It is constantly dividing its attention between collecting food and watching out for predators, which it does, adorably, by standing on its hind legs and looking around. An entire ecosystem is built around the Suslik. Many predators feed on it, in particular the Marbled Polecat (see page 88) and birds of prey like Eastern Imperial Eagle and Saker Falcon.

The Suslik or European Ground Squirrel lives exclusively in steppes and pastures with deep soils where it can dig its burrows.

Susliks also play an important part in the turnover of the soil, creating through their digging sandy patches, where plants can germinate and insects can live. The Susliks are (together with some other rodents) the gardeners of the steppes, creating open patches and shifting heaps of seeds of a large variety of wildflowers. Some of them are those that we consider as plants of arable fields, such as Cornflower, Corn Cockle, Eastern Larkspur and Wild Chamomile. These were originally steppe plants and occur here in their native habitat. Their seeds are eaten by Calandra, Short-toed and Crested Larks and Corn and Black-headed Buntings which can be very numerous in the steppes and in grain fields.

Abandoned Suslik burrows are much appreciated by other ground-breeding species. One of them is the Isabelline Wheatear. In fact, the presence of Isabelline Wheatears is a good indication that Susliks are around too.

**STEPPES AND ARABLE LAND**

Another important feature of the steppe ecosystem will become evident when you visit the area in late spring and summer. Thousands of grasshoppers, both big and small, feed on the grasses. Large insects are a key element of the flora and fauna of the steppe. They are important food for Hoopoes, Lesser Grey Shrikes, Rollers, Bee-eaters, Little Owls, Stone Curlews and Lesser Kestrels. Apart from grasshoppers, lizards (mostly Balkan Wall Lizard) and beetles are also important prey for these birds.

## Steppes under pressure

Historically, the Thracian Plain had a mix of ploughed fields and grasslands. Some of these grasslands were communal land where villagers grazed their sheep. Others were patchily distributed between areas with rocks and therefore not suited for ploughing.

In the 20th century, the balance between animal husbandry and crop growing started to shift – and it continues to shift today. Arable farming has intensified and has grown at the expense of sheep and cattle grazing. The ploughing destroys the burrows and kills the Susliks. The ground-dwelling lizards face the same fate. Due to the destruction of its habitat, the Suslik and lizard populations have fallen dramatically over the last few decades (see page 88). Without them, the predators have a hard time surviving, Other small mammals, such as Hares and Hedgehogs do a little better, and now rank high on the menu of these predators. Recent studies revealed that Hedgehogs are at present, the number one prey of Eastern Imperial Eagles in Sakar – that used to be Suslik.

Even fallow grounds that are left undisturbed for years have a vegetation that is very different from that of the natural steppe. It is dominated by annual, pioneer species rather than true grassland plants. Many of the insects of the grasslands disappear with the disappearance of the perennial grasses and wildflowers.

Fortunately, not all is lost. Here and there, larger and smaller patches of grasslands remain. These can vary from saline areas, communal grounds (usually near villages or along small streams), the broader borders between fields, the verges of roads and tracks, pockets of deep-soiled steppe between rocky places, etc. These are the areas where the traditional wildlife of the deep-soiled steppes persist. The highest concentrations of pristine habitat are found on the lower slopes of Sakar, near Ivaylovgrad and locally near Besaparski. Sadly, these places are still considered wastelands that have yet to be transformed for agriculture rather than the valuable and threatened ecosystems they are. There is a case for claiming that these deep-soiled steppes are Europe's most threatened yet least valued ecosystems.

# Rivers and wetlands

> Route 22 to Zlato Pole is the place to visit to explore the Maritsa River, with sites A to E on pages 250-253 visiting the fishponds and lowland reservoirs in the Thracian Plain. Routes 1, 2, 6, 8 and 14 explore the river habitats in the Eastern Rhodopes, with route 1, 5, 6 and site A on page 181 also leading to the reservoirs in the Arda River. One excellent way to enjoy the river from up close is by renting a canoe in Madzharovo – see page 263. For the Byala Reka River, check out route 14 and site D on page 195. and for the Thundzha, drive route 23.
> The rivers of the Western Rhodopes are subject of routes 15, 19, 20 and site B on page 224, routes 15, 17 and 18 explore the rock faces in the higher mountains. Some of the best limestone cliffs here, are the subject of sites A and B on page 222.

For a region that carries the title 'Rhodope Mountains', there is a surprising richness in aquatic habitats. There are wetlands and broad rivers with oxbow lakes in the lowlands, middle sized rivers in the mountains and small shaded mountain brooks. There are even a number of mountain peatlands, which have been described in the chapter on the coniferous forests and mountain meadows (page 24).
In the previous chapters we 'armchair-travelled' from the Sub-alpine peaks of the Western Rhodopes down the slope, crossing various forest

The Arda river near Madzharovo (route 1).

**RIVERS AND WETLANDS**

types and scrubland to reach the open, steppe-like expanses in the Thracian Plain. In this chapter, we make the journey in reverse, but this time we follow the rivers and their associated wetlands.

## The wetlands of the lowlands

The Maritsa is the largest river of the Thracian Plain but certainly not the only one. The lowlands aren't flat. Between the hills numerous small and often seasonal streams drain the region. Some of them are dammed to form reservoirs which then have a very attractive wildlife.

Historically, there were some large wetlands as well, fed by these local streams. They were drained to create fertile land or deepened to make fishponds. The latter have dense reedbeds and retain water year-round, ideal for waterfowl and reed-dwelling species. Most small reservoirs have wide, shallow margins with little vegetation where, waders and herons can be seen. Black-winged Stilt, Stone Curlew and even Collared Pratincole breed here locally.

Particularly around Plovdiv, there is a high concentration of fishponds, reservoirs and rice paddies that form artificial wetlands. Combined with the Maritsa river, they make a great aquatic ecosystem with a rich wildlife. It is first and foremost, the birdlife that makes a visit to the lowland rivers and wetlands worthwhile. The majority of the European wetland birds are present. There is a plethora of herons and ducks. Both Black and White Stork are numerous, while Glossy Ibis, Dalmatian and White Pelicans are more local delights whose numbers have been increasing in the few last decades. Many of them breed (although not yet the pelicans), but even more birds spend the winter here. Northern ducks, geese and both pelicans can be found during the cold months. In spring and autumn, migrating birds rest and to fatten up on their journey to or from the north. In spring, a large number of migrants follows the Turkish west coast up to the Maritsa (or Evros) Delta on the Greek-Turkish border and then follow the river upstream into the Thracian Plain. When you visit the Maritsa wetlands in April and May, you'll find the wetlands alive with terns, waders and a variety of raptors.

## The Maritsa

The Maritsa river itself, plus some of its tributaries, are the true gems of the Thracian Plain. The Maritsa is a meltwater-fed river. It springs in the mountains and its waters rise as the snow starts to melt early in spring. During its peak discharge, water is everywhere and the current is strong. The flow easily widens and deepens existing channels and even digs out

# RIVERS AND WETLANDS

new ones. As the water drops again and the dissolved sediments sink down, some of these channels silt up, creating a patchwork of riverbeds, still backwaters, islands, sand and pebble banks are revealed.

Ribbons of thick, mature swamp forest line the river and its backwaters. This lush, green woodland type sports big trees that form a sharp contrast with the adjacent dry slopes clothed in scant vegetation. The riparian forest consists of variety of species like White and Black Poplars, White and Crack Willows, Black Alder, Narrow-leaved Ash and various oaks and elms, all of which take advantage of the permanent presence of moisture and nutrients. These forests are heavily draped with climbing plants.

When you think of it, this sprawl of biomass is hardly surprising. The river sediment is full of nutrients and fresh water is in continuous supply. The climate is generally warm and sunny, so growing conditions, at least in spring and summer, are ideal. The plant life in the riverine forests shows adaptation strategies reminiscent of those in wet tropical forests. Water and nutrient supplies not being restricted, all energy is employed in a race to beat the neighbours in the struggle for sunlight. Vines, such as Hop, Silk-vine and Ivy, use the stems of trees to climb up to the canopy. Those plants that remain on the forest floor produce large leaves to catch as much of the remaining sunlight as possible. The damp atmosphere and the loud, fluting songs of Nightingale and

The Maritsa River near Zlato Pole (top; route 22). The Squacco Heron can be quite numerous in the lowland marshes (bottom).

LANDSCAPE

Golden Oriole add to the tropical experience, as do the numerous Aesculapian and Grass Snakes, European Pond Terrapins and – in some places – fresh-water crabs.

A rather special type of riverine forest, dominated by Oriental Planes, is unique to the eastern Mediterranean and reaches its northernmost distributional limit in southern Bulgaria. The Oriental Plane is a long-lived tree, reaching heights of over 25 metres and growing massive trunks – probably the thickest of any of the European trees. You'll find this forest type in the valley of Byala Reka and the Thundza, but also near Dobrostan. It is easy to catch a glimpse of the riparian lowland forests from any of the bridges that cross the Maritsa, but a more thorough exploration is quite hard. The very best location to really get into this habitat is at the Zlato Pole reserve (route 22), which is an oxbow lake – a former river channel, now cut off from the main river that flows directly beside it.

The birdlife is again the main attraction of the riparian forest. Most in evidence are the Golden Orioles, Bee-eaters, Rollers, Hoopoes and Kingfishers which occur in (very) high numbers in this habitat. Zlato Pole is magnificent in this respect.

Riverine forests are of great importance for breeding birds. The larger birds, such as Black Stork, Lesser Spotted Eagle, Black Kite and (rather scarce) White-tailed Eagle, use the crowns of big trees in which to build their nests. The true highlights here are two south-eastern birds that reach their north-western limit along the Maritsa but occur nonetheless in good numbers: the Levant Sparrowhawk and the Masked Shrike (see page 105).

Birds are by no means the only attractions along the Maritsa: from Golden Jackal to European Pond Terrapin and from Eastern Spadefoot to the glider butterflies (*Neptis*) – there is a wealth of wildlife to discover here. And with few naturalists really exploring these parts, you may very well make some new discoveries.

## The Arda and tributaries

In the Eastern Rhodopes, the river Arda and its tributaries snake through wide valleys down to the Greek border and beyond, where it merges with the Maritsa/Evros. The Arda and tributaries (e.g. Krumovitsa, Borovitsa and Varbitsa) collect water from large areas of the Rhodopes, but since snow is uncommon or restricted to a short winter period in much of this catchment, the water levels depend on rainfall rather than snowmelt. Rain is common in winter but rare in summer. Hence, the 'middle section rivers' are gentle and shallow for half of the year, but rise and occasionally

## RIVERS AND WETLANDS

even become diabolic currents after heavy rains. When water levels are low, shingle banks, river grasslands and patches of riparian woodland form a collection of habitats which have a lot to offer naturalists.

The Arda and its tributaries are faster flowing than the Maritsa. The fine sand and clay particles that form the soil in the Maritsa valley, remain suspended in the stronger currents of the middle-section rivers. Rather than fine sand, you'll encounter coarse sand and pebble banks along the river. In damper spots, there are also some meadows and thickets of willows, poplars, elms and oaks along the streams.

The Arda itself is a collection of habitats rather than a single unity, with small sections of rapids that alternate with isolated, still pools. These shallows vary in depth, temperature, the amount of shade, and whether they carry water permanently or only seasonally. This variation is reflected in a large biodiversity. Besides rich in wildlife, these rivers are also simply very scenic. They are largely undisturbed, with shingle banks and sandy banks where Bee-eaters, Kingfishers and Sand Martins breed. The broad ribbons of willow and poplar woods with Golden Oriole, Lesser Grey Shrike and Roller.

The shingle banks are a specialty of these middle-section rivers. They warm up quickly on the surface, yet beneath the pebbles it remains cool and moist. They host a special flora of pioneer plants that can withstand periodic flooding. Perhaps more remarkable, even the insect life survives the frequent flooding. The rarest species here is undoubtedly the Small Bath White, which occurs only on shingle banks in a couple of river valleys in the southern Balkans, including the Arda.

The rivers hold plenty of fish, which attract many fish-eating species. Otters are common, if, as ever, difficult to see. Black Storks though, are almost as numerous as anglers on the Istanbul bridge. They can be seen in small groups hunting, wings flapping as if gesticulating, in the middle of the river. Dice and Grass Snakes are also very common, especially in the smaller rivers like the Armira and Byala Reka.

If you look at the distribution maps of some of the dragonflies and reptiles you'll notice an interesting phenomenon – the Arda, Byala Reka and

Black Storks are common breeding birds of the river valleys of the Eastern Rhodopes.

**LANDSCAPE**

**RIVERS AND WETLANDS**

Tundzha function as gateways of Mediterranean fauna and flora. The damselfly Odalisque serves as an example of this, just like the Worm Snake, Sand Boa and Kotschy's Gecko. All are Mediterranean species that have spread via these river valleys into Bulgaria yet still remain restricted to these river valleys and the hills directly around.

## Reservoirs

Heading further west and upstream along the Arda, the Mediterranean influences diminish. Several reservoirs, built in the 1950s and '60s, have changed the character of the Arda river. One is east of Madzharovo (route 1); there is another one between Studen Kladenets (the village and dam; see route 8) and Kardzhali (route 5) and there is a third one west of Kardzhali (route 6). These reservoirs have undoubtedly destroyed a lot of valuable habitats, but have also created new opportunities for wildlife, in particular for birds, to flourish. The lack of human habitation and the closeness of rocks and cliffs has made the Studen Kladenets reservoir a haven for wildlife: vulture cliffs, high concentrations of Black Storks, Otters, Deer, Jackals and Wolves all find the peace to rear their young in this area. The large game reserve on the south slope of the Studen Kladenets reservoir owes its existence to the reservoir, as it was the flooding of the area that cut off transport links and forced local inhabitants to move away, leaving the area largely deserted.

Over the last decade or so, the reservoirs have begun to develop a special birdlife, with some unexpected guests like Dalmatian Pelican, White-tailed Eagle, Ruddy Shelduck and Goosander (see page 111).

Wildlife photography on the thickly wooded banks of the Tundzha River (route 23).

## The Byala Reka and Thundza

The Byala Reka river valley has a very different character from that of the Arda. This remote and unspoiled river flows through a more densely forested, narrow valley, not far from the Greek border. Besides a wildlife with a distinctly Mediterranean flavour, it harbours some species that are exclusive to a few isolated sites in the Eastern Rhodopes. One of them is the Bulgarian Emerald (see page 128 and 192).

Equally exciting, is the Tundzha river in the most eastern part of the area covered in this book. It separates the Sakar hills from the lowland still further east that eventually rise again to form the hilly region on the Black Sea Coast known as Strandzha.

The lower Thundzha valley is a nature reserve and, due to its remoteness, one of the hardest rivers to get to. A small section near the village of Srem is easily accessible though (route 23) and gives the impression of a heavily wooded, slow-flowing river with masses of dragonflies and birds.

## Brooks

Before continuing our journey further up the mainstream into the Western Rhodopes, it pays to explore the numerous side streams that run down from the hills of the Eastern Rhodopes.

When visiting the Eastern Rhodopes in spring after a wet winter, you will encounter small streams at pretty much every little depression in the hillsides. At such times, it may be hard to appreciate that nearly all these streams are 'winterbournes', which dry up completely in the summer. Only those few places that are fed by permanent underground reservoirs, retain a steady flow of water during the summer.

The latter obviously are welcome and vital to aquatic animals like terrapins, water snakes and fish retreat in the heat of summer. They also harbour many attractive dragonflies, of which the Turkish Goldenring is perhaps the most typical.

But even the streams that do lose their water in summer, still function as ecological oases. The little floods in spring deposit fertile soil around these streams – a fairly rare situation in a region where thin infertile soils are the default condition. Even these small trickles of water allow larger and more leafy trees to grow up alongside them, thus creating cool and damp valleys for many birds, mammals, reptiles and wildflowers.

## Mountain streams

The higher into the mountains that you follow the rivers, the more 'central European' your surroundings become. The ecological conditions and the

## RIVERS AND WETLANDS

species found near streams in the Western Rhodopes are quite similar to those you find in the hills and mountains of Romania, Slovakia or Austria. Grey Wagtails and Dippers move from rock to rock in the stream and you can look for the beautiful black and yellow Fire Salamander below trunks and rocks on the streams edge. The water frog you frequently encounter here is the Balkan Stream Frog, a Balkan endemic that is closely related to the familiar Grass Frog.

The high mountain streams are rich in oxygen and fish. They also form a ribbon of nutrient-rich soil in an otherwise rocky and rather nutrient-poor environment. This is immediately visible in the plant life – the massive leaves of butterbur line the streams and there are many plants that are elsewhere either absent or, if present, much smaller. This is, for example, the sole domain of the Rhodope Toothwort (see page 70). The Eastern Spotted Orchid* (*Dactylorhiza saccifera*) is nowhere as numerous and tall as in the river valleys.

Also typical of river valleys, are the trees. Various species of willows and Trembling Aspen grow here and are the food plant of several species of butterflies. Interestingly, there seem to be as many or perhaps even more, butterflies tied to these mountain streams than there are dragonflies. Poplar and White Admirals are frequent here, and more locally, there are Common Gliders and Large and Eastern Tortoiseshells.

The brooks high up in the Western Rhodopes are enchanting places, with a rich flora.

# Crags and cliffs

> Routes 1, 2, 4, 5, 8, 11, 21 explore the crag-and-cliff habitat in the lower mountains. In the Western Rhodopes, routes 15, 17 and 18 explore the rock faces in the higher mountains. Some of the best limestone cliffs here, are the subject of sites A and B on page 222.

The previous chapter neglected an essential element of many river valleys in both the Eastern and Western Rhodopes, rocky slopes and cliffs tower over many parts of the river. Even though it is hard to find two habitats that are ecologically more different from one another than a riverbank and a rock face, they are often found right next to one another. In fact, many of the greatest wildlife sites in the area feature both of these extremes in the same place. This fact was brought home to us one day when we stood on the cliffs of Monyak (route 5), looking at a Rock Nuthatch through the binoculars that stood out beautifully against the white mass of a flock of pelicans on the river below where the river disgorges into the reservoir.

The Black Stork embodies, as no other animal, the link between cliffs and rivers. It needs both habitats as it breeds on the cliffs above the river where it feeds. Many rock plants in the Western Rhodopes enjoy the constant dampness rivers provide. Conversely, in the Eastern Rhodopes, many warmth-loving reptiles occur exclusively along the river valleys, where they survive on the south-facing cliffs. In short, rivers and cliffs are intrinsically linked, not least because it was usually the river that cut the gorge and thereby created the cliffs.

Cliffs form a strange habitat. They have wildly varying, but always extreme, environments. Permanent dampness and deep shade are as much an environmental condition of cliffs as its opposite – extreme drought full exposure to the sun.

The gravity makes it nearly impossible to live on rock walls unless you have tenacious roots, are a good climber or able to fly. Yet this inaccessibility is a quality that makes the habitat a safe retreat from predators and herbivores. Birds find a safe place to nest and roost, while many plants thrive on cliffs, well out of reach from the hungry mouths of deer and sheep.

The birdlife and plant life of rocky slopes is particularly striking. Some of the rarest, most attractive and most sought-after species are found on cliffs. The same goes for the reptiles and the butterflies, but for different reasons. They need the sun to warm up and the exposed rocks form the perfect places to do so.

CRAGS AND CLIFFS

The cliffs of the Yumruk Kaya seen from the hunting reserve near Kardzhali (site A on page 183).

## Flora and fauna on cliffs

The broad-winged birds form undoubtedly the most striking fauna of the cliffs. Many of them, such as Griffon and Egyptian Vultures, Golden Eagle, Black Stork and Eagle Owl, strongly favour rock ledges for nesting and roosting. Besides safety from predators, the strong upward drafts help them to take off.

Aerial feeders like Alpine Swifts, House and Crag Martins nest here too as their short legs makes them vulnerable to predators elsewhere. The cliffs and scree slopes also provide feeding and nesting sites for Rock Nuthatch, Rock Bunting, Rock Thrush, Blue Rock Thrush and Eastern Black-eared Wheatear. Indeed, the rocky environment is a true birding hotspot, particularly in the Eastern Rhodopes.

This being said, these mountains are not blessed with cliffs. This habitat occurs most abundantly where rivers have carved gorges through soft bedrock and more locally where there are volcano craters (e.g. the famous Kovan Kaya cliffs near Madzharovo) or at the eroded peaks of the oldest ranges in the region. This localised character means that cliff species are predictable in their occurrence. Unfortunately, it also makes them vulnerable for disturbance by human activities like paragliding and climbing. Therefore, more than any other habitat in the Eastern Rhodopes, cliffs enjoy a high level of protection. Nearly all activity on rock faces are banned.

The flora of cliffs and rock slopes is, like the birdlife, distinct and attractive. Slopes appear rather bare at first glance, but on closer inspection they can be seen to support a wealth of wildflowers. They include various species that are restricted to this part of the world. The first that comes to mind is the flashy Rhodope endemic Haberlea – a remnant of the Tertiary era (see page 70), but both Dwarf and Reichenbach's Irises* (*Iris reichenbachii*) belong in this category too (see page 78 for a longer list of cliff flora).

## History

The Rhodopes and adjacent Thracian Plain have a very long and rich history of human settlement, dating back to at least the 7th millenium BC. There is evidence that present-day Plovdiv was already inhabited in the 6th millenium BC, making it older even than Athens or Rome. The Thracians settled the area in the 2nd millenium BC but it's not until the 5th century BC that we have any written information about them (and then only from Greek sources).

### The Thracian period
The area covered by this guide roughly coincides with the heartland of historic Thrace. We use the term 'heartland' because its boundaries never were precise and the region was, like most of southeast Europe, never very stable. The history of Thrace is complicated, in part, because there many different Thracian tribes and because they left no written evidence. The ancient historian Herodotus describes the Thracians as one of the most populous people and claims that if not for their constant feuding, the Thracians would be invincible.
After Greco-Persian wars in the early 5th century BC, the Rhodopes and Sakar became part of the Odrysian kingdom – the largest and most powerful Thracian realm and the first large political entity of the eastern Balkans. Throughout much of its early history the Odrysian kingdom was an ally of Athens and even joined the Peloponnesian War on its side. What knowledge we have about ancient Thrace largely dates back the 7th century BC when they are mentioned by Greek sources.
The Thracian tribes in the mountains were herdsmen and gold miners. The economic prospects of the many gold mines attracted people from all over the region, so the mountains were quite densely populated at the time. In fact, Europe's oldest known gold mine was located in Rhodope Mountains.

## HISTORY

Judging from Greek sources, the mountain tribes had a reputation for being barbaric, savage, disloyal and incapable of speaking decent Greek. The inhabitants of lowland Thrace (both on the coast and in the Thracian Plain) had a better reputation. They were seen as peaceful and sophisticated, besides being famous for their ability as horsemen, their military prowess, their craftsmanship in working with precious metals, their music and their poetry.

There are many Thracian remains throughout our region, in particular tombs. The Thracians honoured their leaders with burial rituals. The more important a person, then the more elaborate the burial site. All over the Eastern Rhodopes and Sakar there are dolmens. Most of them are just somewhere on a bushy slope out in the countryside, and one must develop an eye for them in order to recognize them as a Thracian remains. However, there are several of them that are close to the road and clearly signposted (e.g. route 21). A cliff on the shore of the Arda River contains hundreds of niches, most likely carved out by Thracians (route 8) and there are many more all along the Arda river valley.

A magnificent Thracian (and Byzantine) site is undoubtedly Perperikon near the town of Kardzhali (site C on page 183), which dates back to more than 1000 BC, much older than the first Greek arrivals. It is thought to be a town and place of worship and is considered the largest megalithic site in the Balkans. Later, it became a temple dedicated to Dionysos. Legend says that in 334 BC, the oracle of Perperikon famously prophesised that Alexander the Great would conquer the world. Nearby, Tatul (site D on page 183) and the tomb of Aleksandrovo are two other exquisite Thracian archealogical sites.

### The Roman and Byzantine empires

As prophesised, Alexander the Great did conquer the much of the then-known world including, around 340 BC, Thrace itself. After his death, the Odrysian kingdom revived, but the Roman influence increased and in the 1st century CE, Thrace became a Roman province (Thracia). It included today's European Turkey, coastal Greece and part of modern Bulgaria. The Thracian culture was (partially) romanised. Within our region Roman remains are found particularly in Plovdiv. Near Ivaylovgrad lie the

The Thracian Empire around 430 BC (in green). The thin grey lines show the present-day borders between Bulgaria, Greece and Turkey.

# HISTORY

Perperikon is one of the most important Thracian relicts.

ruins of a Roman villa (the Armira villa; route 13) and near the village of Dolni Glavanak (near Madzharovo) there is a Roman road.

In 395, the Roman Empire was divided into a Western and an Eastern Empire. Emperor Constantine, who is considered the founder of the eastern Roman Empire, moved his capital to Byzantion (or Byzantium) which was renamed Constantinople in his honour (now Istanbul). Hence Thrace then became a province that was near the centre of power. Most historical remains found today are from the Byzantine times.

## The Bulgarian Empires

Although the Goths had repeatedly attacked the Roman Empire in the 3rd century AD, during much of the 4th century, the border along the Danube between Rome and the Goths was stable and peaceful. It was, most likely, a change of climate deep in central Asia that sparked an event that changed this situation and so kindled the Bulgarian state. In short, a drought there worsened the living conditions of a local nomadic people, the Huns. They moved westwards and, being formidable warriors, pushed the peoples in western Asia into Europe to seek shelter within the Byzantine Empire. The Goths were one such group. The Goths were welcomed at first but being treated as second-class citizens, aggregated by famine, they soon started to revolt. The ensuing wars culminated in 378 with the battle of Adrianopolis (present-day Edirne).

The Goths were victorious and secured a degree of autonomy within the Byzantine Empire. In the years that ensued, the Byzantine Empire had increasing problems on all of its borders, but not too many in our region. The Goths and Romanised Thracians lived here with increasing

# HISTORY

numbers of Slavic tribes who settled here from more northerly areas. This changed in the 7th century when a new nomadic group started to migrate south-west from what is now Ukraine. The lands north of the Azov Sea were known as Great Bulgaria after the largely nomadic inhabitants, the Bulgars. In the late 7th century, the Bulgars moved into what is today called Bulgaria where they were absorbed by the local Slavic majority who they conquered. The Bulgarian Khan Asparuh (ruled 668–695) concluded a treaty with the Byzantine Emperor in 681, which recognised Bulgaria for the first time as an independent state.

By the 9th century, under Boris I, the Bulgarian elite had adopted Eastern Orthodox Christianity, aiding internal unity but at the price of increasing Byzantine influence. It was then too that St Cyril and St Methodius created Slavonic alphabet. Later, the Bulgarian Tsar Simeon I (893–927), who had studied in Constantinople, and the Byzantine Emperor started to quarrel. A series of disputes would eventually lead to the growth of the Bulgarian power at the cost of Byzantine land. Interestingly, the current borders between Bulgaria and European Turkey still reflect the borders between the Byzantine and Bulgarian powers (on either side of the border Edirne (Adrianopolis) and Plovdiv (Puldin) still remain important centres). The Rhodope mountains, although close to both seats of power, very much remained a borderland.

Under Tsar Simeon I, the Bulgarian Empire extended rapidly towards the north into Dacia (present-day Romania), the west (Serbia) and the south, where the Bulgarian tsar marched all the way to the Peloponnese. These victories were short-lived however, and in 1018 the empire dwindled and returned under Byzantine rule again. In 1204, in an act of unparalleled betrayal, the 4th Crusade plundered Constantinople and installed Count Baldwin of Flanders as Emperor, fatally weakening the rump of the Byzantine Empire. At the Second Battle of Adrianople (1205), the Bulgarians under Tsar Kaloyan (1196 -1207) crushed a force of Crusaders firmly establishing the Second Bulgarian Empire. The battle was fought near the castle ruins of Vulekon at Matochina (route 21) which date from this period. Under Kaloyan's nephew, Ivan Asen II (1218-1241), the Bulgarian Empire expanded and its power was consolidated ushering in another period of great cultural prosperity in the region. The town Asenovgrad and nearby Asen's Fort (route 15) are named after Ivan Asen II.

## The Ottomans

In the 13th century, Europe faced another crisis, probably induced by Central Asian climate change. Again, it led to westward migrations and

sparked war. This time it was the Mongols (later known as the Tartars) who moved rapidly westwards and turned central Europe into a bloody battlefield. In 1240 they swept into the Balkans and, although the Bulgarian Empire wasn't threatened directly, the war and unrest weakened the position of the country that already faced a crisis after Asen II's death (1241). In the end it were the Ottomans that took advantage of this.
The Ottomans invaded the region in 1352, striking a fatal blow to the dwindling Byzantine Empire, and conquering the Bulgarian Empire. By 1396 Bulgaria had become an Ottoman vassal state and confirmed the Ottomans as the ultimate power in the region. Although the capture of Constantinople occurred generations later in 1453, by then the great city and its empire was a shadow of its former self. The ethnic groups that populated the Thracian mountains converted to Islam and today this remains an important religion in the Rhodopes, as is witnessed by the many mosques all over the villages in the mountains.

From the 14th century onwards, the Ottoman Empire pushed deep into Europe, but the tide turned with their defeat at the gates of Vienna in 1683. After that, the power of the Ottoman Empire gradually waned but it wasn't until 1923 that the modern borders were established by the Treaty of Lausanne (see below).
The five centuries of Ottoman rule in the region, ended less than a century ago. It is no wonder that the Turkish influence on the local culture is still very strong (see also text box). Under the Ottomans, religion was more important than ethnicity in determining a person's status. A Muslim of Turkish descent had the same obligations and privileges as a Muslim of Bulgarian descent. Although the Ottomans probably did not impose Islam on the people, there were considerable privileges for Muslims, which, in part, explain the mass conversions to Islam that took place.
The final decades of the Ottoman Empire transformed Bulgaria. The anarchy that followed the gradual collapse of the empire at the end of the 18th and beginning of the 19th century was dangerous for the citizens of the region. Robbery and looting by (former) Turkish soldiers was commonplace and rekindled the Bulgarian nationalist spirit. This led to one of the darker pages in Bulgarian history: the April Uprising in 1876. This insurrection of Bulgarians against the Ottoman rulers was ruthlessly crushed. In particular, the Plovdiv area was badly hit by the bands of Bashi-bazouks, a type of irregular mercenary force raised by the Ottomans. They were known for their merciless violence – a reputation that was more than lived up to during the April Uprising.

HISTORY

> **A mix of peoples**
> One of the striking features of the Rhodopes is the mix of different peoples – Orthodox Christians and Muslims, ethnic Bulgarians, Turks and Roma. Each part of the mountains has its own mix of people, which greatly contributes to the different atmosphere in each of these areas.
> One thing to appreciate is that religious groups do not completely overlap with the ethnicity. Islamic people are an ethnically diverse bunch. During the Ottoman rule, most the local Bulgarian-Slavic people in the mountains converted to Islam and they are known as Pomaks. They are found throughout the mountains, but particularly in the valleys near Kirkovo in the Eastern Rhodopes (route 12) and Trigrad and Smolyan in the Western Rhodopes. Additionally, there are many other Muslim peoples, consisting mainly of Turkic groups (for example Karaman and Shia). What they mostly have in common is that they have more liberal cultural and religious habits than what is generally regarded as 'Muslim'. For example, the Bulgarian Muslims don't necessarily follow religious prohibitions on drinking alcohol or eating pork.
> In the lowlands, people of Bulgarian descent are more typically Christian-Orthodox with, besides the main cities, the Bachkovo monastery near Asenovgrad being a major centre.
> The Ottoman Empire was huge and did not come about without bloodshed. One strategy to subjugate unruly people was to forcefully move them from one end of the empire to the other. This way, people of Turkish descent from the eastern part of the Ottoman Empire were actively deported to the Rhodopes, where over centuries, they became part of the mix of peoples of the Rhodopes. These Turkish descendants are found a lot around Kardzhali and Momchilgrad. Originally, they formed the main inhabitants of the small villages and hamlets scattered in the mountains here. In recent decades, many of them have moved to the towns in the region. Kardzhali especially has a thriving Muslim community of people of Turkish descent.
> Additionally, there are many more (traces of) other ethnicities in the region, ranging from Roma to Albanian, Greek and even Georgian peoples. In short – this is a fascinating region, not only for its wildlife but also for its people.

There were protests at this all over Europe against ruthless Ottoman repression of the Bulgarians (between 30,000 and 100,000 were massacred). The strongest and most concrete response, however, didn't come from western Europe but from Russia which regarded itself as the leader of the Pan-Slavism movement. Russia started the Russo-Turkish war in a coalition with Slavic Ottoman vassal states - Bulgaria, Romania, Serbia and Montenegro. Russia and the Balkans states won and the Ottomans withdrew. The new lines on the map were made official in the San Stefano treaty in 1878 on March 3 – Liberation Day in Bulgaria.

## The Rhodopes as a border land
Instead of peace, a new period of turmoil began, known as the Balkan Wars. In the First Balkan War (Oct. 1912-May 1913), the Balkan League (Bulgaria, Serbia, Greece and Montenegro) defeated the Turks who surrendered much of its territory in Europe. It was in this period that many Muslims of Turkish descent left Bulgaria. This had a big impact across the Rhodopes, especially in the Western Rhodopes. During the Ottoman period, the Western Rhodopes had a much more open landscape, with meadows and karstic grasslands, grazed by cows and sheep. Forests were mainly inaccessible, or in areas set aside as hunting reserve by the nobility, or remained untouched because there was a place of worship nearby. This radically changed during the Balkan Wars. With the disappearance of the farmers and their herds, the grasslands turned to forests.
In the Second Balkan War, Bulgaria and Greece found themselves at loggerheads. In the outcome of this war, Bulgaria was defeated by a combination of Greek, Serbian, Romanian and Turkish forces, and had to give up a large part of its territory. In the First World War, which followed right after the second Balkan War, Bulgaria sided with Germany and Austria-Hungary. During the Second World War, Germany forced Bulgaria to ally with them. After WWII, Bulgaria came in the Russian-communist sphere of influence. Greece on the other hand, sided with the western allied forces in WWII and later came under the American-capitalist sphere of influence. In short, from the second Balkan War in 1913 up until the fall of the Iron Curtain in 1989, Greece and Bulgaria were most of the time part of opposing power blocs – their border running right across the high ridge of the Rhodope mountains. This is quite a contrast with all the time before, when the Rhodopes were a mountain range within an empire, whether it being Thracian, Roman, Byzantine, Bulgarian or Ottoman.

## Traditional life and land use
Before turning the page to the next chapter in Rhodopean history, it is good to take stock and look at what the region looked like at the beginning of the 20th century.
During most of the Ottoman rule and afterwards, the Rhodope life was a rural one. Small hamlets were dotted over the scarcely accessible countryside, and for the larger part, the economic activity consisted of livestock rearing and crop growing.

## HISTORY

The people that have lived here over the last centuries were a colourful mixture of Slavic and Turkish ethnicities (see page 54). During the summers, they took their flocks of sheep and herds of goats and cattle up into the mountains. In winter, they stayed at one place and fed their livestock with branches that had been cut from the trees. Trees were pollarded for centuries to provide pasture for livestock and to provide both fodder and firewood, and were scattered in the pastures. The gentler hillsides and ridges were heavily grazed, resulting in open patches and meadows, whereas the steeper hillsides, especially those facing north, were clad in thick woodland – this pattern is still visible today.
Traditionally in the Rhodopes, like in many parts of Europe until relatively recently, cattle roamed free and unrestricted by fences. What is special about the Rhodopes is that, unlike elsewhere, this tradition continues. As you drive the backroads of the Eastern Rhodopes you'll soon notice cows standing lazily by the road (although this is less pronounced in the Western Rhodopes). The cows simply fend for themselves, staying in small family groups. Some return to the farmhouse in the evening, lured by some fresh hay, but others remain in the mountains.
There, the cows both browse in the forests and graze the grassy and bushy slopes, and are a natural sculptor of the mountain landscape. Locally (often near farms), woodlands are overgrazed, but elsewhere they are undergrazed and everything in between, creating, with help from wild animals, a wonderful, natural patchwork of more open landscapes, which combined provide a home to a rich wildlife. There are various breeds of cattle in these mountains, but the most common one is endemic to this region: the Rhodopean Shorthorn.
The broad river valleys and fertile hills in the Thracian Plain have a perfect climate and soil for growing crops. Together with the Danubian plains, this is the main agricultural region of Bulgaria. Since ancient times, wheat, barley and millet have been the main cereal crops. From the 13th century onwards, grapes, fruit orchards and vegetables gradually became more important. In the mountains and foothills, crops were grown on a smaller scale. Tobacco became an important cash crop. Especially in the mountains many households depended on tobacco for their income. For a long period, silk production was another important economic pillar in the mountains. Cattle rearing however, was the main agricultural activity.
At the end of the 19th and the beginning of the 20th century, the landscape of both the Western and Eastern Rhodopes was very different than it is today. Over the entire mountain range, there were less forests and a lot more pastures. The density of both people and livestock was higher

# HISTORY

during the Ottoman period than it is today. The salient landscape story of the 20th century is one of people moving away, particularly farmers, and one of scrubland and forest returning. This exodus of people and change in agriculture did not happen all at once but in a series of events, each for their own reasons.

One important moment was the collapse of the Ottoman Empire in the first Balkan War. During the Ottoman rule, there was no strict border between the Aegean lowlands and the mountains, and a system of transhumance existed, particularly in the Western Rhodopes. Transhumance is the seasonal migration of livestock from the summer pastures in the mountains to the winter pastures in the lowlands. It made it possible to keep large numbers of animals. When there is snow in the mountains, it is the growing season in the coastal plain. When the food runs out in the lowlands, the meadows in the mountains are juicy and nutritious again, so people and livestock moved up the mountains again.

When the Turks were defeated and the Christian forces took over, part of the Muslim population left the mountains, fearing to be associated with the former Ottoman rulers. At the same time, the new borders were formed, cutting off the transhumance drover routes between the mountains and the lowlands. Transhumance became impossible, which was a blow to the stock breeders in the higher mountains, who had keep the animals in stables and feed them with hay – a much more costly affair.

All in all, many farmers abandoned their fields and meadows and many of today's forests grow where once their cattle grazed.

Traditional agriculture is not just a means to support a rich biodiversity; it is also part of a rich culture that is valuable in its own right. These haystacks are placed on poles to prevent feral cattle from reaching it – a typical practice in the Kirkovo region.

## The Rhodopes in communist times

After the Second World War, Bulgaria further developed in a communist regime under Soviet influence. Over a short period, many things changed

# HISTORY

radically in the Rhodopes, and they did so in two opposite ways. On the one hand, the Rhodopes became a fortified border region. Along a broad strip on either side of the border, people other than the military were not allowed. For wildlife, especially the bigger animals, this depopulated zone allowed populations to increase. Woodlands that would elsewhere be exploited, were able to develop towards old-growth woodlands. This is how the Beech forest of the Gyumyurdzhinski Snezhnik reserve (route 12), maintained its pristine state.

Under communist rule, agriculture was centralised and, where possible, expanded. Dams and reservoirs were created in the Arda River to produce electricity. Since studies found that erosion would cause the reservoirs to silt up, a huge re-afforestation programme, using non-native conifers, was implemented to resolve this problem. Today, you can still see these dull pine plantations in some places of the Eastern Rhodopes. Most of them are dying, as the climate is unsuitable for them (and is getting worse as the climate is changing).

Extremely old, pollarded trees in a much younger forest, such as this superb Hornbeam are a sign that this land was much more intensely used than it is today.

The new centralised agricultural regime made it increasingly hard to earn a living by traditional livestock rearing. The oncelarge herds further diminished and many open grasslands became overgrown with shrubs and ultimately turned into young oak forest. This is also the landscape you see everywhere today in the Eastern Rhodopes – a transition from open pastures to scrubland and woodland. At present, this mosaic makes it a truly rich region in terms of wildlife and biodiversity. However, woodland is growing at the cost of open landscapes and threatens this diversity. It is with this in mind that the Rewilding Rhodopes project aims to go back to grazing animals, both wild and domesticated, in the Eastern Rhodopes. In this way, these mountains can retain their unique mosaic landscape and the biodiversity that comes with it.

The communists created large ore mines in the Rhodopes. Zinc, lead, copper and other metals were mined on an industrial scale up until the 1990's. Mining is what made Madzharovo, with the subsequent abandonment of the industry, the near-ghost town it is today.

## The EU and the free market

Drive down the A1 from Sofia to Haskovo and you are greeted with an endless row of billboards that make it clear that Bulgaria has embraced the free market with enthusiasm. Many of them advertise agricultural machinery, from drones and combines to fertilizers and pesticides. The ideology of a modern, rational and centrally planned agriculture was a pillar of communism, but it was taken to a next level when Bulgaria entered the EU. The Thracian plains have been largely converted to large crop fields. Although these retain a richer biodiversity than its counterparts in western Europe, the wildlife of the plains is under great strain.

### Madzharovo – a communist mining town

The small town of Madzharovo is right at the touristic heart of the Eastern Rhodopes. It is the logical first base for any nature-minded visitor. It is, however, quite easy to stay in the accommodation somewhere around the town and never really visit the place itself. And that would be a great shame, as Madzharovo is likely to be one of the strangest places you've ever visited.

First there is the setting: spectacularly located within an old caldera whose remains form the mountains and cliffs that surround the town. It sits close to, but not quite on, what is probably the most scenic stretch of the Arda river. It just couldn't be better. And then there is the town: a small collection of drab communist flats, most of them deserted, some of them derelict state. There is a bar, hotel and even a dance club, all of which look as if no-one has set foot in them in 20 years. At night, wildlife takes over Madzharovo, with Scops Owls everywhere and Jackals roaming the streets. Madzharovo looks like a little Chernobyl set in a scenic mountainscape... until you pass the high school, which looks shiny and new, with happy kids shooting hoops on a fancy blue-floored basketball court. What is going on here?!

Madzharovo was in the communist days a lively mining town of approximately 10,000 inhabitants, all living in the few blocks of flats that together make up Madzharovo. The people all worked in the lead and zinc mines, but they closed down in 1997 and today the population has shrunk to fewer than 700 people. Nonetheless, it remains the administrative centre of the region and as such it has a school where the youth of all surrounding villages attend. Since Bulgaria entered the EU, the school, being the only one in the municipality, obtained a special protected status and funding, which explains the rather unexpected state-of-the-art building in the middle of a near-abandoned town.

## NATURE CONSERVATION

One of the problems (from an ecological point of view) is the ploughing of the grazing ground, made possible as more and more land change from communal to private ownership. The sheep and the susliks both need this communal grazing ground, and with them comes an entire ecosystem from wildflowers to birds of prey.

Sadly, the EU subsidies play a dubious role. On the one hand, Europe provides money for nature conservation, but on the other hand it also finances (with a much bigger purse) the ploughing of grazing land and (in the Rhodopes) the mass clearing of scrub. Much of the conservation money is spent minimise the problems caused by other EU funds!

In the mountains, grazing is an issue too, but here, fortunately, most of the land has not been privatised. One of the great perks of the Rhodopes, in fact of pretty much all mountains in Eastern Europe, is the near absence of fences. With the exception of some sensitive ecological sites, you are free to go as you like in the countryside. Just park besides the road where it looks good and stroll into the pastures or the woodlands. In that sense, this really is the land of the free – who would have guessed that as a heritage of the communist era!

## Nature Conservation

The Eastern Rhodopes is one of those European regions where the rich landscape of traditional grazing and wood cutting – activities that have over centuries greatly enhanced biodiversity – has been well preserved. But this is not to say that the big changes in the 20th century have left the region unaffected. The creation of reservoirs has destroyed part of the Arda river and surrounding lands. The planting of pine woods, instead of native woodlands, takes yet another bite out of the pristine fabric of the Eastern Rhodopes. Fortunately, there are no plans for new plantations. However, there are plans for big wind turbine parks on the mountain peaks on both sides of the border. These parks present a particularly tricky problem for conservationists, on the one hand, the increasing use of renewable energy sources is to be applauded, but, on the other hand, the chosen locations have a very negative effect on birds of prey, migratory birds and bats. They are also such a blemish on the natural landscape, that they provide a key focal point for Bulgarian conservationists.

Power lines are another major threat to birds in general and raptors in particular. An investigation carried out by the Bulgarian Society for the Protection of Birds (BSPB) found that whilst White Storks and Common

## NATURE CONSERVATION

Buzzards were the main victims, globally threatened species such as Egyptian Vulture and Imperial Eagle were also electrocuted. Finally, hunting and poaching continues to be a big problem. Poisoning also happens although it is not as big a problem as across the border in Greece where in 2010 the entire Griffon Vulture and Golden Eagle populations in the Nestos gorge were wiped out by illegal poisoned bait. This was shocking news, but the explanation behind this act made it even worse: it wasn't even meant to kill the birds, but wolves.

Indeed, herdsmen on both sides of the border see Wolves as important enemies of livestock, and poisoned bait is regarded as a good way to get rid of them. Eagles and vultures are collateral damage. There are already compensation schemes for damage to livestock in place, but they are either not sufficient, not adequate or not well enough known. Despite damage being hardly reported, poisoning is still taking place.

### Nature conservation efforts

In Bulgaria almost 34 percent of the land is currently protected in the Natura 2000 network of protected areas. After Slovenia and Croatia, this is the highest amount in the European Union!

As far as the Eastern Rhodopes are concerned, many parts of the region are also under official Natura 2000 protection. Great stretches of the Arda river system and that of the Byala Reka are covered by Natura 2000 and are nationally protected areas as well.

Various national and foreign nature organisations are active in the

Traditional grazing with sheep has diminished enormously and with it, wildlife is disappearing too. In particular the species of steppe-like landscapes, such as Susliks and birds of prey are under pressure.

**LANDSCAPE**

## NATURE CONSERVATION

region, including WWF, Green Balkans, BSPB and Rewilding Rhodopes. We teamed up with the latter to write this guidebook. The BSPB/BirdLife is fighting for a more sensible deployment of wind energy and opposes the building of wind turbines in the areas key for birds. The organisation was very successful in their efforts to recover the vulture population in the Rhodopes. The population of Griffon Vultures increased from about 15 pairs to more than 110 pairs and the Egyptian Vulture population stabilised. Black vultures are being reintroduced in 2022-23 by Rewilding Rhodopes (see text box).

In collaboration with the power grid operator EVN and with support from the EU LIFE program, BSPB/Birdlife insulated thousands of dangerous electricity poles in Eastern Rhodopes and Sakar thus contributing to the recovery of the national Imperial Eagle population from about 15 to 41 pairs.

In 2022, BSPB/BirdLife started a large forest and grassland restoration project along the Green belt from Eastern Rhodopes to the Black Sea supported by the Cambridge based Endangered Landscape Program. In Sakar, the Green Balkans works together with the German-European NGO EuroNatur in a project to reintroduce and secure the population of Lesser Kestrels.

Rewilding Rhodopes works in the Eastern Rhodopes where it develops sustainable initiatives that promote and combine nature conservation, green business and education. This is an encompassing approach, typical of rewilding projects in general: the notion that a robust and healthy ecosystem ('wild nature' in terms of Rewilding Rhodopes) should be the basis of a sustainable society and actually supports the economy, culture and general well-being of the people that live in and visit the area. Supported by Rewilding Europe, the Rewilding Rhodopes does all of its work with local stakeholders, be they hunters, farmers, the tourism business,

In order to retain the traditionally grazed landscape, Rewilding Rhodopes has brought back different species of grazing animals. The impressive European Bison roams the Eastern Rhodopes again since 2013 and can, with a little luck, be seen in the mountains near Potochnitsa (route 9).

## NATURE CONSERVATION

officials or a combination of them. One focus is on restoring the grazing regime that once sustained the patchwork landscape of the Rhodopes. With the (gradual) disappearance of the herds of sheep and – to lesser extent – cattle, Rewilding Rhodopes turns to wild grazers to supplement the domesticated grazers. Red Deer, Konik Horses and European Bison have been introduced, which, combined, will maintain the semi-open landscape and in the meantime provide an income in the form of hunting and ecotourism. The grazers also create a niche for predators and scavengers like vultures and eagles which, in turn, also improves the region's attraction as a tourism destination. It is this kind of interplay between people and their surroundings that create a mutual benefit that enables both people and wildlife to thrive.

Ecotourism – that means you – is thus one of the trump cards of nature conservation in the region. It gives value to nature, economically by generating income for the local communities and ethically and culturally by showing that nature has an intrinsic value – a value that is great enough to draw visitors from all over Europe to the region. On page 258 you can see what you can do to support conservation of the area.

**Rewilding Rhodopes**
The non-profit organization Rewilding Rhodopes strives to support and strengthen the region's biodiversity. One of the threats that face the Eastern Rhodopes is the gradual encroachment of shrubs and forests due to the decrease of livestock. Therefore, Rewilding Rhodopes is introducing various species of native grazing animals which together should maintain a half-open landscape.
The Rewilding Rhodopes' team has reintroduced over 50 Red Deer and 600 Fallow Deer. In 2011, the first twelve Konik Horses were set free in the mountains. Currently over 100 Wild Horses roam the slopes (of both the Konik and Karakachan race). Similarly in 2013, a small herd of five European Bison was brought to the area of Studen Kladenets. Ten years later their population has grown to 16. Currently, the team is analysing grazing practices in the Eastern Rhodopes and preparing recommendations for more sustainable grazing systems.
Between 2016 and 2021, as part of a LIFE project, Rewilding Rhodopes together with Bulgarian and Greek partners worked on stabilizing and growing the Griffon Vulture population in the Rhodope Mountains. Building upon that experience in 2022 the organization released 14 Black Vultures, as part of a new long-term reintroduction programme that aims to establish a second colony of Black Vultures on the Balkans, besides the one that is present in the Greek Dadia forest.

# FLORA AND FAUNA

The flora and fauna of the Eastern Rhodopes, Sakar and the Thracian Plain form one big, fascinating cabinet of natural curiosities, comprising many species unfamiliar to most Europeans. There are, of course, the raptors and vultures for which the area is famous, but you can also come across subterranean worm-like lizards, curiously shaped orchids, hill-roaming jackals, dwarf irises, paradisiac lilies, gigantic predatory bush crickets and a myriad of other strange insects. If the oddities of this part of the world were presented in a single catalogue, you'd be amazed by such diversity of life in such a small area.

There is no single reason explaining this abundance, but the varied topography certainly is one positive contributor. On the one hand, there are rugged hills and mountains with large forests and cliffs of an overall impenetrable and wild character and on the other, there are open plains. These consist of fertile soils that support numerous different species providing prey for the many raptors. The wide range of habitats, from wetlands to scrubland, various types of forest, karstic plains and agricultural land, offer a home to a wide variety of species.

One major factor that positively influences the natural diversity of the region is its position in the contact zone of several of the main biological regions. The Rhodope Mountains support plants and animals that are well-known throughout central Europe (like Beech trees and Fire Salamanders for example). Higher up in these mountains, you encounter sub-alpine boreal species; those that are typical of the coniferous forest zone of the central European mountains and northern Europe. Examples are Capercaillie, Ghost Orchid and the Apollo Butterfly). If you look carefully, you'll find many other species in these realms that are unique to the Balkan countries. Particularly among the flora and insect fauna, there are many uniquely Balkan species, such as and the Balkan Fir* (*Abies borisii-regis*) and the Rhodope Avens* (*Geum rhodopeum*). A few of them are even restricted to the Rhodopes themselves, such as the Bulgarian Emerald (a dragonfly) and the Rhodope Lily.

Species of open woodlands and small-scale agricultural land, such as this Hoopoe, do well in the Rhodopes.

INTRO

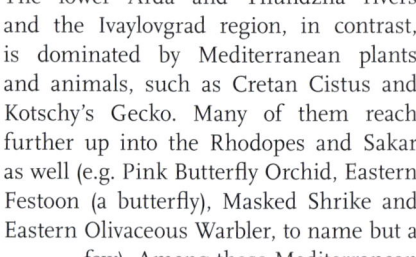

The lower Arda and Thundzha rivers and the Ivaylovgrad region, in contrast, is dominated by Mediterranean plants and animals, such as Cretan Cistus and Kotschy's Gecko. Many of them reach further up into the Rhodopes and Sakar as well (e.g. Pink Butterfly Orchid, Eastern Festoon (a butterfly), Masked Shrike and Eastern Olivaceous Warbler, to name but a few). Among these Mediterranean species are several distinctly eastern ones, which just reach this region. Examples are highlights like Bronze Bush-cricket, Sand Boa and Spurred Helleborine (an orchid).

And then there is the Pontic element – species proper to the steppes and steppe woodlands of the Black Sea region and further east. The 'Pontics' are the cherry on an already pretty well decorated cake, and include the likes of Suslik, Isabelline Wheatear and both pelicans. Time to dig in!

In the Rhodope Mountains, various biogeographical regions meet. It is here that you can find together the Red-back Shrike of central Europe (top), the Lesser Grey Shrike of eastern Europe (second), the Woodchat Shrike of southern Europe (third) and the Masked Shrike of southeastern Europe.

## CLIMATE HISTORY AND SPECIATION

**Temperate European**
Yellow-bellied Toad
*Bombina variegata*
Brooks, pools

**Pontic**
Suslik
*Spermophilus citellus*
Deep-soil Steppes

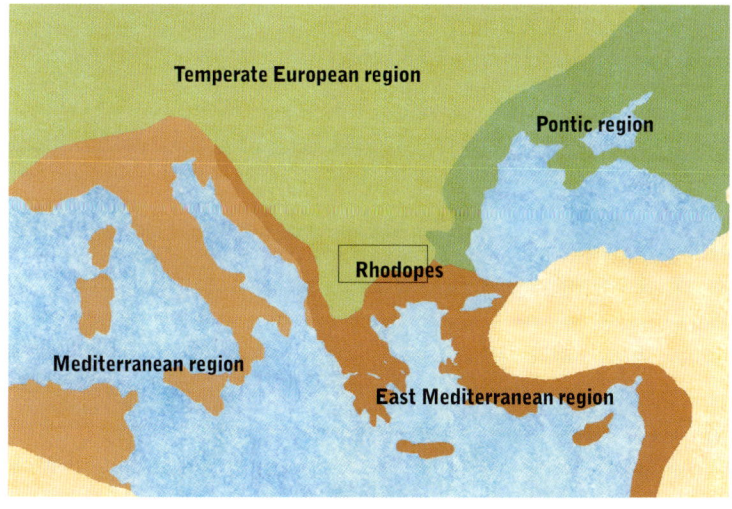

**Alpine**
Apollo
*Parnassius apollo*
Karst plateaux

**East Mediterranean**
Olive-tree Warbler
*Hippolais olivetorum*
Christ-thorn scrub

**Rhodopes Endemic**
Rhodope Lily
*Lilium rhodopaeum*
Subalpine meadows

**FLORA AND FAUNA**

## Flora

> Routes 1, 3, 4, 8, 23 and 24 and site E on page 224 have an attractive flora of lowland scrub, rocky grasslands and warm oak woodlands. Additionally, routes 23 and 24 and the sites B an C on pages 194 consist largely or partly of warm limestone slopes, with an excellent flora, containing all sorts of steppe plants and many orchids. In the Western Rhodopes, routes, 16, 17, 18 and 19, plus sites A and E on pages 222 and 224 are of particular botanical interest.

Close your eyes and imagine open, sun-speckled forest floors, grass-fringed streams, dotted with fritillaries and wild tulips. Further on, there is some warm, rocky scrubland, covered with a blanket of pinks, anemones, orchids, toadflaxes, asphodels, grape-hyacinths and other wildflowers. Now add a cliff face laden with colourful irises and Haberlea and you have a pretty accurate image of the flora in the Eastern Rhodopes during spring (April-May). Of course, it is not so idyllic in other seasons, but from late March to mid-June, the region has a lot to offer. Further into summer, the wildflower show carries on in mountain grasslands in the Western Rhodopes.

In terms of botanical species, the Rhodopes are among the richer areas in Bulgaria. However, until quite recently, information on this region was very limited due to its remoteness from the centres of botanical science, the difficulty of access and the poor infrastructure.

Today, the region rejoices in an increased level of attention, and new populations of wildflowers are regularly found. Bulgarian botanists now turn their attention to another, up until recently very little visited area: Sakar. Sakar has a lower diversity than the Rhodopes, but being right on the edge of the Pontic (steppic) and Mediterranean realms it has a unique microclimate and is poorly studied, making it easy to find new things. One such recent discovery was the pretty toadflax *Veronica multifida*, a rare species that extends from Iran over northern Turkey and just reaches Sakar (see route 23).

The fact the flora is still so unknown makes this region an exciting one for wildflower hunting. There is still so much to discover! Unfortunately, it also means that there are few good books on the area which makes a study of the area difficult (see page 260 for suggestions on literature).

In this chapter, we focus on those species that are unique, striking or commonly encountered, with special emphasis on those species that can be identified with the present literature. In the boxes at the end of each par-

## FLORA

agraph, we give a more detailed list of species present. Still, this is but a small cross-section of what you might find.

The flora is a mixture of species from various ecoregions (see page 67) including those predominantly found in temperate Europe, the east and those belonging to the Mediterranean region. Most numerous are plants that are typical for the transition zone between the Mediterranean and temperate European flora – the so-called sub-Mediterranean species. True Mediterranean vegetation, such as evergreen forests and maquis, is not found in the region, but does occur nearby, on the southern foothills of the Rhodopes in Greece. A good number of species that thrive in such vegetation do make their way into southern Bulgaria though, as is evidenced by the occurrence of Mediterranean orchids like Horned Woodcock Orchid and Long-lipped Tongue Orchid (see page 82).

The flora of the region is supplemented with plants from two other botanical regions. The first are wildflowers that are found in Balkan mountain chains. These are – predictably – found in forests, meadows and pastures higher up in the mountains. The second set of wildflowers to spice up the flora is that of the Pontic and the Anatolian (steppe) region. Plants belonging to this botanical region are mostly present in the lowlands and Sakar.

It is amazing what a colourful show of wildflowers the thin volcanic soils manage to produce. But to appreciate it, you need to be here in spring.

## FLORA

### Special plant species of the Rhodope Mountains

Many of the most remarkable plants are endemic to the region. These species are found only in the southern Balkans or even smaller ranges, such as the Eastern and Western Rhodopes. The vast majority of them belong to familiar plant families like aster (*Asteraceae*) and pea family (*Fabaceae*).

#### Haberlea (*Haberlea rhodopensis*)

is a special kind of endemic. The plant, one of the few relatives of the *Gesneria* family in Europe, is a survivor of the Tertiary period. During this era, when a subtropical climate dominated the region, it grew in many parts of Europe and Asia, but it disappeared at the beginning of the ice ages. Haberlea managed to survive in secluded warm gorges on limestone soils using the special survival technique called 'anabiosis' or 'fake death'. For exceptionally long periods, the plant is able to stop growing without dying off. When

growing conditions are more propitious, it can completely revitalise as if it never experienced such a harsh environment. Haberlea is locally common in the Eastern Rhodopes, but only found on northern exposed, calcareous and volcanic cliffs.

#### Rhodopean Toothwort (*Lathraea rhodopea*)

is a South Balkan endemic preferring damp forests. This beautiful pink flowering plant, belonging to the broomrape family, is a parasite which attaches itself onto the roots of other plants. The plant lacks green leaves completely, and obtains its nutrients from the host.

**Rhodope Lily (*Lilium rhodopaeum*)** endemic to the beech forests of the Rhodopes, is a flashy species with big yellow flowers. Most occur in the western Rhodopes, but even here it is largely confined to a few populations, mostly in the eastern half of the Western Rhodopes, close to the Greek border.

**Three-lobed Crabapple (*Eriolobus trilobatus*)** is one of the rarest trees occurring in Greece and Bulgaria. The small tree is found in open, mixed pine and oak woodlands. The East Mediterranean species extends from Lebanon, through Minor Asia into Europe, where it is restricted to the Eastern Rhodopes and adjacent Greece.

## Flora of sub-Mediterranean scrubland and open woodland

A sub-mediterranean scrubland and woodland dominate the hills of the Eastern Rhodopes. Besides the many oaks found here (see page 28) there are plenty of other shrubs and bushes. In fact, there are few places in Europe with such a diversity of wild shrubs and small trees. Common species you'll encounter here are Wild Lilac, Wild Jasmine, Christ's-thorn, Cretan Cistus, Montpellier Maple, Smoke-tree, Judas Tree and Turpentine Tree.

The closed oak forests often have a very rich understory. In spring thousands of Perfoliate Alexanders and Common Grape-hyacinth colour the forest floor. Drifts of bright pink Peacock Anemones form a cheerful note, but for the delicate green bells of the Pontic Fritillary, you'll need to search a little harder. Not that this is a rare species, quite the contrary – it is just that it is an inconspicuous plant.

As a plant-hunting habitat, the oak forests pose a daunting task, for they are extensive and many parts are, quite frankly, not that exciting. This is because most woodlands are young, shrubby and dense. The most attractive wildflowers grow in the older, more developed parts, especially where

FLORA

Wandering Peony is quite frequent in open oak forests (top). Grecian Foxglove is a south-east European species that is quite common in all sorts of bushy places (bottom).

the undergrowth is regularly cleared. Typical spring wildflowers here are Laxmann's Bugle* (*Ajuga laxmannii*), Wandering Peony* (*Peonia peregrina*), Rose Campion and the local relative of the Spring Pea. Usually, there are orchids around as well, especially on the little glades that are so numerous in these woods. White and Narrow-leaved Helleborine and Monkey, Lady, Roman and Violet Bird's-nest Orchids are the most frequently encountered.

Roadsides and glades in the forests are the realm of a dazzling number of mulleins (*Verbascum*). This region is a hotspot for different species of this group but it takes an expert eye to tell all the different species and microspecies apart. Later in spring, the Grecian Foxglove becomes a very common sight in open patches in the forest. This species, endemic to south-eastern Europe, is easy to recognise, being the only foxglove with greenish-white flowers.

## Flora of dry grasslands and fields

The woodlands seamlessly merge into dry grasslands and vice versa, creating the mosaic landscape that is so typical of the lower parts of the Rhodopes. The flora just as fluently changes in composition, with the shade-loving woodland plants gradually making way for the drought-tolerant and heat-loving grassland species.

> **Typical species of scrubland and open woodland**
> **Trees and shrubs** Prickly Juniper (*Juniperus oxycedrus*), Judas Tree (*Cercis siliquastrum*), Smoke-tree (*Cotinus coggygria*), Silver Linden (*Tilia tomentosa*), Cretan Cistus (*Cistus creticus*), Christ's-thorn (*Paliurus spina-christi*), Oriental Hornbeam (*Carpinus orientalis*), Almond-leaved Pear (*Pyrus spinosa*), Turpentine Tree (*Pistacia terebinthus*) Hungarian Oak (*Quercus frainetto*), Sessile Oak (*Quercus petraea*), Turkey Oak (*Quercus cerris*), Manna Ash (*Fraxinus ornus*), Bladder Senna (*Colutea arborescens*), Oriental Hornbeam (*Carpinus orientalis*), Hop Hornbeam (*Ostrya carpinifolia*), Montpellier Maple (*Acer monspessulanum*), Wild Service-tree (*Sorbus torminalis*), Wild Jasmine (*Jasminum fruticans*), Wild Lilac (*Syringa vulgaria*)
> **Herbs** Peacock Anemone (*Anemone pavonina*), Wandering Peony* (*Paeonia peregrina*), Purple Clematis (*Clematis viticella*), Ivy-leaved Sowbread (*Cyclamen hederifolium*), Pale Birthwort (*Aristolochia pallida*), Rose Campion (*Lychnis coronaria*), Perfoliate Alexanders (*Smyrnium perfoliatum*), Orlaya (*Orlaya grandiflora*), Creeping St. John's-wort* (*Hypericum cerastoides*), Cowslip (*Primula veris*), Red-topped Sage (*Salvia viridis*), Laxmann's Bugle* (*Ajuga laxmannii*), Grecian Foxglove (*Digitalis lanata*), Purple Gromwell (*Buglossoides purpurocaerulea*), Yellow Gromwell (*Neatostema apulum*), Knautia orientalis, Tassle Hyacinth (*Muscari comosum*), Common Grape-hyacinth (*Muscari neglectum*), Yellow Asphodel (*Asphodeline lutea*), Lesser Yellow Asphodel (*Asphodeline liburnica*), Pontic Fritillary (*Fritillaria pontica*), Roman Orchid (*Dactylorhiza romana*), Early-purple Orchid (*Orchis pinetorum*), Balkan Lizard Orchid* (*Himantoglossum caprinum*), Pink Butterfly Orchid (*Anacamptis papilionacea*), Narrow-leaved Helleborine (*Cephalanthera longifolia*), Mammose Orchid (*Ophrys mammosa*)

Your average thin-soiled grassland sports a variety of stonecrops, thymes and pinks. Proliferous Pink, Common Grape-hyacinth and Tassel Hyacinth are common, Creeping St. John's-wort* (*Hypericum cerastoides*), the sheep's-bit scabious *Jasione heldreichii* and the familiar Cornflower which occurs here in its natural habitat. Later in spring, you'll encounter masses of Orlaya, Yellow Scabious and *Knautia orientalis*, which at first glance doesn't look like a scabious at all (see photo on page 79). Two common herbs from the borage family are Yellow Gromwell (with small yellow flowers) and the purple Dyer's Alkanet. A little easier are the various species of yarrow (*Achillea*), both white and yellow-flowered, and most with woolly leaves and stems – and adaptation to drought. All these are conspicuous spring flowers, but are, of course, just the tip of the botanical iceberg.

Species-rich dry grasslands are natural habitats in both the Pontic and Mediterranean ecoregions, where the hot and dry summers combined

**FLORA**

Old oak forests which' undergrowth is regularly cleared (bottom), boast a very attractive flora. Drifts of Peacock Anemones (top) are usually found here.

with the high grazing pressure is tough on trees and shrubs, leaving grasslands as a natural climax vegetation. The Mediterranean grassland plants are largely dormant during summer but grow in winter, while the continental Pontic species are dormant in winter and are able to withstand the hot summers. Since the Eastern Rhodopes and Sakar are where these two biomes meet, you'll find Mediterranean and Pontic species together. What grows where depends greatly on the type of bedrock and on how much topsoil lies on top of it. In many places, there is more rock than soil on the surface, and the flora has more in keeping with a rock garden than with a grassland.

Deeper soils, which can be found scattered through the region, sport a different flora. It is here that you may encounter orchids like Pink Butterfly and Green-winged Orchids, and, less frequently, Three-toothed, Mammose, Horned and Monkey Orchids (especially on limestone soil). Another species very often found here is the deep red Sainfoin Milk-vetch* (*Astragalus onobrychis*) and the large, pink-flowered milkwort *Polygala anatolica*.

Roadsides offer a special type of grassland, somewhat similar to the grasslands with deeper soils. Here you'll find, besides the afore-mentioned mulleins and Orlaya, several sages. The small Red-topped Sage is a very common along roads in steppe-like areas, where it often grows together with the large and showy Clary Sage. More locally, you'll encounter Silver Sage (with very large, white flowers) and Mediterranean Sage (small white flowers). The tall but small-flowered Italian Viper's-bugloss is another typical roadside plant. The roadsides are again a good place to look for orchids, especially in limestone areas. Balkan Lizard, Monkey, Pink Butterfly and Mammose Orchids are the most usual species in the lowlands.

In many ways, the flora of thin grasslands resembles

## FLORA

that of arable fields, which is quite understandable when you visit these places in summer and see how relentlessly the sun scorches and desiccates the thin layer of soil. These conditions favour annual plants which finish their growth cycle in spring and survive the summer as seeds. This is a similar strategy to that required in fields that are chopped up and ploughed every year. Indeed, these soils are the natural home of those flowers we have come to associate with man-made habitats like fields and waste places. Fields are interesting areas for wildflower hunting even though most of them belong to common species that are widespread in the Balkan and (eastern) Mediterranean region. They are the pioneers – specialists in the quick colonisation of vacant gaps in the vegetation. They are capable of swift, widespread dispersal and have a short life cycle that can be completed before bigger, more competitive plants arrive. However, fields are in a perpetual open state, so pioneer plants can quickly and massively disperse over large areas.

The flora of the fields contains many strikingly colourful plants. Poppies can turn entire fields deep red. The 'default species' in the region is the Common Poppy which is found throughout Europe but is much more brightly coloured here.

Some fields may have a yellow wash that one usually associates with buttercups. Upon closer inspection, however, this turns out to be Hypecoum, an odd-looking relative of the poppy family, which is confined to the Mediterranean and Pontic regions. It often grows alongside Large Venus's-looking-glass, a species of arable fields that has become rare in western Europe.

Creeping St.-John's-wort* (*Hypericum cerastoides;* bottom) – a very common wildflower of dry grasslands and rock slopes.
Hypecoem (top) is a Mediterranean field weed and relative of the poppies.

## FLORA

> **Typical species of fields and steppes**
> **Arable fields** Common Poppy (*Papaver rhoeas*), Hypecoum (*Hypecoum imberbe / H. procumbens*), Large Blue Alkanet (*Anchusa azurea*), Brown Nonea (*Nonea pulla*), Italian Viper's-bugloss (*Echium italicum*), Ground-pine (*Ajuga chamaepytis*)
> **Steppes** Field Love-in-a-mist (*Nigella arvensis*), Southern Larkspur* (*Delphinium fissum*), Proliferous Pink (*Petrorhagia prolifera*), Sand Catchfly (*Silene conica*), Sainfoin Milk-vetch* (*Astragalus onobrychis*), Creeping St. John's-wort* (*Hypericum cerastoides*), Purple Mullein (*Verbascum phoeniceum*), Clary Sage (*Salvia scalarea*), Drooping Sage (*Salvia nutans*), Felty Germander (*Teucrium polium*), Blue Bugle (*Ajuga genevensis*), Cornflower (*Centaurea cyanus*), Silvery Scabious* (*Lomelosia argentea*), Immortelle (*Xeranthemum annuum*), Large Venus's-looking-glass (*Legousia speculum-veneris*), Jassione heldreichii

The steppes share some of the plant species of the fields, but the number of perennial plants is much greater than annuals. Usually, the steppes are simply open, dry low altitude grasslands.

### Flora of cliffs

For the plant enthusiast, rocks and cliffs are one of the most exciting habitats to explore. Plenty of attractive wildflowers are found here, often with odd adaptations to survive in the harsh environment. The plants here are subjected to a direct impact of a harsh climate, determined by huge seasonal swings in temperature, strong solar radiation and, depending on the direction the cliff is facing, either a very high or very low humidity.

Hence, there is not a single cliff vegetation. There are a multitude of communities, ranging from those with species adapted to surviving extreme heat and drought, to those living with constant shade and humidity. The first extreme is restricted to the Eastern Rhodopes, while the second is found mostly in the Western Rhodopes, where, with increasing altitude, the cold plays another role.

It's difficult to do justice to this diversity in this short text, so we'll limit ourselves here

The Purple Clematis is a climbing plant that often grows in bushes, such as Christ's-thorn.

to some of the extremes. In the very exposed areas, one of the first plants to catch the attention in spring is the dwarf iris *Iris reichenbachii*, which grows here with its slightly taller look-alike *Iris suaveolens* and, according to some sources, *Iris pumila*, making this one of the more challenging species groups to identify. All these species have both a purple and a yellow form, which often grow side by side. Some flowers have a mix of both colours.
Common wildflowers accompanying the irises are goldendrops (with in the Western Rhodopes the endemic *Onosma rhodopea*), Lingulate Bellflower, Sticky Catchfly and Mount Olympus* (*Hypericum olympicum*) and Creeping St. John's-worts* (*Hypericum cerastoides*). On rocks along the Arda two endemic mulleins with deeply lobbed leaves are found: *Verbascum rupestre* and *Verbascum roripifolium*. Rather local are the early-flowering Yellow Asphodel (*Asphodeline lutea*) and Lesser Yellow Asphodel (*Asphodeline liburnica*), two tall, yellow-flowering plants of the lily family. Rather more delicate and later-flowering is the Balkan Harebell* (*Asyneuma limonifolium*), which forms small, blue spikes of flowers and is most commonly found on limestone rock faces in the Western Rhodopes. A final fascinating species of exposed rocky limestone in the Western Rhodopes is the tall, thistle-like *Morina persica*, an odd one out of the honeysuckle family and a fabulous plant of central and Western Asia which reaches into the Balkans.

Reichenbach's Iris grows in two colour forms – purple and yellow.

As said, the shady and damp side of the cliffs, host a very different flora. It is patchily distributed in the Eastern Rhodopes (e.g. near the Devil's Gorge, route 8, both sun and shade-loving cliff vegetations can be found), but much more common in the deep gorges in the Western Rhodopes.
The key species is the remarkable *Haberlea rhodopensis*, which can form large colonies, mainly on damp, north-facing cliffs. Its pretty flowers can turn entire cliffsides purple. *Haberlea* is remarkable for a number of reasons. First, it is an endemic of the Rhodope Mountains, where it is common in the Western but rather local in the Eastern Rhodopes. Second, this plant

## FLORA

> **Typical species of cliffs**
> **Silicate rocks** Bulgarian Cinquefoil* (*Potentilla regis-borisii*), Proliferous Pink (*Petrorhagia prolifera*), Creeping Sweet-William Catchfly* (*Silene lerchenfeldiana*), Dense-flowered Catchfly* (*Silene compacta*), Sticky Catchfly (*Silene viscaria*), Haberlea (*Haberlea rhodopensis*), Yellow stonecrop (*Sedum ochroleucum*), Needle Rockrose* (*Fumana procumbens*), Olympus St. John's-wort* (*Hypericum olympicum*), Uneven-leaved Goldendrops* (*Onosma heterophylla*), Scented Iris (*Iris suaveolens*), Reichenbach's Iris* (*Iris reichenbachii*)
> **Limestone rocks** Bladderpod (*Alyssoides utriculata*), Golden Alison (*Aurinia saxatilis*), Haberlea (*Haberlea rhodopensis*), Golden Navelwort (*Umbilicus erectus*), Evergreen Saxifrage (*Saxifraga sempervirens*), Burning Bush (*Dictamnus albus*), Linum capitatum, Broomleaf Toadflax (*Linaria genistifolia*), Rhodope Golden-drops* (*Onosma rhodopea*), Balkan Betony* (*Stachys scardica*), Balkan Woundwort* (*Stachys plumosa*), Silver Sage (*Salvia argentea*), Clary Sage (*Salvia scalarea*), Catnip (*Nepeta cataria*), Morina (*Morina persica*), Balkan Harebell* (*Asyneuma limonifolium*), Clustered Bellflower (*Campanula glomerata*), Lingulate Bellflower (*Campanula lingulata*), Yellow Leek (*Allium flavum*), Burnt-tip Orchid (*Neotinea ustulata*), Pyramidal Orchid (*Anacamptis pyramidalis*), Fragrant Orchid (*Gymnadenea conopsea*), Bug Orchid (*Anacamptis coriophora*)

cannot be confused with any other plant. It is a member of the *Gesneriaceae*, a plant family that has many representatives in South Africa, and only a few in the European Mountains. But above all, it is, like the handful of European relatives, relict species of the Tertiary era – the historic period from before the ice ages. *Haberlea* found refuge from these cold periods in the secluded, humid valleys of the Rhodopes, where it still occurs today. Here it grows with many other plants, such as Golden Navelwort* (*Umbilicus erectus*; on very shady places), Rock Crane's-bill and a variety of ferns and saxifrages. Higher up in the mountains you'll encounter several species of saxifrage, including the Balkan endemic *Saxifraga sempervivum*, which has typical drooping inflorescences with purple flowers in spring.

### Mountain flora

The true mountain flora is reserved for the Western Rhodopes and the area of the Veykata peak in the Eastern Rhodopes on the border with Greece (route 12). Here, the forests, meadows and karst plateaux each have their own specific set of wildflowers. As in many places, the bulbous plants (the orchids, lilies, irises, tulips and others) form the true eye-catchers, but it is the trees and shrubs that are from an ecological point of view of greatest interest.

**FLORA**

The lowest zones are reserved for the oak forests (see page 28) which contain a great number of different species that are exclusively reserved for the Balkans and further east, into northern Turkey along the southern Black Sea coast. The Sessile and Hungarian Oaks are the dominant oak trees here, but Hornbeam, Hop-Hornbeam, Silver Linden, Manna Ash, Common and Norway Maple are widespread as well. More local are Montpellier and Balkan Maples, endemic to the Balkans and West Asia.

Higher up, Scots Pine woods gradually take over on south facing slopes whilst Beech woods do so on the north slopes. Mixed in with the Beech trees is the rather uncommon Greek or Heldreich's Maple, an endemic tree of the Balkans.

Coppiced woodlands, especially on limestone, are dominated by various maples, hazel, horn-beam and Hop-hornbeam. It is in these woodlands that you'll find a splendid spring flora, with Wood and Yellow Anemones, Dog's-tooth Lily, Common and Red Lungworts, Asarabacca, Mezereon, Bulbous Comfrey, Coral-root Bittercress, wild strawberry and many, many more. This is also a good place to look for orchids in May and June, with various helleborines, Twayblade and Eastern Spotted Orchid* (*Dactylorhiza saccifera*) usually present in large numbers (see also page 82). The flora in these woodlands is its richest in places

Dry limestone grasslands are a hotspot of wildflowers. Two commonly encountered species are the Silver Sage (top) and the scabious *Knautia orientalis* (bottom).

with some moisture and sufficient light on the forest floor. This helps a quick turnover of the leaf litter, making nutrients available for the plants, The process is further aided by the calcareous soil and the fact that the leaves of these particular trees decompose very easily.

Conspicuous plants you see very often in such places, as well as in forest glades, are Dotted Loosestrive, Martagon Lily, Green-flowered Foxglove* (*Digitalis viridiflorus*) and the Sticky Sage. The latter three are worth a

## FLORA

The Dog's-tooth Lily is common on the Veykata ridge (route 12), but to find it in flower, you need to be here in April.

closer look. The Martagon Lily is a widespread species in Europe, but the local variety has smaller and darker flowers; more purple than pink. The foxglove has small but very pretty green flowers and is endemic to the Balkans whereas the Sticky Sage has large, pale yellow flowers, large, sticky leaves and is widespread in the central-European mountains. In similarly nutrient-rich habitats along streams and rivers, the Rhodopean Toothwort isn't rare. This tall, strange-looking parasitic plant flowers from early April to early June, depending on the altitude.

Higher up there are spruce and fir forests of the montane to subalpine zones. Here too, the trees themselves are very interesting. Although the diversity is not great, there are a number of species that remained here after the last ice ages and evolved into local species, unique to the Balkans. The Balkan Fir* (*Abies regis-borisii*) is one example of such a local species.

The spruce and fir forests form another botanical gem, at least locally. The older forests with a well-developed forest floor are definitely the most attractive. Within these forests, it is the presence of light and moisture that form the

### Typical mountain species

European Yew (*Taxus baccata*), Wood Anemone (*Anemone nemorosa*), Bird-in-a-bush (*Corydalis solida*), Hollow-root (*Corydalis cava*), Coralroot (*Cardamine bulbifera*), Rhodope Avens (*Geum rhodopeum*), Red Avens (*Geum coccineum*), Bloody Crane's-bill (*Geranium sanguineum*), Rock Crane's-bill (*G. macrorrhizum*), Lathyrus laxoflorus, One-sided Wintergreen (*Orthilia secunda*), Green Wintergreen (*Pyrola chlorantha*), Biting Stonecrop (*Sedum acre*), Large Milkwort (*Polygala major*), Shrubby Milk-vetch* (*Astragalus angustifolius*), Green-flowered Foxglove (*Digitalis viridiflorus*), Somerset Skullcap (*Scutellaria altissima*), Large Skullcap (*Scutellaria columnae*), Rhodopean Toothwort (*Lathraea rhodopea*; rivers throughout), Green False Helleborine (*Veratrum lobelianum*), Herb-paris (*Paris quadrifolia*), Martagon Lily (*Lilium martagon*), Dog's-tooth Lily (*Erythronium dens-canis*), Lady's-slipper (*Cypripidium calceolus*), Elder-flowered Orchid (*Dactylorhiza sambucina*), Heart-lipped Marsh-orchid (*Dactylorhiza cordigera*), Eastern Spotted Orchid* (*Dactylorhiza saccifera*)

CROSSBILL GUIDES • RHODOPE MOUNTAINS

## FLORA

better locations for Whorl-leaved Salomons-seal, Herb-paris, Willow Gentian, Green Wintergreen and One-sided Wintergreen. Locally, particularly in the darker parts, there are parasitic plants like Yellow Bird's-nest, Bird's-nest Orchid and Ghost Orchid.

The meadows in the higher zones, some of which peaty, attract again different plants, including various endemics, such as Rhodopean Avens* (*Geum rhodopaeum*), with its large orange flowers, not to be confused with Red Avens* (*G. coccineum*), which grows in similar terrain but has scarlet flowers. Other wildflowers to look out for in these Alpine meadows are Green False Helleborine* (*Veratrum lobelium*), the bellflower *Campanula moesiaca* (like a tall, pale-flowered version of the Clustered Bellflower), Betony, Rhodopean Lousewort* (*Pedicularis leucodon*) and Winged Greenweed. There are orchids too in these meadows, in particular Heart-flowered Marsh-orchid* (*Dactylorhiza cordigera*) and Fragrant Orchid, but also Bug and Burnt Orchids.

Two delights of damp meadows in the Western Rhodopes: the Rhodopean Avens (Geum rhodopensis) top) and Green False Helleborine (Veratrum lobelium; left).

The Rhodopean Lily is the crown on the high mountain meadow, almost literally given the shape of the flower. This showy yellow lily occurs only in meadows between approx. 800 and 1500 metres in the Rhodopes, There is only a limited number of populations known, all of them occurring near the Greek border between Trigrad in the west and Vejkata mountain in the east.

Two wildflower habitats in the western Rhodopes stick out in diversity and rarity of species: the cliffs, described on page 47, and the karstic grasslands.

Karstic grasslands are found only in the few limestone regions of the Western Rhodopes, which are the plateaus of Trigrad-Yagodina, Zabardo and Dobrostan. All these areas feature on routes in this book precisely

## FLORA

because these karstic grasslands are so attractive. From (late) spring deep into the summer, these karst plateaux are a riot of colour from all the different wildflowers that occur here. The species composition in a specific spot depends on altitude and the relative position of the sun, the depth of the soil and the presence of shade-giving canopies and bushes, creating a large number of micro-climates, each with its own specific qualities. In the deeper soils, a meadow-like grassland with Dropwort, Spanish Catchfly, Wild Gladioli and Downy Woundwort. In the drier and rockier parts, there are simply too many species to list here. Some rather common and conspicuous ones are Cowslip, Tassel Hyacinth, the Rhodope endemic goldendrop Onosma rhodopea, the aforementioned Balkan Harebell, Bloody Cranesbill (foodplant of the Geranium Blue), Yellow Scabious and St Bernard's Lily, plus of course, a wide range of orchids, including Fly, Bee, Pyramidal and Green-winged. A special type of karst vegetation is found on the northern edge of the Dobrostan mountain, which is lower and more exposed, and therefore has a typically warm and dry microclimate. This is the location of the blood-red Rhodope Tulip* (*Tulipa rhodopaea*), which is one of the few species here that can rightly be called a 'narrow-endemic' – a plant whose entire population is limited to a very small area. In the case of the Rhodope Tulip, this range is restricted to the warm, open slopes of Dobrostan and direct surroundings at an altitude of 500-800 above sea level. It is a critically endangered species.

### Orchids

A little over 50 species of orchids are found in the region, which makes the Rhodopes and Sakar reasonably attractive to orchid aficionados. Although there are clearly more diverse regions in Europe, this region has two great trump cards – first the occurrence of a good number of species found only in south-eastern Europe and second the fact that this is an underexplored region where you can easily discover new populations and perhaps even new species. This not only reflects the fact that still few botanists visit this extensive region, but also the role of climate change. Several Mediterranean orchids are present on the Aegean coast in Greece and Turkey, but not (yet) known to occur a little further north, in Bulgaria. It is quite possible that they will be discovered one day in the lower parts of the Rhodopes. And some recently have, such as the exciting find of the Reinhold's Orchid in the city park of Madzharovo (route 3). A little more recently, in 2021, there was an (unconfirmed) sighting of a Yellow Bee Orchid in Sakar – a potential first for Bulgaria.

These are all exceptions of course. The majority of the orchids found

## FLORA

in the region are the species that are widespread in warm-temperate Europe. Additionally, though, there are species that are unique to the Balkan Peninsula, often replacing the closely related species found in the same climatic zone in western Europe. Good examples are the Balkan Lizard Orchid, replacing the familiar Common Lizard Orchid, the Heart-flowered Marsh-Orchid (*D. cordigera*) replacing the Broad-leaved Marsh-Orchid and the *Dactylorhiza saccifera*, which we'll call Eastern Spotted Orchid in this book, is a close relative to the Common Spotted Orchid.

In Sakar and the Eastern Part of Europe, these species are complemented or replaced by East Mediterranean species, such as Mammose and Horned Woodcock Orchids, while the higher reaches of the Western Rhodopes, particularly those on limestone, support some species that are familiar from the central European mountains. Many of these are rare and threatened, but there are still some populations left of Ghost and Lady's Slipper Orchids. Due to their vulnerability to illegal collection, the locations of the latter are not disclosed in this guide.

Around Ivaylovgrad on the eastern edge of the Rhodopes, and again near Topolovgrad and Shtit in Sakar, there are limestone grasslands and light forests with a (sub)Mediterranean climate. These are highly attractive places for orchid lovers. Monkey, Three-toothed and Pink Butterfly Orchids are among the more common and eye-catching species, but among them are also good numbers of Horned Woodcock and Mammose Orchids – two species of the Bee Orchid genus that are quite widespread here. The first is like a Woodcock Orchid but the extensions of the lip look like the

The most abundant orchid of the Eastern Rhodopes is the Green-winged Orchid. There are places where it washes entire meadows purple. This meadow is part of site E on page 184).

FLORA

### Orchids

**Eastern Rhodopes and Sakar** Spurred Helleborine (*Cephalanthera epipactoides*; rare), Narrow-leaved Helleborine (*C. longifolia*), Three-toothed Orchid (*Neotinea tridentata*), Monkey Orchid (*Orchis simia*), Lady Orchid (*O. purpurea*), Eastern Early-purple Orchid* (*O. pinetorum*), Provence Orchid (*O. provincialis*), Bird's-nest Orchid (*Neottia nidus-avis*), Violet Bird's-nest Orchid (*Limodorum abortivum*), Roman Orchid (*Dactylorhiza romana*), Mammose Orchid (*Ophrys mammosa*), Horned Orchid (*O. cornuta*), Reinhold's Bee Orchid (*O. reinholdii*; rare), Balkan Lizard Orchid* (*Himantoglossum caprinum*), Long-lipped Tongue Orchid (*Serapias longifolia*), Pink Butterfly Orchid (*Anacamptis papilionacea*), Loose-flowered Orchid (*A. laxiflora*), Green-winged Orchid (*A. morio*).

**Western Rhodopes** Lady's Slipper (*Cyprepidium calceolus*), Red Helleborine (*Cephalanthera rubra*), White Helleborine (*C. damasonium*), Marsh Helleborine (*Epipactis palustris*; rare), Twayblade (*Listera ovata*), Ghost Orchid (*Epipogium aphyllum*), Bog Orchid (*Hammarbya paludosa*), Greater Butterfly Orchid (*Cephalantera chlorantha*), Lesser Butterfly Orchid (*C. bifolia*), Fragrant Orchid (*Gymnadenia conopsea*), Elder-flowered Orchid (*Dactylorhiza sambucina*), Macedonian Marsh-orchid* (*D. kalopissii*), Eastern Spotted Orchid (*D. saccifera*), Heart-flowered Marsh-orchid (*D. cordigera*), Burnt-tip Orchid (*Neotinea ustulata*), Fly Orchid (*Ophrys insectifera*), Bee Orchid (*O. apifera*), Pyramidal Orchid (*Anacamptis pyramidalis*), Bug Orchid (*A. coriophora*).

Monkey Orchid is common in the Eastern Rhodopes.

horns of a Longhorn bull (photo on page 195). Especially in roadsides, Balkan Lizard Orchid and Pyramidal Orchid can be quite frequent. More locally, mostly around Ivaylovgrad, but also near Madzharovo and the Byala Reka, the Long-lipped or Ploughshare Tongue Orchid is found – the only representative of the Atlantic-Mediterranean genus *Serapias*.

In the woodlands, there are Lady Orchid, Violet Limodore and White and Narrow-leaved Helleborines. One of the greatest rarities in the region is undoubtedly the Turkish Helleborine. This handsome orchid species reaches its north-western limit of its predominantly Turkish range.

Heading into the Eastern Rhodopes, the orchid flora becomes somewhat unpredictable. The great diversity of soils and the small but important fluctuations in microclimate make that some of the aforementioned species still occur (e.g. Balkan Lizard, Pink Butterfly, Horned Woodcock and Mammose Orchids and Violet Limodore), but they are now joined by other species, such as Bird's-nest Orchid, and the south-eastern cousin of the familiar Early Purple-orchid, *Orchis pinetorum*. Green-winged Orchid can be very common in the grasslands, while the pretty but very early-flowering Roman Orchid graces the forest floors. Roman Orchids, known from Italy and the Balkans, come in two colour forms – the rosy-red form is the most common, but there are plants with yellow flowers as well. Much less widespread, but locally numerous is the delicate yellow Provence Orchid, a plant of older oak forests in which the undergrowth is regularly cleared.

The Western Rhodopes have a very diverse orchid flora. With the exception of the Heart-lipped Marsh-orchid, which is common on damp, acidic meadows, the orchid action in the Western Rhodopes takes place in the limestone regions. Green-winged, Elder-flowered, Pyramidal, Greater Butterfly and Fragrant Orchids are all widespread in limestone grasslands. Locally they are joined by Fly and Bee Orchids. The Bug Orchid, which has suffered great losses in many parts of Europe, is still quite common in the meadows around Trigrad.

Light woodlands are the realm of Lady Orchid, White and Red Helleborines and Common Twayblade. The most numerous orchid here, flowering in late June and July, is the Eastern Spotted Orchid. It grows everywhere where there is some limestone (and even when there isn't) and can grow very tall.

In addition to the above-mentioned. the Western Rhodopes has a good number of rarities that reach the edge of their range here, where they occur on just a few spots. The aforementioned Lady's Slipper and Ghost Orchids serve as good examples. The latter is very local but occurs (in good years – this species is notorious for being very rare in one year, and numerous in the next) in good numbers near Trigrad (route 19). Even the tiny Bog Orchid grows very locally in these mountains, while in calcareous swamps on the edge of Dobrostan, the very rare Balkan endemic marsh orchid *Dactylorhiza kalopissii* grows, together with Marsh Helleborine.

Reinhold's Bee Orchid is essentially a Greek species, with only very few locations in Bulgaria. However, it is slowly increasing, probably a result of climate change.

MAMMALS

# Mammals

> Jackals and the other smaller predators are present especially in the Eastern Rhodopes, Sakar and along the Maritsa – your best chances are being out at dusk or dawn and you need to be a bit lucky to find them. Suslik are present on routes 5, 13, 21, 22 and 22. They are active during sunny days. Look for deep soil steppes and patiently scan them. The larger ungulates (Bison, Konik Horses, Red and Fallow Deer) are most numerous around the game reserve (site A on page 181 and routes 9 and 10). For Bear and Wolf watching excursions, see site F on page 225).

The Rhodopes are home to a high variety of mammal species. There are steppe animals like Suslik (a species of ground squirrel) and even the great carnivores Brown Bear and Wolf are present in the mountains. Unfortunately, this does not imply that these animals are easy to spot.

The great mammal diversity is again explained by the variety of largely undisturbed habitats on the crossroads of the western, eastern and southern realms. Therefore, animals of western Europe (e.g. Chamois), the east (e.g. Suslik) and the southwest (like Golden Jackal) occur in close vicinity of one another.

Although Wolves are rarely seen, they are actually quite common in the Eastern Rhodopes.

## Predators – great and small

With the (surprising) exception of the Lynx, all large European carnivores are present in the region. There is a healthy population of Brown Bear in the Western Rhodopes, while Wolf occurs throughout the mountain range. The Brown Bears are protected but were fiercely hunted in the past and poaching is still not exceptional, so they fear people and are not easily located although evidence of their presence, their footprints or faeces, can be found. The Golden Jackal by contrast can often be heard howling or seen crossing the small roads, especially at dusk. This small dog

## MAMMALS

species (in size Jackals are somewhere between Wolves and Foxes) is quite common, particularly in the Eastern Rhodopes, but also in the Maritsa Valley and Sakar. In contrast to the forest and fielddwelling Wolves and Foxes, the Jackal prefers open scrubby country, including marshes.
Amongst the smaller predators, Wild Cat, Badger, Stoat, Weasel, Pine Marten and Beech Marten are all present. All rivers have thriving populations of Otters, and on the Arda (routes 1 and 8) you might just be lucky enough to spot one.
None of these animals are easy to find, but if personal experience is any indication, the chances of just stumbling upon one or more of these species along a back road is higher than in most European areas. On our trips we've seen Wild Cats like this on several occasions, and also Beech Marten, Otter and even Wolf.

### Large grazers
Since most of the herds have left the mountains (see page 55) it is up to the wild ungulates to maintain the half-open landscape. In the Eastern Rhodopes, Roe Deer and Wild Boar are very numerous and, together with the Rhodope Short-horn Cattle they do a fair job. However, their foraging alone is not enough, so over the last two decades, new species of grazing animals have been (re)introduced. Some of them were originally present in these hills, and others, such as the Konik Horses, are close relatives to the now extinct original fauna.
Red Deer and Fallow Deer are both native to the Rhodopes, but went extinct and were subsequently reintroduced in the Rhodopes for hunting. Red Deer is native to the region, but was extirpated in the last century. It occurs mostly in the hunting reserve (see site A on page 181), an unfenced part of the Eastern Rhodopes near Studen Kladenets. Whether Fallow Deer is native, is under debate. Large groups occur in the same hunting reserve. As noted, Konik Horses have been introduced and have

Red Deer is one of the big grazers that is part of the indigenous fauna of the Rhodopes, but was extirpated. It is being reintroduced in the Studen Kladenets game reserve (site A on page 181).

MAMMALS

been joined by European Bison which roam the Eastern Rhodopes, again in the general vicinity of the hunting reserve.

The grazing fauna of the Western Rhodopes is less diverse. Besides Wild Boar, Roe Deer and Red Deer, there is one other ungulate in this region: the Balkan Chamois. This animal is closely related to and virtually indistinguishable from the Alpine Chamois, and roams the mountain forest glades, roughly above 1,000 metres.

## Suslik and Marbled Polecat – mammals of the steppes

Mammalian life in the steppes is quite different from that of wooded parts of the country. Although 'true steppes' are rare in the region (see page 35) but the open grasslands and fields with sufficient soil to make burrows form a good substitute. Because this is open country with great all-round visibility, the ability to hide underground is vital. The Suslik (or European Ground Squirrel) does precisely that – creating elaborate burrows in steppes and other terrain where they are found. They reproduce quickly and can, in suitable habitat, be very numerous. Susliks feed on seeds and herbs and always remain close to the burrows, because there are plenty of predators around that have Suslik on the menu – Saker Falcons, Long-legged Buzzard, Montagu's Harrier, Imperial and Lesser Spotted Eagles – they all love to eat Susliks. And so does the Marbled Polecat. This panther-patterned version of the Polecat shares the Suslik's habitat but unlike the birds of prey, they can enter the suslik burrows to hunt these rodents down.

In a healthy steppe ecosystem, Susliks form an important food source for these predators. Sadly, the numbers of Suslik have dropped hugely over the last few decades. Without doubt, the intensification of agriculture and the transformation of grazed steppes to ploughed fields are major reasons for the Suslik's decline in the Thracian Plain. However, it is likely that there are other, yet unknown, causes for the low numbers, especially in the Rhodopes. Here, many apparently good Suslik territories are not inhabited and there seems to be a

Suslik

## MAMMALS

link between the decline in sheep grazing and the disappearance of the Suslik. Additionally, the isolation of the deep-soiled areas in the otherwise rocky terrain prevents recolonisation of former breeding sites. Most sites inhabited sites in the Rhodopes are in or close to the Arda and Amira River valleys. In the Thracian Plain and especially around Sakar, there are much larger populations.

Susliks and Marbled Polecats are by no means the only steppe mammals. Hares and Hedgehogs are common and close to river valleys, there are plenty of Golden Jackals.

### Mouse-tailed Dormouse and Mole-rat – some rarities

The list of rodents and small insectivorous animals is too long to describe fully, but there are two odd ones we wish to highlight here. The first is Roach's Mouse-tailed Dormouse, a mouthful of a name for a small and inconspicuous species. The story behind this small rodent is fascinating. It is one of those animals with an extremely secretive lifestyle and very specific habitat requirements. It lives only in European Turkey, a few isolated places in the very western edge of Anatolia and south-east Bulgaria. This animal is so rare that it has been considered extinct in Bulgaria. The last sighting was in 1978, but in 2017, it was suddenly rediscovered. Or more precisely, its remains were discovered in owl pallets, after which a more thorough search found populations in Sakar, locally in the Eastern Rhodopes and in Strandzja. Like all (European) dormice, the Mouse-tailed climbs in bushes and trees (where it needs holes to sleep and nest in), but in contrast, mostly feeds on the ground.

The second is the Lesser Mole-rat, a very strange rodent that, like a mole, lives almost exclusively underground. Only after heavy rains it leaves its burrows and may suddenly be seen crossing the road (which happened near Madzharovo when we were exploring routes for this book in 2022).

It is these latter two animals (and the great diversity of mammals in general) that has generated a lot of interest recently among mammal researchers in the Rhodopes and Sakar.

Roach's Mouse-tailed Dormouse is perhaps our continent's least known mammal. It has a very small distribution range, but it may not be all that rare in the Eastern Rhodopes and Sakar.

FLORA AND FAUNA

BIRDS

# Birds

> The best birdwatching routes are 1, 5 (both cliff and wetland birds), 8, 9, 11 and site A on page 181 (river and scrubland birds, raptors), 17, 18, 19 and 20 (all for the birds of subalpine forest), site A on page 222 (for Wallcreeper primarily), 21, 23, 24 and site C on page 249 (for the birds of steppes and dry grasslands) and route 22 and sites A to E for wetland birds. For a species-specific account of where to watch birds, see the list on page 264.

The Rhodopes and adjacent plains rank among the top birding sites in Europe. This area matches the famous birdwatching destinations of Spain, Southern France and Eastern Poland. Within a 10 day to two week visit at the peak time (2nd half of May) it is possible to see such delightful species as Masked Shrike, Levant Sparrowhawk, Olive-tree Warbler, Eastern Imperial Eagle, Western Rock Nuthatch, Sombre Tit, Dalmatian Pelican, Wallcreeper, Pygmy Cormorant and Rose-coloured Starling – to name just a few of the highlights.

Again, the fact that this region is the meeting point of temperate, Mediterranean, Pontic and Alpine species makes it also the meeting point for species from different regions. Classic Mediterranean species like Bee-eater, Squacco Heron, Blue Rock Thrush and Roller are present here mixed in with eastern specialties, Isabelline Wheatear, Olive-tree Warbler and Eastern representatives of Subalpine, Olivaceous and Orphean Warblers. Some of them reach in the Eastern Rhodopes the western end of a range that stretches out over Turkey into the Middle East, like Western Rock

The Eastern Sub-alpine Warbler is locally common in shrubby areas on the warm slopes of the Eastern Rhodopes and Sakar.

CROSSBILL GUIDES • RHODOPE MOUNTAINS

Nuthatch, Masked Shrike, Chukar and Levant Sparrowhawk. These are understandably among the most attractive species for birdwatchers from western Europe.

Due to the Rhodopes' eastern position in Europe, the temperate birds have a distinctly eastern flavour. The mountain woodlands support Grey-headed and White-backed Woodpeckers (a misnomer here as the local race, *lillfordi*, has a barred back), while Syrian Woodpecker, Barred Warbler and Lesser Spotted Eagle breed in the lower areas. Even the passage migrants are often distinctly 'eastern', wintering in East Africa or the Middle East and having an east-European or Siberian breeding range. Examples are Marsh Sandpiper and White-winged Tern, which can be seen in the area on spring migration with relative ease.

The dry, steppic lowlands form another birding hotspot with Pontic-Pannonian specialities such as Lesser Grey Shrike, Rose-coloured Starling (in some years), Eastern Imperial Eagle and Isabelline Wheatear. The cherry on this already well-decorated cake is found in the higher regions of the Western Rhodopes, where a number of northern and Alpine species are present, such as Capercaillie, Three-toed Woodpecker, Wallcreeper, Nutcracker, Tengmalm's Owl and Pygmy Owl.

It is not just the mix of different biological regions though, that makes this region so rich in birds – it is also the large number of different bird habitats and the generally great condition they are in. Birds of small-scale agricultural land that are rapidly disappearing in Europe –shrikes, Little Owls, Ortolan Buntings and Turtle Doves are still doing relatively well here, although they are now declining in the intensified and subsidised large-scale farmland areas in the Thracian Plain.

The best bird habitats are the cliffs and rocky slopes in the Eastern Rhodopes, the shrubby pastures with their scattered oaks and woodlands, and the river floodplains in the mountains. This is where a large number of the highlights are found. Additionally, however, there are a number of generally small marshes and lakes, mostly in the Thracian Plain, which combined support almost all of the wetland species of south-eastern Europe – nearly all European herons, Glossy Ibis, Pygmy Cormorant, Great White and Dalmatian Pelican – even Collared Pratincole is present.

All this paints a picture of the Rhodopes as a birdwatcher's nirvana, but this is not entirely true. Before going into detail about the different bird regions, it needs to be said that finding the full range of specialties is not an easy task. Some sought-after species occur in very specific places and for them, you need to know exactly where to go. With this guidebook, that should be easy. Many others are simply scattered thinly over suitable hab-

## BIRDS

itat and an element of luck is involved in finding them. This goes for the raptors, but also for many of the passerines, which are by far easiest to find when they sing. Knowing their songs and being present in the season and at the hour they are most vocal are important means by which you can increase your chances of finding them. Hiring a local guide for a day or two is another excellent option for finding some of the more difficult local specialties (see page 263).

The region covered in this book lies close to but not on a major bird migration route. Migratory birds in spring overwhelmingly follow the Turkish coastline north and reach Europe in the Evros (Maritsa) delta that forms the border between Greece and Turkey. Some travel upriver from there and pass along the marshes of the Thracian Plain for a bit – waders, terns, swallows and passerines can be seen in large numbers in this period. However, the majority of the broad-winged migrants maintain a course along the coast, flying north along the great lagoons along Bulgaria's Black Sea coast. Some of the species mentioned here as very scarce passage migrants (e.g. Spotted Eagle, Pallid Harrier) are in fact much more numerous on the coast, which is one of the reasons many birdwatchers combine a visit to the Rhodopes with birdwatching on the Black Sea coast.

### Raptors and Owls

Of all the bird groups of the region, the raptors are arguably the greatest attraction. The Arda River Valley in the Eastern Rhodopes, Sakar and the Thracian Plain, in particular, have a joint reputation of being amongst the most raptor-rich areas in Europe (together with the Dadia forest just across the border in Greece). In terms of species diversity, this is certainly the case. No less then 23 out of 38 raptors of the European mainland breed in the area, and a few more winter or pass through. The diversity of raptors is impressive, but the majority of them are not very common and some are downright rare. If you have been watching raptors in Spain, you should realise that even though the diversity of birds of prey in southern Bulgaria is higher, the numbers are lower.

The vultures are, perhaps, the most striking and visible. Griffon and Egyptian Vultures occur in good numbers – For both of these cliff-breeding species, this region is the stronghold in eastern Europe. A census in 2022 on the Bulgarian side of the Rhodopes revealed 111 pairs of Griffon Vultures, with another 50 or so unpaired birds. Close to 20 pairs of Egyptian Vulture are known from the Bulgarian Eastern Rhodopes. These birds form a single, large Rhodopean population that stretches out across the Greek border where a smaller number of both these vultures breed. The situation is reversed with the Black Vulture, which breeds on the Greek side (Dadia forest) and is regularly seen in the Bulgarian Eastern Rhodopes. However, in summer 2022, the Black Vulture was also reintroduced to the Bulgarian Eastern Rhodopes in the vicinity of Madzharovo, so by the time you are reading these lines, it is much more likely that you'll be able to see these majestic birds on your trip (the Black Vulture is, with a wingspan of almost 3 metres, the world's largest bird of prey after the condors).

Eagles are the next big draw. Golden, Eastern Imperial, White-tailed, Lesser Spotted, Booted and Short-toed Eagles are all frequent. However, the numbers seen on a spring trip vary from year to year – in some years you'll see plenty, while in others they are, for some reason, quite scarce.

Sakar is the best location for eagle-watching. The key species is the Eastern Imperial Eagle, of which 30 pairs breed (out of a total Bulgarian population of about 40 pairs). Impressive numbers, especially when you consider that this doesn't even make it the most common eagle (that would be the Lesser Spotted). The Imperial Eagle hunts for rodents in open flat or slightly hilly terrain. Classically, Hares and Susliks are its main prey; and the disappearance of the sheep herding and conversion to ploughed fields is a major threat to the Suslik and therefore to this superb raptor. Interestingly, in recent years, the Imperial Eagles of Sakar are focussing more and more on another prey: hedgehogs!

You will have little difficulty observing Griffon Vultures at the cliffs along the Arda or from one of the photography hides in the Eastern Rhodopes (see page 263).

## BIRDS

There are also good numbers of Lesser Spotted, Booted and Short-toed Eagles, both in Sakar and the Eastern Rhodopes. Lesser Spotted Eagle is most numerous in Sakar and in the area around Ivaylovgrad. The foothills of the Western Rhodopes, in particular the Besaparski Hills, support good numbers of Lesser Spotted, Booted and Short-toed Eagles. The Golden Eagle is the classic mountain eagle and together with Short-toed the only species found in the Western Rhodopes. It is however most common in the Eastern Rhodope mountains. Golden Eagles are versatile hunters and the reason they're doing well in the Eastern Rhodopes is because of the large numbers of tortoises here. The eagles grab the tortoises, fly up and drop them on the rocks to break the carapaces – a rather brutal but effective way to hunt. The White-tailed Eagle is rather scarce, but breeds in increasing numbers along the region's lakes and reservoirs.

Other exotic species are found among the smaller raptors. The Levant Sparrowhawk (a southeastern species in Europe) breeds close to the rivers. Again, the Arda River and particularly the Maritsa (Zlato Pole; route 22) are favourite haunts. The Long-legged Buzzard is another flagship species of the Balkans. It is a scarce breeder of the Eastern Rhodopes and a little more common in Sakar, where it hunts over the fields and steppes. However, it is a lot less frequent than the Common Buzzard which occurs here in two forms. The migratory Steppe Buzzard is considered to be the most numerous form in the eastern part of the region with the sedentary Common Buzzard more frequent in the Western Rhodopes. However, the distinction between these two forms is not always clear and DNA analysis suggest there is little difference between them. Black Kites breed in the wider river valleys, mainly the Arda in the Eastern Rhodopes and the Maritsa in the Thracian Plain.

The harriers are birds of the Thracian Plain and not very common. Marsh Harrier is seen most, frequenting the local marshes in spring and summer. Montagu's Harrier, traditionally a bird of arable fields and steppes, is much scarcer than the habitat would suggest, but does occur around Sakar and Besaparski, as well as scattered through the Thracian Plain. Pallid Harrier is a migrant, but as it mainly passes along the coast, it is rather scarce in our part of the Thracian Plain. Hen Harrier is a widespread winter visitor.

A similar story holds true for the Red-footed Falcons. They breed further north in the Danube plain and pass through mostly along the coast. However, lower numbers do occur and Red-footed Falcons have recently bred in the Thracian Plain (and were much more numerous several decades ago). In late spring and early summer, you may encounter Eleonora's Falcons.

## The eagle and the tortoise

One of the more spectacular features of the region form the large numbers of birds of prey. Their diet is rich and varied, but centred around a single and surprising prey: the tortoise. Both Spur-thighed and Hermann's Tortoises occur in abundance and form the bulk of the menu for Golden Eagles. Buzzards, Lesser Spotted Eagles and Egyptian Vultures are also known to appreciate a bit of turtle meat (or gut). An old and presumably rather rough-and-ready estimate is that 10,000 tortoises, perhaps 2% of the total population, are eaten each year in the Dadia region. Unfortunately, the gradual change of the landscape (see page 51) has caused the tortoise population to decline. This is thought to be a major reason for the decrease in raptors over the last decades in North-east Greece. In Bulgaria, the local habit of some ethnic groups to eat tortoise meat is another threat to the population.

Golden Eagle

Tortoises are characterised by their tough, boney armoured body with the back protected by the carapace and the belly by the plastron. This armour is obviously a problem for raptors, none of which have a bill big or strong enough to break it, but gravity helps where bills fail. Occasionally you stumble on bloody, broken tortoise shields when you are in the field. If you are lucky, you may actually see the spectacle itself: an eagle that snatches a tortoise, soars up high to unceremoniously drop it to its doom on the merciless rocks. This way of hunting requires eagles to fly a bit lower than when they were hunting rabbits, providing you with first class views of Golden Eagles, flying like a harrier over the steppe-like terrain.

Tortoise-dropping appears to be an ancient trick. According to legend, Aeschylus (525 BC – 455 BC), the famous founding father of the Greek Tragedy, met his tragic end when his shiny bald head was mistaken for a rock and an eagle dropped a tortoise on it. (This happened on holiday in Sicily, apparently, not in Thrace). This unfortunate but above all painfully trivial ending of a great person's life shocked his contemporaries, although the humorous side of the story was recognized as well. What are, after all, the odds that such a tragedy happens to the very person who invented tragedy? Later on, Aeschylus' close encounter with the tortoise became a more serious lesson about life – however hard working and responsible a person you may be, the important things in life are beyond control.

BIRDS

This elegant falcon has a curious life cycle. It winters in Madagascar and the nearest breeding colonies are on the Aegean Islands but it doesn't nest until autumn, when its main prey, migrating songbirds, are readily available. They arrive rather late in the area, around mid-May and regularly undertake hunting raids over the mainland, including the Eastern Rhodopes. They have their favourite haunts here, and are seen especially in the region of the Arda and Krumovitsa confluence (route 8). Dark birds are distinctive, but pale examples, and particularly young birds resemble large, long-tailed Hobbies – a species of falcon that is quite common along the rivers all over the region.

Among the larger falcons, the Peregrine is the most common species, breeding on rocky areas in both the Western and Eastern Rhodopes. In fact, it is together with Golden Eagle, Kestrel, Goshawk, Sparrowhawk, Buzzard and Honey Buzzard, the only raptor of note in the Western Rhodopes.

The other two large falcons, Lanner and Saker, are both very scarce. Lanner breeds in very low numbers in the Eastern Rhodopes and is rarely seen. It seems to breed in the remote parts near the Greek border. Saker, by contrast, is found on the northern end of our region. It was recently reintroduced to an undisclosed site in the Thracian Plain where, if you are lucky, it may be seen. Like the Eastern Imperial Eagle, it has Susliks on its menu. By far the most common falcon in the region is the familiar Kestrel, which occurs in any open or half open types of landscape, including the meadows and karst plateau high up in the Western Rhodopes. The Lesser Kestrel by contrast, is very rare. It is a migratory bird that lives in colonies around

Egyptian Vulture

the Mediterranean (and further east) in steppe-like environments where it feeds mostly on large insects. A reintroduction program was set up in the village of Levka in Sakar to bring back this species. Here it is easy to see this magnificent bird (route 23).

Thus far, we painted an image in which the Eastern Rhodopes, Sakar and the Thracian Plain are the target area for watching diurnal raptors. This is a little different when it comes to the owls. In the lowlands, Little Owl and Scops Owl are the common and widespread species, the latter even breeding in the tiniest of village parks. Little Owls prefer agricultural and steppe-like habitats, often on the outskirts of villages, and are regularly seen during the day. At night, it is the Barn Owl that you encounter here. Long-eared and Tawny Owls are widespread, but for Eagle Owl, Tengmalm's Owl and Pygmy Owl you need to search more closely. The latter two occur only in the coniferous forests of the Western Rhodopes, while Eagle Owl breeds on cliff faces all over the Rhodope mountains.

## Birds of open woodlands, scrub and small-scale agricultural land

If you have never visited the Rhodopes, it may sound odd to lump the birdlife of such different habitats as woodland, scrub, and hedgerow-lined fields in a single paragraph. Yet a simple glance on the landscape of the Rhodopes (or, for example, the photo on page 8) makes it clear that these habitats are not neatly divided as they often are in northern Europe. Agricultural land divided by hedgerows is often abandoned and invaded by Christ's-thorn bushes and seamlessly merges with the 'true' scrublands. The division between open, oak woodland and scrub is just as arbitrary as drawing a line between the open woodlands and denser forests.

This gradual merging of one habitat into another is reflected in the birdlife; a single location may hold bird species typical of a variety of habitats. The birdlife in most spots is not a matter of kind, but of degree. Scrubland birds like Eastern Subalpine Warbler or Black-headed Bunting may be found in open woods, while open woodland birds like Eastern Orphean Warbler and Woodlark, may appear in shrubby places.

**Key birds of the open woods and scrublands**
Black Vulture (reintroduced), Lesser Spotted Eagle (mostly Sakar), Eastern Imperial Eagle (mostly Sakar) Booted Eagle, Short-toed Eagle, Honey Buzzard, Turtle Dove, Scops Owl, Middle Spotted Woodpecker, Black Woodpecker, Syrian Woodpecker, Woodlark, Nightjar, Red-backed Shrike, Woodchat Shrike, Lesser Grey Shrike, Masked Shrike (uncommon), Eastern Olivaceous Warbler, Olive-tree Warbler, Sombre Tit, Barred Warbler, Lesser Whitethroat, Eastern Orphean Warbler, Eastern Subalpine Warbler, Sardinian Warbler, Hawfinch, Spanish Sparrow, Ortolan Bunting, Black-headed Bunting, Corn Bunting, Cirl Bunting

## BIRDS

The Syrian Woodpecker (left) is the only woodpecker that occurs in almost treeless areas. It is the most common woodpecker in the Thracian Plain. The Sombre Tit (right) is one of the birds of shrubby, open woodlands.

In a similar fashion, birds of the Mediterranean realm may dominate over birds of temperate Europe in the one place, but the reverse may be true just a kilometre further along the road. And sometimes they simply occur together. Red-backed (more associated with temperate Europe) and Woodchat Shrikes (a typically Mediterranean species) are often found side by side on the same shrubby field (or is it open scrubland?).

This woodland-scrub-fields 'habitat' dominates the landscape in both the Eastern Rhodopes and Sakar and is stunningly diverse. Typical species you can find here are Corn, Cirl, Ortolan and Black-headed Buntings (plus Rock Bunting in rocky areas), Sombre Tit, Red-backed and Woodchat Shrikes (and occasionally Lesser Grey and Masked, although these are more frequent elsewhere), Barred, Sardinian, Eastern Orphean, Eastern Subalpine, Eastern Olivaceous and Olive-tree Warblers, Woodlark, Whitethroat and Lesser Whitethroat. Volunteers doing bird censuses in the Eastern Rhodopes have come up with some extraordinary bird counts. They have found – not infrequently – Woodchat, Lesser Grey and Red-backed Shrikes all within one square kilometre. There are territories of Ortolan Bunting, a typical bird of open woodlands, within 100 metres of a pair of Tawny Pipit, which prefers steppe-like environments. Sometimes it seems as if any combination of birds is possible in this type of habitat.

The landscape also offers a challenge to 'read', as experienced birdwatchers are used to do. It is not as easy to predict which species a particular hillside may harbour. Could there be Ortolan Bunting? Sure, quite likely – it is a common species here. Black-headed Bunting? Yes, most likely if there is open agricultural land. Eastern Subalpine Warbler? More difficult to predict.

# BIRDS

Predicting the presence, or absence, of bird species is further complicated by the 'edge effect'. A number of bird species whose range is centred in the Mediterranean, temperate Europe or western Asia approach the extreme limit of their range in this region. At these limits, the birds are generally more thinly distributed and may show odd or unpredictable distribution patterns. Eastern Subalpine Warbler for example is quite common around Madzharovo, but for some reason, it is often absent in seemingly equally suitable habitat elsewhere.

This being said, there are some patterns to discern, which can be helpful with the most sought-after species. For example, Olive-tree Warbler prefers open country with scattered small trees and Christ's-thorn bushes and is most numerous in Sakar. Ortolan Bunting prefers scattered trees mixed with open fields, while Black-headed Bunting (a late arrival) occupies trees and hedges in agricultural land.

It is within this half-open landscape that most villages and farmsteads, which will be the starting point for many bird walks, are found. Besides, the houses, sheds and the agricultural land close to the villages adds some more extras to the landscape. Small orchards, some grazing land, gardens and vegetable gardens, stone walls, drinking basins, some chickens and perhaps a few cows that provide the necessary manure that attracts insects and makes the grass grow. All this attracts birds. The classic 'villagers' are Collared Dove, Barn and Little Owls, Starling, House Martin, both Barn and Red-rumped Swallows and both Pallid and Common Swifts, White Storks and sparrows. Every village has its stork's nest, and usually more than one. The nest is usually a big pile of branches forming a platform for the storks to nest on. However, that tangle of branches is like a tower block for sparrows with both House and Spanish Sparrows in residence.

Hawfinches frequent the oak forests, both in the Western and Eastern Rhodopes.

The somewhat wilder gardens and orchards are the places where you'll hear and see Hoopoes during the day and Scops Owl in the evening. The latter is remarkably numerous in the region, not only in the lower areas, but also in the villages higher up in the Western Rhodopes. Scops Owls are easily detected by the simple one-syllable call they constantly utter, like the ping of a sonar. A stroll on a warm spring evening should provide a glimpse of them in the darker corners on the

**FLORA AND FAUNA**

BIRDS

edge of the village – and sometimes on the telephone pole in the main street!

The outskirts of the villages are also the best places to find Syrian Woodpeckers. This look-alike of the widespread Great Spotted Woodpecker is especially numerous in the lowlands, where it is often more common than Great Spotted. Syrian Woodpeckers even occur in very open landscapes, where the trees along a country road or some low orchards are enough for them to make a living. Additionally, this is where you'll find the birds that we discussed at the beginning of this section: Black-headed or Ortolan Buntings, a Lesser Whitethroat and a Red-backed Shrike. The latter often attracts nesting Barred Warblers which increase their breeding success from having a more aggressive neighbour to chase away predators. In addition, an Isabelline Wheatear may be hopping around in a dry field – in short, the birding nirvana starts at the end of the village; splendid for a pre-breakfast stroll on a fine spring morning.

The villages in the Western Rhodopes have a different birdlife. It is also rich, but the species are more familiar with those in central Europe. Serins, Goldfinches (which are also in the lowlands), Black Redstarts, Red-backed Shrikes and Yellowhammers make up the bulk of the birds with swallows (including Red-rumped) and swifts (including Pallid) also present in the finer West Rhodopean villages.

In the box on the following page, we divided the more attractive bird species of the Eastern Rhodopes into their preferred habitat, but keep in mind that many of them are not entirely exclusive to these habitats.

## Birds of cliffs

All over the Rhodopes, both west and east, there are cliffs. In the Eastern Rhodopes they are mostly of volcanic origin, whilst in the Western Rhodopes, the limestone regions have the tallest cliffs. The dry and hot Sakar region and the Besaparski hills do not have few natural cliffs, but quite a few (abandoned) quarries. In all these three regions, the cliffs support a great birdlife.

Most famous and fabulous are the rock faces along the Arda river in the Eastern Rhodopes. From Kardzhali to Kovan Kaya (east of Madzharovo), there are isolated mountains with steep cliffs facing the river. It is on these that the region's great vulture colonies are found. Griffon Vultures, in particular, are numerous and most of the rocks have at least a few pairs of these spectacular birds. Egyptian Vultures are frequent too, particularly between Studen Kladenets and Madzharovo. They don't form colonies like the Griffons, rather they are more scattered over the

area, also breeding on smaller cliffs, just like Golden Eagles which are also found all over the area. Peregrines, Ravens and Black Storks are present on most of cliffs in the Eastern Rhodopes, while Eagle Owl occurs more sporadically.
Watching cliff birds is obviously much easier than searching the thickets or woodland canopies, but it can nevertheless be tricky to find the birds when they are sitting still. One can spend many pleasurable hours with binoculars (or better, a telescope) scanning the cliffs of Kovan Kaya or Monyak in search of vulture, eagle or Black Stork nests.

> **Key birds of cliffs and quarries**
> Black Stork, Griffon Vulture, Egyptian Vulture, Golden Eagle, Peregrine, Raven, Eagle Owl, Chukar (Eastern Rhodopes), Rock Partridge (Western Rhodopes), Western Rock Nuthatch, Alpine Swift, Crag Martin, Red-rumped Swallow (also common in villages), Eastern Black-eared Wheatear, Rock Thrush, Blue Rock Thrush, Rosy Starling (quarries in Besaparski Hills), Rock Sparrow (quarries in Besaparski Hills), Rock Bunting

In places where you can approach the rocks, you'll be able to find many more birds. Alpine, Pallid and Common Swift are all quite common cliff breeders, as are Barn and Red-rumped Swallows, House and Crag Martins. Rather less numerous are some of the sought-after species like Blue Rock Thrush (frequent), Rock Thrush (rather scarce), Black Redstart (uncommon but more frequent in the Western Rhodopes), Rock Bunting (rather scarce), Eastern Black-eared

Two specialists of cliffs: the Western Rock Nuthatch (top) and the Blue Rock Thrush (bottom).

## BIRDS

Wheatear (frequent) and Western Rock Nuthatch (rather scarce). The latter is again one of these south-eastern specialities that are here at the northern edge of their mostly south-eastern range (although it is found westwards up to the Croatian coast). All these species not only breed on cliffs, but also find their food here. Many of them can be found foraging on nearby rocky slopes. Such places are also the favoured haunt of the Chukar, a species of partridge with a large, predominantly Asian and Middle-Eastern distribution range, that reaches its western limit in the Eastern Rhodopes. It does not occur in the Western Rhodopes. In the Western Rhodopes the Chukar is replaced by the Rock Partridge – a look-alike that occurs throughout the south European high mountains. But Chukar and Rock Partridge are not easy to track down – you may hear them or just stumble upon them when you are walking the trails through rocky grasslands.

The birdlife of rocky slopes in the Western Rhodopes is not nearly as rich as in the east, but it has its attractions. The great raptor community that is such a big draw in the east is not present here, although Golden Eagle is still a widespread bird. Crag Martin, Red-rumped Swallow, Alpine, Common and Pallid Swifts are all still there, and also Peregrine and Eagle Owl occur, although uncommon as in the Eastern Rhodopes. The great attraction of the Western Rhodopes cliffs is the Wallcreeper. This grey bird with its long down-curved bill is often called the butterfly bird because has such beautiful rounded, white-spotted red wings and a very slow, fluttering and butterfly-like flight. When sitting on a cliff (it always creeps along vertical rock faces) it constantly flickers its wings, showing off its red markings. In the Western Rhodopes, the Wallcreeper is probably widespread but scarce in the steep limestone gorges in the area, but that doesn't matter as there is one locality where it is very easy to find, and usually present at eye-level. For truly spectacular views you should head to the Trigrad gorge (see site A on page 222).

The cliffs in the quarries of the Sakar and Besaparski are worth mentioning as they hold a few species not present in the Eastern Rhodopes. Besides the Ravens, Eastern Black-eared Wheatears and Blue Rock Thrushes, Besaparski has two other birds: the Rock Sparrow and the Rose-coloured Starling. It is this second bird that will be most interesting for birdwatchers but you have to be lucky. Rose-coloured Starlings are nomadic birds, wintering in India and breeding on the steppes of western Asia, usually in Kazakhstan, southern Russia and the Ukraine. Where they stop to build their nests depends strongly on the rains. If the weather is bad, they just move on further west, to the Black Sea coast of Romania, Bulgaria, the Thracian Plain and sometimes further down into Greece and Turkey. If the weather is excellent further east, they don't come all the way to Bulgaria, and if they do during a rainy spell, they will move on. But with a little luck (the long-term average is about 50%) they will nest in the region and for some reason, they always pick the same quarry in the Besaparski Hills where they breed in a big colony.

## Birds of steppes and large-scale agricultural land

The region this book covers is at the periphery of the large steppe plains of the East, which are known as the Pontic (steppes surrounding the Black Sea) and the Anatolian regions (central Turkish uplands). Traditional agriculture created extensive grasslands and fields, grazed by sheep, which sufficiently resemble the 'true' steppes to support some of the typical steppe birds. The best example of this is the Isabelline Wheatear, which is common only in these Pontic and Anatolian ranges, and just sneaks into our region, where it is locally quite common, such as near Ivaylovgrad, Kardzhali, Sakar and in some places in the Thracian Plain. Isabelline Wheatears are strongly tied to the presence of Susliks, in whose abandoned burrows they breed (see page 88).

Black-headed Bunting

Key to the birdlife of these areas is the presence of sufficient seeds and large insects, and the absence of pesticides and herbicides – in other words, traditional agriculture and grazing instead of modern, intensive farming (see page 35). However, the transition to

**Key birds of steppes and agricultural land**
Long-legged Buzzard, Common (Steppe) Buzzard, Booted Eagle, Short-toed Eagle, Eastern Imperial Eagle (Sakar), Lesser Spotted Eagle (Sakar), Lesser Kestrel (Sakar), Sakar (rare; reintroduced), Quail, Grey Partridge, Stone Curlew, Collared Pratincole, Great Spotted Cuckoo (rare; Besaparski), Hoopoe, Bee-eater, Roller, Tawny Pipit, Black-headed Wagtail, Calandra Lark, Short-toed Lark, Crested Lark, Skylark, Northern Wheatear, Isabelline Wheatear, Lesser Grey Shrike, Black-headed Bunting

## BIRDS

The Isabelline Wheatear is so named because of its colour. Isabelline colours are drab yellowish-brown, named (legend has it) after the colour of Queen Isabella's underwear who had sworn not to change it until the Siege of Ostend finished. The siege lasted over 40 years...

intensive agriculture is painfully visible in the numbers of steppe birds present. Typical birds of the 'good' places (read: traditional agriculture and grazed land) Stone Curlew, Tawny Pipit, Lesser Grey Shrike, Roller, Little Owl, Lesser Kestrel, Eastern Imperial Eagle, Lesser Spotted Eagle, Long-legged Buzzard, Short-toed Eagle and Hoopoe – all birds that eat large insects, lizards and small rodents.

Calandra, Crested and Short-toed Lark depend on invertebrate food sources in the summer, but even typical seed eaters like Corn Bunting and Black-headed Bunting depend on this source of protein to raise their young. More intensive farming, by using a range of pesticides, reduces the invertebrate fauna thus causing a decline of these birds – here and elsewhere in Europe.

The large-scale agricultural land, particularly that near the wetlands such as north of Plovdiv, have a few attractions of their own. The Grey Partridge for example, which has declined so tremendously in central Europe, is still quite common here. Quails, Pheasants, Skylarks and Black-headed Wagtails are common too, as are (in damper areas) Lapwings. There are several colonies of Collared Pratincoles near the small reservoirs in the region and they can be seen flying over the fields and open marshes in spring.

### Birds of the rivers

The river valleys of both the Arda and its tributaries and Maritsa, have an interesting mix of dense, tall and lush vegetation and open landscapes, the latter consisting of natural open places like pebble banks and regularly flooded plains, and fields and riverine grasslands grazed by sheep. The river valleys thereby combine the very open with the very dense, which suits a specific set of birds. Syrian and Green Woodpeckers, Golden Orioles, Turtle Doves, Rollers, Hoopoes and Bee-eaters are more numerous here than elsewhere. The Black Kite is a classic raptor of the riverine forest, but the tall trees with their large crowns also provide nesting sites for other raptors. Most species of eagles have a strong presence along the rivers. However, the raptor that is most strongly tied to the riparian habitat is the Levant Sparrowhawk. Along the Maritsa river, in particular, it reaches high densities and can be seen hunting over the nearby fields.

The second great draw of the riverine habitat, next to the Levant Sparrowhawk, is the Masked Shrike. This handsome species reaches the north-western limit of its rather small breeding range (which extends over Turkey into Syria and Iran) in the Thracian Plain. Here it can be surprisingly numerous in the more open woodland patches along the river. Furthermore, it is thinly scattered in all sorts of woodlands and scrublands in Sakar and the Eastern Rhodopes. It is often found close to rivers, including poplar plantations, but also in open oak woods. Masked Shrikes are known for their more secretive lifestyle compared to the other shrikes, which usually perch on prominent venture points on tops of bushes.

The colourful Bee-eater forms colonies, sometimes of hundreds of individuals. They breed in holes they dig themselves. Hence loamy slopes, such as along roads and rivers, are their favourite haunts.

# BIRDS

Golden Orioles are very numerous in the riparian forests throughout the area.

Although this may be true sometimes, this is by no means exclusively a skulking bird. We've found Masked Shrikes singing prominently on the top of willow trees in Zlato Pole for example.

Among the smaller passerines, it is the Eastern Olivaceous Warbler that reaches its highest densities along the river.

On the river itself, it is probably the Black Stork that is most conspicuously present. It can be found in spring along all major river courses. In early spring and particularly in late summer, Black Storks congregate in the marshes along the Maritsa river. One August in Zlato Pole (route 22), nearly 50 Black Storks were counted together in a single pond. Kingfishers breed in sandy banks along the river, as do Bee-eaters and Sand Martins. Dipper and Grey Wagtail also occur, but only higher in the mountains, which means that they are limited mostly to the Western Rhodopes.

Few birds breed on the shingle banks of the rivers, but there are a few. Little Ringed Plover and Common Sandpiper can be found throughout in low numbers, as well as Stone Curlew. The latter is mostly found on the broad, shallow margins of reservoirs. Finally, a special mention should be made about what is probably the most unexpected river bird and one that is only found on the Maritsa River: the Oystercatcher! The bird that is so familiar for visitors from north-western Europe was until recently strictly coastal, occurring in salt marshes of both the Black and Aegean Seas, but has colonised the Maritsa river in the last few decades.

**Key river birds**
Black Stork, Levant Sparrowhawk, Kingfisher, Little Ringed Plover, Green Woodpecker, Turtle Dove, Hoopoe, Bee-eater, Roller, Golden Oriole, Masked Shrike, Eastern Olivaceaous Warbler

## Birds of oak and beech forests

Whereas the bird diversity of the open oak woods is superb, the numbers go down where the forest becomes denser. This is not to say that these are of little importance to the region's birdlife. On the contrary, the denser patches, especially those with old trees, are of great importance as breeding areas, especially for the broad-winged species like raptors and Black Storks. Also, the smaller species that you look for in half-open landscapes often seek out the nearby thicker woodlands to breed. However, when you are into one of the larger oak or beech stands, you'll notice that these are not the greatest places to see many birds.

There are exceptions though. Most of the widespread central European species – the tits, the nuthatches, Robins and Chaffinches, reach the highest densities in the forest. In the oak forests, there are also many Hawfinches, Golden Orioles and woodpeckers. Middle Spotted Woodpecker is, whilst not terribly numerous, widespread in the older oak stands, where it occurs together with Lesser Spotted, Great Spotted, Green and Black Woodpeckers. The older stands with sufficient dead wood are generally the richest. Another typical bird of oak forests that is restricted to the Eastern Rhodopes and (locally) Sakar, is the Eastern Bonelli's Warbler.

Other birds of Oak forests include Hawfinch, Golden Oriole, the common tits and chaffinches, Cirl Bunting, Lesser Spotted, Middle Spotted, Great Spotted, Green and Black Woodpecker (the latter everywhere). Among the typical forest raptors, the Honey Buzzard, Sparrowhawk and Goshawk stand out.

There are absentees in the oak forest as well – birds you'd expect as they are present in oak forests in central Europe, but are rare or absent in these hot and dry Bulgarian woodlands. Short-toed Treecreeper and Wood Warbler for example. These are in the Rhodopes much more tied to the Beech forests.

As a birdwatching habitat, the beech forests are of the Rhodopes are complicated. There are three highly sought-after species here: Grey-headed Woodpecker, White-backed Woodpecker and Semi-collared flycatcher. All three, however, are fairly to very scarce and, in case of the woodpeckers, they occupy large territories. Since Beech forests occur mostly on steep slopes, hearing a Grey-headed or White-backed by does not

> **Key birds of Beech and Oak forests**
> Honey Buzzard, White-backed Woodpecker, Middle-spotted Woodpecker, Grey-headed Woodpecker, Black Woodpecker, Golden Oriole, Semi-collared Flycatcher (scarce), Eastern Bonelli's Warbler, Wood Warbler, Cirl Bunting

## BIRDS

mean you are going to see it and it is hard going down or upslope to find them. Moreover, these birds call most early in spring, when these forests are largely inaccessible due to snow or, during the thaw, mud. Nonetheless, the birds are there and could be seen. The Grey-headed is the most numerous of the three and is not strictly confined to these forests and altitudes. We've also found it in tall riparian forests along mountain streams. The Semi-collared Flycatcher by contrast is truly scarce, occurring in much higher numbers in the eastern part of the country.

### Birds in the high parts of the Western Rhodopes

Above approximately 1000 metres, the coniferous forests of pine and spruce are starting to take over from the oak and beech woods of the low slopes. These forests range from dense, closed forests to open stands, mixed with meadows and karstic dry grasslands. The birdlife of this zone consists of a mix of 'classic' Alpine species, mixed with birds that are familiar to visitors from central Europe.

The most frequently encountered birds in the coniferous forests are Chaffinches, Dunnocks, Robins, Mistle Thrushes, Crossbills, Bullfinches, Chiffchaffs, Siskins, Tree Pipits, Firecrests, Goldcrests and a large number of tits.

Coal and Crested Tits are the most numerous, but you may find Willow and Marsh Tits too. In fact, the latter two form, together with Sombre Tit, an interesting triplet of similar-looking species with a partially overlapping distribution. Sombre Tit prefers the warm oak woods and lowland riversides of the Eastern Rhodopes and Sakar. The optimal habitat for Marsh Tits are the temperate oak and mixed woodlands in the lower parts of the Western Rhodopes but is found in low numbers in the (mixed) coniferous woodlands, while Willow Tit prefers these highest zones.

Besides the Wallcreeper (which we discuss in the section on cliff-breeding birds), Tengmalm's and Pygmy Owls, Three-toed Woodpecker, Nutcracker, Ring Ouzel, Capercaillie and Hazel Grouse are the major attractions of the coniferous forests of the Western Rhodopes. The owls, the Capercaillies and Hazel Grouse cover large areas and are very hard to find. You really need a guide to show them to you, or just tremendous luck, as we had at Zabardo, when we stumbled upon a Pygmy Owl. This sparrow-sized bird is a ferocious hunter of 'crests and tits at dawn and dusk. During the day, the roles are reversed and the owls are often mocked by the small songbirds that form their prey at night.

# BIRDS

Capercaillies and Hazel Grouse feed on the buds of trees, with Capercaillie preferring the old, open pinewoods and Hazel Grouse searching out the wet valleys with birches and alders.

> **Key birds of the Subalpine zone**
> Capercaillie, Hazel Grouse, Rock Partridge, Corncrake, Tengmalm's Owl, Pygmy Owl, Eagle Owl, Alpine Swift, Rock Thrush, White-backed Woodpecker, Three-toed Woodpecker, Grey-headed Woodpecker, Black Woodpecker, Nutcracker, Wallcreeper, Ring Ouzel

Much easier to find are the Nutcrackers and Ring Ouzels, which you most often discover on the edge of spruce forests or in the more open stands. To see Nutcrackers, it greatly helps if you know their call (somewhat reminiscent to that of Jay). Finally, the Three-toed Woodpecker is a notoriously difficult bird to find. It prefers the very old spruce stands, with lots of dead snags. It occurs through the coniferous forests but reaches its highest densities in the gorges where dead wood accumulates and unlogged trees tend to be older.

The open areas are not to be missed either. In the scattered trees and bushes on the meadows and on the karstic plains, there are Yellowhammers, Serins, Tree Pipits, Woodlarks and Red-backed Shrike. Where there are rocks, there are Black Redstarts and Dunnocks, whilst around farms, you'll come across the nests of Crag and House Martins and Swallows. Even Red-rumped Swallows still breed here. Skylarks sing high above the flower-rich meadows where, in some places, Rock

The Capercaillie is quite numerous in the coniferous forests of the Western Rhodopes.

BIRDS

Partridges and Corncrakes can be found as well. The latter is, as ever, very hard to see, but its comb-rasping call is very much a part of these mountains. When it suddenly shuts up, look up to the sky as there's a good chance that a Golden Eagle has silenced it.

## Wetland birds

For a region that is not known for its wetlands, the Rhodopes and particularly the adjacent Thracian Plain has a splendid range of wetland birds. They all occur rather locally, but many are nonetheless quite easy to find. The wetlands are all rather small and most of them are artificial: reservoirs, both in and outside the mountains and fishponds are what you mostly encounter. None of these have the full range of wetland species; rather, they each have their own specialties.

North of Plovdiv there are a few shallow reservoirs with reedy margins and a number of fishpond complexes (sites A-E on pages 248-251) that combined have a great range of wetland birds. The herons are the first to catch the eye: Little Bittern, Little and Great White Egrets, Night and Squacco Herons can be found in good numbers. Recently, Glossy Ibis has started to breed here as well and in keeping with this species' range expansion, it is likely that it will become a much commoner bird in the near future.

There are not many ducks here but there are a few, mostly Pochard, Garganey, Gadwall and Mallard plus Ferruginous Duck. Great-crested Grebe and Little Grebe are both common as well. Breeding waders include Black-winged Stilt.

Further east there are two reservoirs (site E on page 251) that are used as cooling water for nearby nuclear plants – not the prettiest of sites, but they do have wintering Dalmatian and White Pelicans, as well as, in some years, White-headed Duck. White-tailed Eagle breeds here too. Within the Eastern Rhodopes, the reservoirs along the Arda river are the main wetland sites. Most of these reservoirs are rather deep and the soil at their margins is too rocky for reeds. Such places are pebbly or have grasses, and are home to Stone Curlews, Little Ringed Plovers and Black-headed Wagtails. Besides Grey Herons and Cormorants, these deeper reservoirs are also home to two unexpected

**Key wetland birds**
**Breeding** Squacco Heron, Night Heron, Little Egret, Little Bittern, Pygmy Cormorant, Black-winged Stilt, Collared Pratincole (rare), Glossy Ibis (uncommon)
**Passage** Dalmatian Pelican, Great White Pelican, Whiskered Tern, Black Tern, White-winged Tern, Red-throated Pipit, Moustached Warbler

species of wildfowl that have recently started to breed here. The first is the Ruddy Shelduck, native to wetlands on the steppes of Anatolia from which it has colonised this region. The second is Goosander. This large, fish-eating duck species is a breeding bird of northern and central Europe, but colonised the great Prespa and Ohrid lakes (on the border of Greece, North-Macedonia and Albania) after the last ice age, where it remains a relict population. This population started to expand recently and Goosander is now a breeding bird of the Arda reservoirs.

Not yet breeding there but occurring in increasing numbers are Dalmatian and White Pelicans. The latter is most likely restricted to being a winter bird and passage migrant, but Dalmatian may well start to breed here. In summer, Greater Flamingos are frequent near Kardzhali. Within this town there's a small wetland on the Arda with a large heronry. From the bridge you look at the birds on their nests – a spectacular sight. Little Egrets, Night Herons and Pygmy Cormorants are the most common species here.

Dalmatian Pelicans (top) are present troughout much of the year in the Studen Kladenets reservoir (route 5) and at the reservoir of Galobovo (site E on page 253). Pygmy Cormorants breed near Kardzhali (bottom; route 5).

The area lacks places with extensive reedbeds or flood forests, but there are many small patches with this habitat. Here Great Reed Warblers are numerous. Penduline Tit, Reed and Marsh Warblers are less frequent while Savi's and Sedge Warblers are scarce. Cetti's Warbler is scarce as well at the time of writing but increasing.

## Reptiles and Amphibians

> The best routes for warmth-loving reptiles is route 1, 2, 3 and 8 (Arda river), 13 and 14 and site A-D on pages 193-195, plus routes 23 and 24 (Sakar). These are the best routes for Kotschy's Gecko (also in Madzharovo), Worm Snake, Dahl's Whip Snake, Glass Lizard, Snake-eyed Lizard and Sand Boa, plus many other, more widespread species, such as the tortoises and Nose-horned Viper. Balkan Terrapin is exclusive to route 23 (and hard to find). Routes 4, 8, 9, 10 and 12 have drinking basins where in spring Yellow-bellied Toads can be found. For Fire-bellied Toad and Syrian Spadefoot, look for suitable sites an routes 22 and sites A-C on page 248-250.

The Eastern Rhodopes boasts, together with adjacent Greece and European Turkey, the highest diversity of reptiles and amphibians in the whole of Europe! A total of 14 amphibians and no less than 28 species of reptiles are known in this region.

Obviously, the climate and the generally good state of the landscape largely explains this richness, but the climate history also plays a part. Both amphibians and reptiles are susceptible to cold conditions and the series of ice ages has regularly wiped out the herpetofauna (as the reptiles and amphibians are collectively called) in large parts of Europe. The more warmth-loving species found refuge not far away on the Greek-Turkish coast and could easily migrate back to Bulgaria – something that was less easy for their congeners in southwestern Europe, where mountains and seas formed barriers for reimmigration into Europe.

There is no other species group in which the edge-of-the-Mediterranean phenomenon is so visible is with the reptiles and amphibians. About half the species that occur in the area, are exclusively found in the south-eastern part of the region, where the valleys of the Byala Reka, Arda and Thundzha Rivers are the gates through which Mediterranean species just protrude into Bulgarian territory.

The combination of (sub-) Mediterranean and more temperate conditions in the Rhodopes suit a wide array of species. From an ecological perspective, the large areas of intact habitat provide plenty of both prey and shelter, thus forming optimal conditions for reptiles and amphibians. The richest areas are the open forest and traditional farmland found in the foothills and river valleys in the Eastern Rhodopes and Sakar. This bit-of-everything habitat provides shelter under stones and bushes, sunny spots to warm up and shade to cool down.

REPTILES AND AMPHIBIANS

## Tortoises and Terrapins
One of the greatest herpetological attractions of the region are the large numbers of tortoises, or 'land turtles'. Few visitors to the Rhodopes are unmoved by the disarming and all-too-human gaze of the tortoises. These easy-does-it vegetarians really are a joy to watch. As with Blackbirds in a British hedgerow, the rustle of leaflitter in a woodland is a good sign there is tortoise around. If you sit down quietly under a bush, it is not exceptional to hear several of them blundering around you. And in the mating period in spring (April-May) you may be surprised to hear that they are capable of making a whole array of other sounds, matrimonial noises that may be comically (and embarrassingly) familiar ...

Two species of tortoises occur in the region and both are common: Hermann's and Spur-thighed Tortoise. As the name of the latter suggests, they may be distinguished by the presence or absence of a spur on the thighs (particularly on the hind legs). Both species are found in a variety of habitats, including dry and open woodland, scrub and arable land.

Water turtles – terrapins – are frequent as well, albeit more difficult to observe because they are quite shy. There are two species in the region. The European Pond Terrapin is common in nearly all types of freshwater. The Balkan Terrapin is, contrary to its name, an East-Mediterranean species that is restricted to the the river sections close to the Greek-Turkish border (e.g. Thundza, Byala Reka, Armira and Maritsa tributaries).

A Hermann's Tortoise on the forest track to Hisarya (route 4). On hot days, the tortoises retreat in the forest to stay cool.

FLORA AND FAUNA

## Reptiles and Amphibians

### Lizards

Any walk through the dry matrix of woodland, grassland and scrubland will reveal at least a few lizards. Without a doubt, the most frequently encountered reptile in all types of habitats throughout the region is the Eastern Green Lizard. The bright-blue coloured throat makes the males at least easily distinguishable from the Balkan Green Lizard (formerly called Three-lined Lizard), which usually has blue restricted to the neck, the other common big (up to 40 cm) green lizard in the region. The females of the Eastern Green Lizard tend to have brown spots whilst the females of Balkan Green Lizard are uniformly green or brownish. Both are good climbers and can often be seen rushing up a bush or tree. Although there is an overlap in these two species' habitats, the Three-lined Lizard prefers more open, dry and hot terrain than the Green Lizard. It shares this habitat with the big and curious European Glass Lizard (page 31), which occurs exclusively in the warm parts of Sakar and the eastern half of the Eastern Rhodopes. The legless Glass Lizard has an impressive, and to some perhaps even vicious appearance, but is completely harmless. Like a big eel, it slithers through dry grasslands, across arable land and along old stone walls. Some specimens measure up to a metre and are as thick as a man's wrist. Like most reptiles, it loves to bask in the sun and often seeks out a sunny road. However, it does not have the agility of snakes because it lacks the ability to move its belly scales, which enables snakes to slither rapidly over smooth surfaces. The Glass Lizard, in contrast, needs vertical intrusions like rocks or vegetation to push itself forward. This is why you will find that European Glass Lizards become 'road kill' more often than snakes. It is the fragility of this species that gave it its name – when hit, it shatters like glass.

Much smaller, but related, is the Slow Worm (note the name), which also has difficulty crossing smooth surfaces. This temperate species is widespread in the higher parts of the Rhodopes.

The region is host to four very similar-looking wall lizards, but since they all seem to prefer a slightly different habitat, not all is lost for those who wish to identify them. Erhard's Wall Lizard and Common Wall Lizard are widespread in the mountains, with Wall occupying the colder areas and Erhard's the warmer parts. The slightly larger Balkan Wall Lizard is most widespread and is the only one that is not restricted to rocky environments. Most specimens of the latter are recognisable by having a distinctive plain and green back. It is the only small lizard in the Thracian Plain. The fourth species is the Meadow Lizard, which belongs to a different genus (*Darevskia*) but is nevertheless not unlike the wall lizards.

**REPTILES AND AMPHIBIANS**

It is a south-east European Lizard, of open patches in the forest. Its distribution is rather exceptional as its main range is both east, north and west of our region and only isolated records in the Rhodopes, mostly in the western part (e.g. Dobrostan and Smolyan).

Just reaching the Eastern Rhodopes in the rolling hills of Ivaylovgrad is the small, brightly coloured Snake-eyed Lizard (or Lacertid). This lowland species of open scrub and stony hillsides is named after its staring snake-like lidless eyes.

The tiny Snake-eyed Skink lacks eyelids too. It is found in dry forests with much leaf litter in which to hide. It can reach high densities, but is not easy to see as they are usually hidden in the leaf litter. It occurs throughout the oak forest zone.

High up on the karstic plateaux of the Western Rhodopes the Sand Lizard can be found.

Geckos are warmth-loving reptiles that occur (within Europe) only in the Mediterranean basin. One species, the Kotschy's Gecko, just makes it into Bulgaria and is easy to find on warm evenings on house walls in villages along the Arda and in Sakar.

The Green Lizard is the most common lizard in the forests of the Rhodopes (right). The Kotschy's Gecko is locally common in the low, warm valleys, such as along the Arda (left).

FLORA AND FAUNA

## Snakes

With 13 species, there is a wide variety of snake species in the region. Only two of them have a poisonous bite. The Nose-horned Viper is with its cat's eye, conspicuous brow and pointy nose an impressive beast. It is quite common, occurring in all dry and rocky areas from the valley up to approximately 1600 metres. It is absent only from the highest areas in the Western Rhodopes, where it is replaced by the Adder. The latter occurs here with the Smooth Snake, both of which are snakes that also occur in central and northern Europe, which again underlines the cool-temperate conditions of these high parts.

The dry scrublands and light woodlands of the Eastern Rhodopes and Sakar are again the hotspots for snakes with the Arda, Maritsa, Tundzha and Byala Reka Valleys being the richest. Five species are confined to these valleys. The Cat Snake, so named because of its vertical pupils (like those of a cat), is essentially a Greek-Turkish species but is also found in the warmest parts of the Arda Valley. It is a rather small species, unlike the Montpellier Snake, which can reach up to two metres and is easily recognizable by its characteristic V-shaped fold between the large eyes. Like the Cat Snake, the Montpellier Snake prefers the warm scrublands and light woodlands of these Mediterranean river valleys. The same goes for the Blotched Snake, the Sand Boa and the Worm Snake. The latter two are special for their partially subterranean lifestyle. The elusive Sand Boa is the only boa species in Europe, killing by wrapping itself around its prey, mainly rodents, and crushing by contracting its strong muscles. Despite its exotic name, it is a relatively small snake, up to 80 cms long, which spends most of its life in rodent burrows. Another strange sub-Mediterranean creature is the tiny Worm Snake. It looks like a shiny earthworm with which it shares

The Aesculapean Snake is rather common and widespread in open oakwoods, especially near rivers.

## REPTILES AND AMPHIBIANS

many characteristics, including the fact that it lives nearly its entire life in self-made burrows underground. It prefers loose soils and is only found on the surface after heavy rains have flooded its burrows.

All the above species, arguably with the exception of the Nose-horned Viper, are not so easy to find as they have either very small distribution ranges or lead hidden lives (or both). Much easier to find are the Caspian Whip Snake and the Aesculapian Snake. Both are large and slender snakes of uniform colour and could be confused when you have only a brief glimpse of them. Upon closer inspection, they are easy to tell apart. The Caspian Whip Snake is yellowish-brown with a dark edge on all the scales, making it look as if wearing a fishnet stocking. The heavy brow, (though not as strong as with the Montpellier Snake) gives it a piercing look, quite unlike the rounded head of the Aesculapian Snake, which looks more friendly. Both snakes are quite aggressive when approached and will hiss and bite, but neither is venomous. They live in warm, open woodlands an are very good climbers. Unfortunately, they often warm themselves on the road surfaces and are often killed by traffic. A third scrubland snake is the beautiful Dahl's Whip Snake. It is smaller and more slender than the other two, and has a relatively long head, with a series of large, round spots just behind the head on an otherwise uniform body. The agile Dahl's Whip Snake prefers stony places and abandoned villages – the same habitat of the Nose-horned Viper.

Two stunning species of snakes you might just find if you are lucky: the Sand Boa (top) and the Nose-horned Viper (bottom).

REPTILES AND AMPHIBIANS

The final two snakes are aquatic and, as they frequently cross streams and ponds, they are most easily seen. The Grass Snake is widespread and common in all types of water, from mountain streams to large rivers. The Dice Snake appears to be more local but can be very numerous. It is a rather dark snake, grey with large and vaguely marked dark spots and large round eyes in an elongated head. It spends most of its time in the water.

## Amphibians

The classic amphibian experience in the Eastern Rhodopes is checking one of the many drinking fountains that are so frequent in the mountains and seeing all the little Yellow-bellied Toads in the drinking basins. They are a joy to watch, especially in spring, when the males are territorial and sometimes fight with one another, which usually ends up in a sort of toad-style sumo wrestling (see photo). The Yellow-bellied Toads are perfectly adapted to living in these mountains as they can survive and reproduce in very shallow waters. Often some puddles on the tracks are enough. Or, as said, the basins of the mountain wells. Sometimes, you can find other amphibians in these basins as well, such as Fire Salamander (in densely wooded terrain) or Smooth Newt.

You can find Yellow-bellied Toads in most puddles of water. In spring you may even see the males wrestle for the females.

Of the 14 species of amphibians, the Yellow-bellied toad is the only species which is most common and easily found in the Eastern Rhodopes. The rest of the amphibians are either lowland species, found most commonly in the Thracian Plain, or upland species with a distribution centred around the Western Rhodopes. A few species, such as the Common and the Green Toad and the Marsh, Agile and the Tree Frog, are found throughout.

The Thracian lowlands are perhaps the most interesting amphibian haunts. The Maritsa Valley, in particular, with its old river arms, fishponds and shallow reservoirs, is the haunt of the Fire-bellied Toad and the Syrian Spadefoot. The first is an east-European species that, like the closely related Yellow-bellied Toad,

## Amphibians and Reptiles of the Rhodope Mountains

| | |
|---|---|
| Fire Salamander | WR; very local ER |
| Alpine Newt | very local WR |
| Danube Crested Newt | all except WR |
| Smooth Newt | all except WR |
| Fire-bellied Toad | Thracian Plain |
| Yellow-bellied Toad | WR, ER, Sakar (local) |
| Syrian Spadefoot | Maritsa and Tundzha valleys |
| Common Toad | throughout |
| Green Toad | throughout |
| Tree Frog | throughout |
| Balkan Stream Frog (Graeca) | WR, very local ER |
| Agile Frog | throughout |
| Grass Frog | WR |
| Marsh Frog | throughout |
| | |
| Balkan Terrapin | Arda, Maritsa, Tundzha, Byala Reka |
| European Pond Terrapin | everywhere, minus high parts WR |
| Hermann's Tortoise | everywhere – west rhod |
| Spur-thighed Tortoise | everywhere – west rhod |
| Kotschy's Gecko | Arda, Maritsa, Tundzha |
| Slow Worm | WR, locally ER |
| Glass Lizard | Sakar, ER, |
| Johannisskink | Sakar, ER, edge of WR |
| Sand Lizard | High parts WR |
| Balkan Green Lizard | Thracian Plain, Sakar, Arda, Byala Reka |
| Eastern Green Lizard | everywhere |
| Snake-eyed Lizard | Byala Reka, Lower Arda and Maritsa |
| Erhard's Wall Lizard | ER |
| Wall Lizard | WR, ER, Sakar |
| Balkan Wall Lizard | ER, Sakar, Thracian Plain |
| Worm Snake | Arda, Maritsa, Tundzha, Byala Reka |
| Sand Boa | Arda, Maritsa, Tundzha |
| Smooth Snake | WR |
| Caspian Whip Snake | everywhere except WR |
| Blotched Snake | Arda, Maritsa, Tundzha, Byala Reka, Thracian Plain partially |
| Dahl's Whip Snake | ER, Sakar |
| Cat Snake | Arda |
| Easculapian Snake | WR, ER, Sakar |
| Grass snake | everywhere |
| Dice Snake | everywhere – west rhod |
| Montpellier Snake | Arda, Maritsa, Tundzha, Byala Reka |
| Nose-horned Viper | everywhere, minus high parts WR |
| Adder | high parts WR |

**REPTILES AND AMPHIBIANS**

The beautiful Fire Salamander is not uncommon in the small streams of the Eastern Rhodopes. Look for the tadpoles in the water, or for adults in the forest on a wet spring day.

prefers shallow water bodies that easily warm up. Only the Fire-bellied Toad occurs exclusively in the lowland and there is hardly any overlap in the range of the Yellow-bellied and the Fire-bellied Toad. The classic environments of the latter are well-vegetated lake margins and oxbows. These handsome small toads are most easily found by listening to their typical call, which sounds a little like the wind that blows over a tube or a piece of bamboo (look it up on the internet). Once you hear it, scan the water – the males are drifting on the surface when calling. The Syrian Spadefoot is a strange and very hard-to-find creature. It lives in roughly the same habitat as the Fire-bellied Toad, but the adults need sandy terrain near the water where they lay their eggs in. This is where the toads dig themselves in during the day and come out on damp, warm evenings and that is how you find them – searching by torchlight on such evenings. These marshes are also rich in Green Toads, Tree Frogs and Balkan Crested Newts, which are also best found on damp evenings.

As noted, the amphibian life in the Western Rhodopes is very different. Here, at an altitude of over 1000 m, there are Grass Frogs and Common Toads in mountain ponds and lakes. In a very few places, the Alpine Newt occurs here as well.

The beautiful black-and-yellow Fire Salamander is quite widespread in the small mountain streams in the forests. Finally, there is the Balkan Stream Frog, a relative of the Grass Frog that lives exclusively in the mountain streams and rivers in the southern Balkans. A frog on the edge of a fast-flowing stream in the Western Rhodopes is most likely this one.

# Insects and other Invertebrates

> Great butterfly routes are 1, 2, 3, 6, 15, 23 and 24 plus sites B and C (pages 193-194) in the lowlands, and routes 16 to 19 in the Western Rhodopes. The best dragonfly haunts are route 1, 6, 14, 22, 23 and 24, site D on page 195 and sites B and E on page 250 and 251. The more spectacular grasshoppers and bush-crickets (including Bronze Bush-cricket and Anatolian Predatory Bush-cricket) are routes 3, 23 and 24, plus site A on page 181.

As you'd expect from a warm and sunny region with many flowery grasslands, the Rhodopes have an overwhelming insect life, both in diversity and in quantity. This as-ever-far-too-short chapter on invertebrates deals with the butterflies, dragonflies and most conspicuous and easily encountered invertebrates of the Rhodopes and Thracian Plain.

## Butterflies of the lowlands and the Eastern Rhodopes

In spring and summer, butterflies are everywhere! Approximately 140 different species of butterflies can be found within the area of this guidebook. And they are on the wing at different periods from April to October. Although there are some spring flying butterflies (e.g. Southern Festoon) and autumn species (e.g. Lang's Short-tailed Blue), the bulk of the species emerge in the second half of May and peak between early June and late August. In summer, temperatures often rise to well above 30° C and most butterflies will then shelter from the heat during the middle of the day. At this time investigate the moist patches like drinking troughs, puddles and the sandy edges of streams, where butterflies gather by hundreds or even thousands to drink from the moist soil.

Dozens of Silver-washed Fritillaries feast on the flowers of Hemp-agrimony – one of the most important nectar flowers in summer.

There are large numbers of butterflies even in the lowlands and in the steppe-like grasslands (habitats that normally don't have a high diversity), but there are clear hotspots. In particular, the flowery grasslands in the Eastern Rhodopes and Sakar sport large numbers, as do the karstic grasslands and meadows at higher altitudes in the Western Rhodopes. A third butterfly hotspot is the collective network of rivers.

## INSECTS AND OTHER INVERTEBRATES

The Eastern Rhodopes are host to many species of blues, fritillaries, coppers and satyrs. Late April and early May is the time for the early spring species. Even though the diversity of butterflies is not as great as it is in late spring and early summer, there are quite a number of the more attractive and sought-after species already active. On the warming grasslands, you'll find Clouded Apollo and Southern Festoon as conspicuous species. Locally, especially near the Arda and Zlato Pole, there are Marsh Fritillaries. Duke of Burgundy, Glanville Fritillary and Weaver's Fritillary are present, mostly on limestone soils. Among the blues, Green-underside and Silver-studded Blues are locally common whereas Eastern Baton Blue is more local, near rocky terrain.

The diminutive Little Tiger Blue, one of the specialties of the area, can be seen near its larval food plant, the Christ's-thorn. It starts to emerge at the end of April. Another specialty, the Small Bath White, is also on the wing already and can be found on the pebble banks along the Arda river. As the month of May progresses, large numbers of new species start to emerge. Since this is also the best season for birdwatchers, it is when most people visit the area. For the butterflies it is an exciting period as everything is just starting to emerge and every day can bring something new that wasn't yet out the day before. In flowery patches along small streams, Chapman's Blue, Common Blue, Scarce Swallowtail, Wood White and Oberthur's Grizzled Skipper should be on the wing on a typical spring day. Both Spotted and Lesser Spotted Fritillaries appear and will become very common in the month to come. From early June both Balkan and Common Marbled White are on the wing (the first most in dry grasslands in the hills; the latter in the valleys). The by now straw-coloured grasslands are alive with butterflies, with Great Banded Grayling, Pearly Heath, Eastern Rock and Woodland Grayling. Inside the oak woodlands, there is another surprise: the Lattice Brown. This Balkan endemic, quite common in the area, rests on tree trunks and you'll frequently see it flying up as you walk by. At first glance it appears a rather uniform, dark butterfly but at closer inspection it has a beautiful pattern and coloration.

Hot secluded places or gullies formed by heavy rainfall constitute a special habitat where many species can be found. Such sunny but wind-free environments are much appreciated by Clouded Apollo, Eastern Dappled White, Balkan Copper, Blue and Mountain Argus, Large Wall Brown and Anomalous Blue. The image conjured up so far is that of the dominant neutral to acidic volcanic and sandstone soils. Calcareous terrain, which is rather uncommon in the area, attracts a different assemblage of butterflies. The limestone areas such as Ivaylovgrad region are the realms of Freyer's

## INSECTS AND OTHER INVERTEBRATES

Grayling, Little Blue and Chalk-hill Blue. The rare Bavius Blue flies locally on similar grasslands in Sakar (route 24).

A final superb location to look for butterflies in the Eastern Rhodopes, is along the rivers and damper places with brambles on forest edges. The Eastern Festoon, larger and paler than the Southern Festoon, starts to fly in May and can be abundant near rivers where Birthwort, its larval food plant grows. It is quite a spectacular butterfly. It is also a good place to look for Purple Shot and Balkan Coppers, Ilex Hairstreak, and, further into the season, for large fritillaries. Silver-washed Fritillary can be very abundant, but also Marbled, Dark-green, and Niobe are present. This is also the place where several species of admirals are found, including two spectacular species of south-

The beautiful Clouded Apollo is very common in spring.

### Special butterflies of the Rhodope Mountains

| | | |
|---|---|---|
| Eastern Festoon | *Zerynthia cerisy* | Conspicuous and common in agricultural land |
| Bavius Blue | *Pseudophilotus bavius* | Very local Balkan species; in our region only Sakar |
| Krueper's Small White | *Pieris krueperi* | Specialist of steep rocky slopes |
| Small Bath White | *Pontia chloridice* | Rare. Dry river beds. Resembles Bath White |
| Powdered Brimstone | *Gonepteryx farinosa* | Difficult to identify. has clear white wing tips. Flies in sheltered places. |
| Grecian Copper | *Lycaena ottomanus* | Usually near scrub, often drinking on bramble |
| Little Tiger Blue | *Tarucus balkanica* | Very small, common around Christ's-thorn |
| Blue Argus | *Aricia anteros* | Widespread, males with steel blue colour |
| Two-tailed Pasha | *Charaxes jasius* | Very rare in Greece, absent in Bulgaria conspicuous |
| Balkan Marbled White | *Melanargia larissa* | Common, bigger and with more white than Marbled White |
| Eastern Rock Grayling | *Hipparchia syriaca* | Shares habitat with Woodland Grayling |
| Freyer's Grayling | *Hipparchia fatua* | Usually on trees hiding in the shade |
| Russian Heath | *Coenonympha leander* | Local beauty in flowery scrubland |
| Lattice Brown | *Kirinia roxelana* | Widespread, flies inside bushy terrain. Hides in shade |
| Sandy Grizzled Skipper | *Pyrgus cinarae* | Local, flies fast and low over the surface |
| Oriental Marbled Skipper | *Carcharodus orientalis* | Widespread. Has clearly contrasting colours. |

## INSECTS AND OTHER INVERTEBRATES

*The Southern Festoon is a common spring butterfly (top). It flies a little earlier than its relative, the Eastern Festoon (bottom).*

eastern Europe: the gliders. Both the Common and the Hungarian occur, although both are quite rare. We found Common Glider not far from Kardzhali, but this beautiful species is bound to occur along many more rivers. Both White and Southern White Admiral occur, although the latter, a Mediterranean species, is limited to the warmer parts of the Arda and the lowlands. The large and impressive Poplar Admiral is found mostly along streams in the Western Rhodopes, where it can be quite numerous, flying mostly in late June and Early July. Of the closely related Emperors, all three species are present – the Large, the Lesser and the Freyer's. All of them have, for them, the so typical, purple gloss in the wings visible when you see them from a specific angle. The Freyer's is a specialty of south-eastern Europe and rather rare in the region. It is primarily known from the Arda river near Madzharovo and the lower Maritsa river but could well occur elsewhere too. It is quite similar to the Lesser Purple Emperor, which appears to be more common in the upper sections of the Maritsa River. The Large Purple Emperor is restricted to the larger rivers in the Western Rhodopes.

All these large and rather spectacular butterflies occur along the rivers in the region and make this an attractive and rather different butterfly habitat than the grasslands. And once you are there, be on the lookout as well for Large and Eastern Tortoiseshells and Camberwell Beauty, all of which occur in varying numbers. In some riverine marshes in the lowlands, you can also find Large Copper and, in drier places, Lesser Fiery Copper. Generally speaking, the Arda basin from Madzharovo to Sredna Arda is the richest stretch of riverine habitat. Some characteristic species

## INSECTS AND OTHER INVERTEBRATES

that occur in this area are Silver-spotted Skipper, Yellow-banded Skipper, Krueper's Small White, Blue-spot Hairstreak, Chequered Blue, Iolas Blue, Delattin's Grayling and Twin-spot Fritillary.

### Butterflies of the Western Rhodopes
All over the continent, mountain grasslands and karstic plateaux are the most diverse butterfly haunts. Both these habitats are present in the Western Rhodopes. Although nearby Pirin and Rila are, due to their higher altitude even richer, the butterfly diversity of the Western Rhodopes is wonderful and matches, if not outcompetes, that of the Eastern Rhodopes. The big difference is, besides the species, the flying time. In the Western Rhodopes, the butterfly season only starts at the end of May and runs all through the summer and early autumn.

Just like in the lowlands and the Eastern Rhodopes, it is also in the Western Rhodopes worth spending some time along the rivers to search for Poplar and White Admirals and, along the broader sections further down, Hungarian and Common Gliders. However, it is the grasslands and rocky slopes in the karstic areas that draws the largest number of species. Naturally, the areas of Dobrostan, Zabardo and Trigrad-Yagodina are the ones that boast the greatest number of species (and is also where we've centred our selection of routes around).

Perhaps the most impressive species here is the Apollo, which often flies together with the slightly smaller Clouded Apollo. The Apollo, one of Europe's largest butterflies, is a typical species of high altitude karstic plateaux and can occur a large numbers. It typically flies together with a large number of other species, including Marbled, Lesser Spotted, Spotted and Marsh Fritillaries, Duke of Burgundy, Chequered Skipper, Pearly and Chestnut Heaths, and Purple-shot Copper and a large numbers of blues, such as Large, Green-underside, Little Blue, Alcon and Geranium Blues. On more rocky terrain, you should look for Mountain Small White, Yellow-banded Skipper, Eastern Baton and Chequered Blues.

Ringlet are a group of true mountain butterflies and although the Western Rhodopes lacks many of the species found in Pirin and Rila, Woodland, (*medusa*), Bright-eyed (*oeme*) and

When it comes to flight behaviour, the Lattice Brown is the Sparrowhawk of the butterflies: instead of flying in the open they go straight through dense underbrush, sometimes resting on shady trunks.

## INSECTS AND OTHER INVERTEBRATES

(near Trigrad) Black (*melas*) Ringlets can be found. Scots Argus, also a species of *Erebia*, flies in the Western Rhodopes too.

Most ringlets fly in the meadows and mountain heathlands rather than the rocky, thin soil of the pastures of the karstic plateaux, although there is a considerable overlap in these habitats. Other butterflies you'll most likely encounter on the somewhat grassier parts are Balkan Copper, Eastern Large Heath, Zephyr Blue, and Twin-spot Fritillary.

### Dragonflies and damselflies

With approximately 50 species, the region ranks amongst the better ones in Europe for dragonflies and damselflies. Besides the widespread European species, there is a large number of rather localised Balkan species (e.g. Balkan Emerald, Turkish and Balkan Goldenrings and several East-Mediterranean specialities (e.g. Odalisque and Eastern Spectre). Additionally, there are a few rare and quite spectacular dragonflies that have recently colonised Bulgaria from the south, most likely the result of climate change. Violet Dropwing and Bladetail serve as two examples. Finally, one of the few European narrow-endemics (that is species with a very small distribution range) occurs in the area: the Bulgarian Emerald. All in all, quite a mouth-watering diversity, the bulk of which is on the wing from late May to late July. Quite unlike the butterflies, the greatest diversity of dragonflies is found in the Eastern Rhodopes and the lowlands. The eastern edge of the Eastern Rhodopes and Sakar, around the Thundzha, Maritsa and Byala Reka rivers plus nearby wetlands, in particular, have the greatest variety.

In a bold attempt to get a grip on the dragonflies and damselflies of the region, we have grouped them in relation to the four major habitats: the fresh and brackish lowland marshes, the major rivers of the Eastern Rhodopes, the small, often temporary stream in the hills, and finally the small, shallow, man-made pools, ponds and puddles that occur pretty much throughout the region.

**Dragonflies of standing waters and marshes in the lowland** The freshwater reservoirs, oxbow lakes and riverine marshes, ditches and puddles in the lowlands are obvious dragonfly haunts. Between June and September, thousands of them can be seen hunting over the wetlands. Blue-eye (or Southern Migrant) Hawker, Vagrant Emperor, Lesser Emperor, Green-eyed Hawker, White-tailed and Black-tailed Skimmers and Red-veined Darter are all common. In May, the Blue Chaser is numerous in lowland marshes, but can also be found far from the water. Although well named as far as the male is concerned, 'Blue Chaser' is a confusing

## INSECTS AND OTHER INVERTEBRATES

name for the females and juveniles which are orangey in colour. Depending on the vegetation, these waters support lots of damselflies like Large Red-eyed, Azure Bluet and Common Bluetail and sometimes also Common Winter Damsel. A very typical dragonfly of small ponds and standing waters is the Broad Scarlet, the males of which are a vivid red.

Small ponds situated in steppe grasslands are very interesting for dragonflies. Their shallowness, thin vegetation and lack of fish make them a suitable habitat for Spotted Darter, Small Bluetail, Migrant Spreadwing and the rare Small Spreadwing.

Dragonflies respond very quickly to climate change, and in the last couple of years, three southern species formerly not known from Bulgaria have settled here. The shallow water bodies are the preferred ones, in particular, the two reservoirs of Galobovo and Ovchi (site E on page 253) are popular as their water is used for cooling the nearby power plants, thus remains relatively warm even in winter. One species to look out for here is the spectacular Bladetail, a relative of the clubtails and pincertails, but larger and with much more slender body that ends in a blade-like appendix. It is quite an impressive species, formerly known from a few large lakes in Greece. Another is the bright purple Violet Dropwing, originally an African species that has colonised the Mediterranean region in the last few decades. The third species is less impressive – the small dark-coloured Black Pennant which is another species that was originally known from several scattered localities in the Mediterranean, mostly coast lagoons.

**Dragonflies of the lowland rivers** The rivers that drain the Rhodopes form another, highly attractive hotspot for dragonflies. Rivers like Arda, Krumovitsa, and Byala Reka provide good conditions for dragonflies throughout their life cycle. Fast-flowing and standing waters are breeding places, while vegetated sand banks provide shelter to newly emerged adults. Small Pincertail and Black-tailed Skimmer are among the most numerous species and are often seen resting on the shores. In spring, hundreds of Common Clubtails fly over the banks of the Arda and other big rivers. Much less common are River Clubtail and Green Snaketail, which are found in scattered colonies along the Maritsa river.

Small, wooded rivers like the Thundzha, Byala Reka and some of the tributaries

The Odalisque, a typical Balkan species, is widespread in the region. We found it to be particularly common along the Byala Reka (route 14 and site D on page 195).

## INSECTS AND OTHER INVERTEBRATES

Turkish Goldenring

of the Arda host different, highly characteristic species. The huge numbers of Banded and Beautiful Demoiselles are the first to catch the eye. Locally, particularly on the lower Thundzha and Byala Reka, they are joined by Odalisque, a very beautiful species of damselfly that looks unlike any other damselfly in Europe. This species is restricted to Greece, Turkey and a few places in southern Bulgaria.

A similar distribution range has the Eastern Spectre, a dragonfly that superficially looks like a miniature hawker, but with very different behaviour, flying slowly and low over shade parts of the water. The large goldenrings are fast insects which use open spaces to hunt for insects. When they catch their prey, they rest on a branch (or other convenient perch), where you can observe them closely to identify them, which is not easy as there are several closely related species. In the small streams of the Eastern

### Special dragonflies of the Rhodope Mountains

| | | |
|---|---|---|
| Odalisque | *Epallage fatime* | Balkan species, local, often in trees near forested streams |
| Eastern Spectre | *Caliaeschna microstigma* | Balkan specialist, along small shady streams |
| Balkan Emerald | *Somatochlora meridionalis* | Balkan species, flies near forested streams and on shady tracks |
| Bulgarian Emerald | *Somatochlora borisi* | Endemic for this region, hunts over small forested rivers |
| Turkish Goldenring | *Cordulegaster picta* | Rare Balkan species, forest streams |
| Balkan Goldenring | *Cordulegaster heros* | Balkan species, sandy forest streams |
| Common Clubtail | *Gomphus vulgatissimus* | Very common on rivers |
| Spotted Darter | *Sympetrum depressiusculum* | Local species of shallow and standing waters |
| Violet Dropwing | *Trithemis annulata* | Mediterranean species, expanding to the north; common in lowland marshes |
| Black Pennant | *Selysiothemis nigra* | Mediterranean species, expanding to the north; local in lowland marshes |
| Bladetail | *Lindenia tetraphyllis* | Mediterranean species, expanding to the north; local in lowland marshes |

## INSECTS AND OTHER INVERTEBRATES

Rhodopes, it is mostly the Turkish Goldenring that can be expected, although Balkan Goldenring is present here too. We haven't heard yet of sightings of the very rare Blue-eyed Goldenring, but there are scattered finds of this species a little north, east and south of our region, so be aware of its existence when identifying goldenrings.

The Balkan Emerald is very specific about its choice of habitat, and can only be found along forest trails or near the shady shores of small streams, where it chases insects. The discovery of the Bulgarian Emerald, a completely new, endemic species, in 1999 (by Milen Marinov) was a spectacular find. Further research has led to the discovery of more populations of this species, and perhaps more will be discovered in the future. The best place to search for this metallic greenish dragonfly is near forested streams, like the Byala Reka.

**Dragonflies of the Western Rhodopes** Although most of the dragonfly action takes place in the lower areas in the eastern part of our region, the Western Rhodopes is not without its odonate attractions. Along the rivers, the classic mountain stream triplet is present – Beautiful and Banded Demoiselles and Small Pincertail. In the lower parts of the river valleys, you may also find Balkan Goldenring. Be aware, however, that Sombre Goldenring is also widespread in the Western Rhodopes although it tends to seek out the smaller streams higher up in the mountains.

Since there are few mountain lakes in the region, the dragonflies and damselflies favouring such habitats are localised. However, the lakes just north of Smolyan (site C on page 223) have several attractive damselflies associated with northern–Alpine environments, such as Dainty Bluet and Spearhead Bluet (formerly called Northern Damselfly). Yellow-winged Darter has been found here as well, just like The Balkan Emerald.

### Other Invertebrates

To many naturalists, the world of grasshoppers, crickets, spiders, millipedes and other 'critters' remain the most obscure chapters in the great book of life. For anyone visiting the Rhodopes between late spring and autumn, this will quickly change as it won't take long before any enthusiastic

The longhorn beetle *Morimus funereus* is common in old Beech forests in summer.

## INSECTS AND OTHER INVERTEBRATES

When you walk along the tracks and trails of the Eastern Rhodopes, you come across many colourful beetles, such as the large, glossy Snail-eating Beetle.

'butterfly-hunter' comes eyeball to antennae with one of the bizarre, beautiful, grotesque or over-sized creatures that inhabit this region. Insects that are so out-of-the-ordinary that they demand an identification.

Spring visitors may come across the large Egyptian Locust, which invades the region from Africa and is one of the few large grasshoppers about early in the season. This biblical species is readily identifiable by its striped eyes. Many more grasshoppers and their allies can be found in the summer months. The largest and most impressive ones are found in the dry hot grasslands of the Eastern Rhodopes and Sakar. One of them is the Anatolian Predatory Bush-cricket* (*Saga natoliae*), often considered Europe's largest insects. It is quite frequent in open Christ's-thorn scrub in summer. It is one of three predatory bush-crickets of the genus *Saga* that inhabit the area (the others being *S. pedo* and *S. campbelli*). It is harmless to humans but a fierce predator of other grasshoppers. One of its victims, surely, is the peculiar Long-nosed Grasshopper. During your walks you are likely to come across one of Europe's largest and bulkiest grasshoppers: the Bronze Bush-cricket (*Bradyporus dasypus*), whose shiny appearance is quite common in Sakar and around Madzharovo from late spring onwards. You may also find mantids (praying mantises) in the summer.

The by now familiar story of eastern and Mediterranean influences upon the fauna of the Eastern Rhodopes clearly explains the origin of the grasshoppers. Turkish and Mediterranean species, include, apart from the above-mentioned, also *Callimenus macrogaster* (another big one), *Acrometopa servillea*, and the aforementioned *Saga campbelli*.

In all dry grasslands, including the karst plateau in the Western Rhodopes, you'll encounter large numbers of owlflies or ascalaphid. It looks a bit like a cross between a moth and a dragonfly, but is actually related to the ant-lions. We found two species to be frequent in the region: the Milky Owlfly* (*Libelloides lacteus*) with bluish-grey wings and the Eastern Owlfly* (*Libelloides macaronius*) with a yellow-and-black wing pattern. More or less related to this family is the conspicuous Spoon-winged Lacewing (or Grecian Streamertail) so called because of its very long wing

## INSECTS AND OTHER INVERTEBRATES

streamers. This impressive creature flies above the dry grasslands and frequently visits flowers (see page 143).

Among the beetles, there are also numerous impressive animals. Two of them we particularly find worth mentioning. First, *Morimus funereus*, is a blue and black longicorn beetle, which superficially resembles a Rosalia longicorn. It is a species of old growth beech woods and we found them in summer in Gyumyurdzhinski Snezhnik, route 12. The second is a big, metallic-blue Snail-eating Beetle, which occurs along the Arda River (e.g. route 6). This species specialises in feeding on snails. Its elongated 'snout' (*pronotum*) has evolved in such a way that it enables the beetle to penetrate snail shells.

Don't miss the huge Great Peacock Moth either. It is Europe's largest moth and is quite common in the oak forests in the Eastern Rhodopes. Look for it on evenings around the streetlights in villages. The lights of the Vulture Centre in Madzharovo (route 1) is a good place for them.

Many grasslands are dotted with cobweb lined holes, large enough to accommodate a mouse. These are the homes of the large Pontic Wolf Spider* (*Geolycosa vultuosa*), a type of tarantula. By carefully sticking a twig into the hole you can tease the tarantula out (she will bite the twig so you can carefully drag her out a little). Do this just once to minimise the disturbance! In rocky areas, you'll frequently encounter the small, bright-red *Philaeus* jumping-spiders, which are no cause for concern. Be careful, though, with the large Scolopendra that hides underneath the rocks. The latter is a big centipede, and has a mean bite, similar to the scorpion's sting!

The impressive carnivorous Anatolian Predatory Bush-cricket* (*Saga natoliae*) is one of the largest insects of Europe, and a mean predator for other insects, particularly grasshoppers and crickets.

# PRACTICAL PART

In this part of the guidebook we recommend routes that are particularly well suited for seeing the many specialities of the area.

The routes are centered in five areas. The first three – Madzharovo, Kardzhali-Momchilgrad and Ivaylovgrad – are situated in the Eastern Rhodopes. The fourth covers the Western Rhodopes and the fifth the large region of the Thracian Plain and Sakar Mountains.

For each of these regions we provide detailed descriptions of walks and car routes, plus a series of other sites of interest. These are not lesser sites. We have chosen to describe them more briefly because they are either smaller, more straight-forward to cover, or because they explore similar habitat, flora and fauna as the more extensively described routes. The map in the inner back cover shows the location of the various regions.

## Routes around Madzharovo

If there is one part of the Eastern Rhodopes that can be called the core area for naturalists, it is Madzharovo. Here all the key elements come together within a small area – the finest stretch of river, the main cliffs with raptors, some marshes, brooks and extensive woods and scrubland. There are some good opportunities to explore on foot, as well as some quiet backroads to drive. Because of this, there is concentration of rural B&Bs, a visitors' centre and a restaurant that are used to cater to naturalists from abroad, plus there are various guides, a bicycle and canoe rental – in short, all you need as a visitng naturalist but all still very low key. The next four routes (1 short car route and 3 walks) are all in the vicinity of the former mining town of Madzharovo, which is worth visiting for its own right (see box on page 59). The Arda River (route 1, 2) and the Kovan Kaya Cliffs (route 1) are definitely highlights of this area and should not be missed when visiting the region. Although the cliffs are part of the car route, you can easily visit them on foot; only 20 minutes from the visitors centre via the quiet road.

You can also explore routes 8 and 9 from Madzharovo as these sites are only a 50 minute drive away.

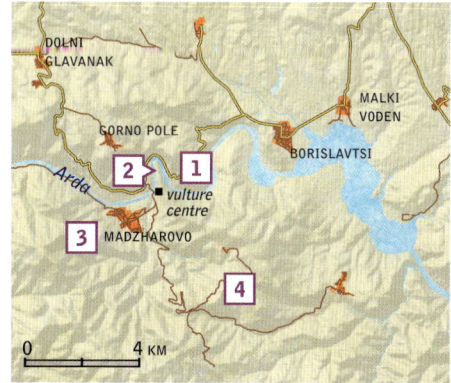

Discovering the Eastern Rhodopes on foot.

ROUTE 1: KOVAN KAYA AND THE ARDA RIVER

# Route 1: Kovan Kaya and the Arda River

**4 - 6 HOURS, 14 KM ONE WAY**

*The famous vulture cliffs of Madzharovo.
Scenic route with a rich birdlife.*

**Habitats:** river, scrubland, stony grasslands, cliffs, oak forest, fields, marshland
**Selected species:** Pink Butterfly Orchid, Jackal, Otter, White-tailed Eagle, Black Stork, Griffon Vulture, Peregrine, Golden Eagle, Western Rock Nuthatch, Blue Rock Thrush, Rock Bunting, Sand Boa, Small Bath White, Russian Heath, Sandy Grizzled Skipper, Freyer's Purple Emperor

The horseshoe river bend of the Arda river with the jagged cliffs of Kovan Kaya is easily the most iconic place of the Eastern Rhodopes. It is where the main vulture colony of the region is to be found and standing underneath the cliff and watching the vultures drift over your head on the one side and the Black Storks feeding in the wild Arda river on the other is a spine-tingling experience.
This scenic route explores this area and then takes you beyond these places and into a broad valley with, for the region, atypical marshlands. Like many routes in the region, the birdlife is splendid, but there is much more. The Arda river functions as a corridor of Mediterranean species that have their Bulgarian stronghold in this valley and in just a few other southern rivers (see page 112).
This route is described as a car route with stops and short strolls. Alternatively, you can easily make the first half of it a walk. There is so much to see that you may want to simply walk up to point 4 along the road, which is usually quiet and has very little traffic.

**Starting point** Vulture centre, Madzharovo (GPS: 41.643198, 25.871804). The centre is situated next to the bridge over the Arda River.

**1** The 'vulture centre' is a nature information centre of the Bulgarian Society for the Protection of Birds (BSPB). It has a small but good restaurant, café and also functions as a small hotel. It is the main hub for nature tourism in the region. Situated on a steep north slope of the river, under the canopy of tall Hungarian Oaks with their large, deeply lobed

## ROUTE 1: KOVAN KAYA AND THE ARDA RIVER

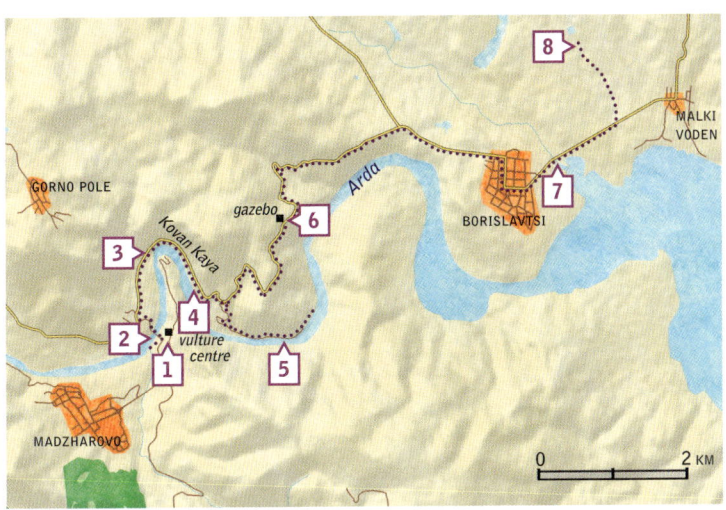

leaves, it is an idyllic spot, especially in hot weather. Local English-speaking ecologists provide up to date information on the area and its species. In the evening, the terrace lights in front of the centre attract many moth species like Cream-spot Tiger, Eyed and Small Elephant Hawk-moth and the impressive Giant Peacock Moth, which often rest on the vegetation near the lamps.

**2** From the vulture centre, walk to the bridge and enjoy the great views of the cliffs of Kovan Kaya and river with its pebble banks and patches of willow and aspen. Scan the shores for Black Storks which are often in the river and you should see the first vultures flying near the cliffs. Just before the bridge there's an open space next to the road. At the western end of it, a trail leads down to the river. This is worth exploring, especially for the endemic Small Bath White, that flies near dried up river-beds.

The river bed of the Arda near Madzharovo.

**PRACTICAL PART**

ROUTE 1: KOVAN KAYA AND THE ARDA RIVER

Cross the bridge and turn right to Borislavtsi.

**3** After 800 metres the tarmac road crosses a dirt road. Park on the left and continue on foot. A small stream has carved a steep little valley through the rocks. The open patch of dry flowery grassland is a butterfly hotspot attracting species like Krueper's Small White, Tree Grayling, Eastern Baton Blue and Southern Festoon. The stream itself supports Yellow-bellied Toad, Southern Crested Newt and Fire Salamander. This area is also a well-known site for the Worm Snake, a very small, blind snake that lives most of its life underground and in ants nests where it finds its food. After rainy spells it may come to the surface and you may then find it under stones. Dice Snake and Grass Snake are frequent here as well.

Kovan Kaya is a great place to watch Griffon Vultures from up close.

Don't forget to look up every once in a while. The vulture cliffs are nearby, so Griffon and Egyptian Vultures drift over frequently. Keep an eye out for Sombre Tit, Eastern Orphean and Barred Warblers here and at the stops ahead.

On the other side of the main road, the dirt track leads down to the Arda river. Look for Grecian Copper and Lattice Brown in the open patches between the trees. Balkan Lizard Orchids are frequent in this area and flower in June and July. Another typical wildflower is a climbing bush with white inflorescences – *Cionura erecta*. It is a species of the eastern Mediterranean growing on cliffs and, surprisingly, sandy coasts.

Continue by car in the direction of Borislavtsi. After another km you find a picnic table on the right side of the road where you can park.

**4** This is a good viewpoint, squeezed between the cliffs and the river. Check the cliffs where the Griffon Vultures breed. Birds of prey here frequently include Egyptian Vulture, Peregrine and Golden and Booted Eagles. Other birds to look for are Black Stork, Chukar (rare), Black-eared

## ROUTE 1: KOVAN KAYA AND THE ARDA RIVER

Wheatear, Blue Rock Thrush, Western Rock Nuthatch, Rock Bunting, Alpine Swift and Crag Martin. On the other side, you have a good view over the river. Apart from the splendid scenery you might be lucky to spot an Otter in dusk or dawn.

Continue and take the first tarmac road to the right, which brings you down to the Arda.

**5** Leave your car at the end of the paved road (beyond it gets sandy and you may get stuck!) and continue on foot. Keep an eye out for fishing Black Stork on the pebble banks, and for Little Ringed Plover, which breeds here. Banded Demoiselles and Common Clubtail are frequent dragonflies in springtime. An early morning visit, in combination with a healthy dose of luck, may produce an encounter with the highly elusive Sand Boa, a European Glass Lizard, an Otter or a Jackal, all of which are seen here on a regular basis. Don't forget to check the cliffs and the sky, for similar birds may appear here as on the previous site.

Retrace your steps to the main road and turn right. After about 5 km you see a wooden gazebo on your left. Park here.

the Kovan Kaya cliffs and the Arda river.

**PRACTICAL PART**

ROUTE 1: KOVAN KAYA AND THE ARDA RIVER

The handsome Little Tiger Blue can be found in the Christ's-thorn scrub along the road.

**6** The reservoir in the valley is part of the Arda River, which is dammed close to Ivaylovgrad. In the area a pair of White-tailed Eagle nests – one of the rarest breeding raptors of the region. They can sometimes be seen hunting over the area although your chances are better of spotting a Black Kite, another raptor that is not common in the region. Explore the Christ's-thorn scrubland behind the gazebo which is a good site for Olive-tree, Barred and Eastern Subalpine Warblers. Among the butterflies, Little Tiger Blue and Sandy Grizzled Skipper often rest on stones in the grassland.

**7** Continue to the village of Borislavtsi and be careful as the road is in bad condition. Drive through the village (Spanish Sparrows breed in the storks' nests) and stop at the first bridge. Scan the marshy grasslands that fringe the northern reservoir for Squacco Heron, Little Egret, Little Grebe and Cormorant. Barred Warbler may be present in the nearby bushes.

Continue over the dam and park on the left just before the next bridge. A 1.5 km walk along the stream leads you to a small lake.

**8** The fields on the left have Black-headed Bunting and Black-headed Wagtail. On your right, you overlook the bushy vegetation lining the stream. This is a good place for smaller songbirds and woodpeckers (Green and Syrian). The small lake at the end of the trail is fringed by marshland and reed beds. This makes this site an excellent one for Marsh Harrier, Kingfisher, Great Reed Warbler and Moorhen. Explore the grassy terrain near the lake for Pink Butterfly and Lady Orchids. Silver-studded Blue and Marsh Fritillary are so common in season that they cannot be overlooked.

Return the way you came.

## Route 2: The horseshoe bend in the Arda River

**2 HOURS, 3 KM ONE WAY**
**EASY**

*The banks of the Arda River, with their butterflies and dragonflies. Breathtaking views of the Kovan Kaya cliffs with its many vultures and other rock-dwelling birds.*

**Habitats:** Christ's-thorn scrub, rocks and cliffs, river banks
**Selected species:** Griffon Vulture, Black Stork, Blue Rock Thrush, Western Rock Nuthatch (rare), Grecian Copper, Small Bath White, Little Tiger Blue, Common Clubtail, Banded Demoiselle

The horseshoe river bend in the Arda river near Madzharovo is the hallmark image of the Eastern Rhodopes. It also graces the cover of this guidebook. Rather than looking over the bend, as you do on route 1, this route explores the pebble bank on the river, with the dramatic cliffs of Kovan Kaya forming the theatrical backdrop of this short walk.

**Starting point** Vulture centre (GPS: 41.643198, 25.871804; see point 1 of route 1).

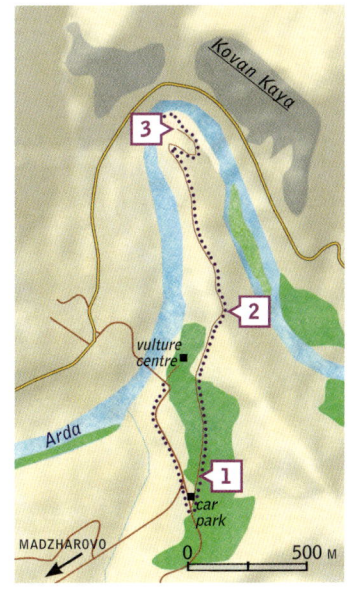

Walk (or drive) along the road in the direction of Madzharovo, but instead of branching off to the right to the town, go straight on towards Senoklas. After 150 metres, go left and make a U-turn on a rough track (If you are still in a car, this is where you park).

**1** This first section leads through dry, rocky scrubland made up of Christ's-thorn bushes, or *Paliurus spina-christi*, so named as allegedly, the crown of thorns that Christ wore

ROUTE 2: THE HORSESHOE BEND IN THE ARDA RIVER

Small Bath Whites fly in spring on the pebble banks of the Arda.

when walking to the cross, was made of this bush. This plant is host to the Little Tiger Blue, a handsome small butterfly with a small distribution range in the Balkans.

**2** The track leads onto the peninsula that juts into the Arda River. Halfway, on the high point, you have wonderful vistas of the river, with many raptors and Black Storks. There are plans to create a vulture feeding station here as well.

You have grand views of Kovan Kaya and its breeding birds. Bring a telescope for good views.

**3** Continue to the bank of the river, from where you have even better views on the cliffs. On the pebble banks, look for dragonflies and butterflies, the latter including the rare Small Bath White in spring.

# Route 3: Momina Skala

**5 HOURS, 10 KM
MODERATE-STRENUOUS**

*Challenging hike over mountainous terrain and through extensive oak forest. Good route for finding reptiles and orchids.*

**Habitats:** rocky grassland, scrubland, sub-mediterranean oak forest, Hornbeam forest
**Selected species:** Sand Boa, Montpellier Snake, Hermann's Tortoise, European Glass Lizard, Early-purple Orchid, Monkey Orchid, Lady Orchid, Laxmann's Bugle, Pontic Fritillary, Grecian Foxglove, Ortolan Bunting, Lattice Brown, Balkan Marbled White, Bronze Bush-cricket, Anatolian Predatory Bush-cricket

If you want to explore the habitats of the Eastern Rhodopes up close and on foot, this is your route. It brings you up to the peak of Momina Skala, which, at an altitude of 750 metres, offers excellent views over Madzharovo and River Arda. Along the way, you come across a variety of typical habitats of the region, each with its own attractive species. The insect life, flora and reptile fauna are particularly rich and you can walk this route multiple times and see different things each time. This route is marked with yellow lines.

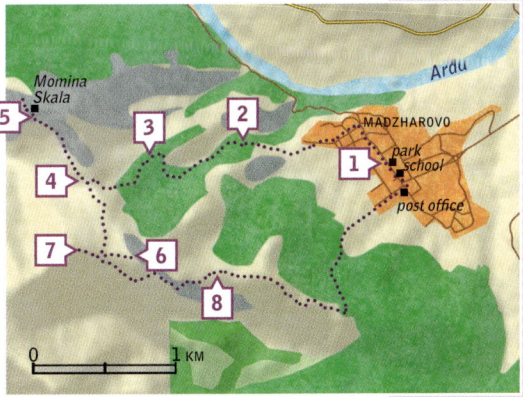

## Starting point Madzharovo

**Getting there** leave your car at the internet café / post office on the main street of Madzharovo. Walk along the main street in a northerly direction (to your right when you stand in front of the post office).

**1** Madzharovo is a unique town with an even more special atmosphere. The run-down apartment blocks and deserted bars

ROUTE 3: MOMINA SKALA

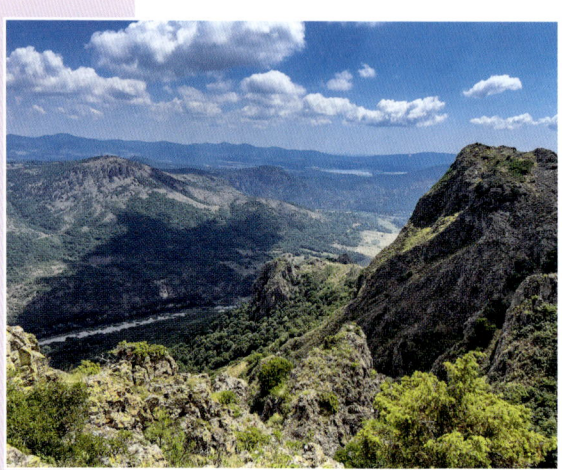

*View from the top of Momina Skala.*

and public buildings would give it a rather neglected air, if it wasn't for the broad boulevards lined with shady trees and beautiful scenery for a backdrop. Madzharovo was built in Stalinist times as a mine workers town and at its peak accommodated almost 15,000 inhabitants. With the closing of the mines, the people left and today, perhaps 500-1000 people remain. Meanwhile, wildlife has crept in. On spring nights, Scops Owls are everywhere (and with a flash light very visible) and in the park on your right just south of the school there are various orchids, including *Ophrys reinholdii* – a species that is very rare in Bulgaria as it is largely restricted to Greece and Turkey. It flowers early – at the beginning of April.

Just before the last flat on the lefthand side, turn left. Go straight at the next crossing and then, where the tarmac bends to the left, continue straight on a concrete track. Another hundred metres further, go left on the first track which leads you through an area of vegetable gardens to the edge of the forest. There, go straight, into the woods.

**2** This is a grazed wood – typical for the Eastern Rhodopes but rare in Europe. Rather than having fenced pastures for their grazing animals, the Rhodope farmers lead them into the communal lands to graze (as was normal during medieval times in Western Europe as well, and there the grazed forest is often referred to by the German word *Hudewald*). As a consequence, the Eastern Rhodopes has a wonderful patchwork landscape of grassland, scrubland and forest. Here look and listen for woodpeckers (Green and all three Spotted Woodpeckers), Hawfinch and Cirl Bunting. There are tortoises in the forest on warm days (at cooler times they prefer the grasslands) and in late spring and summer there are many Lattice Brown (a butterfly).

After 1.3 kms, the track forks. Take the left trail, signposted *Okopa*.

**3** By now you have arrived on the steep section of this trail. It is not very long, but quite tough. Catch your breath in the open sections and look for butterflies. There are easily 30 species to be seen on this walk, but among them are Balkan Marbled White, Green-underside Blue, Spotted, Lesser Spotted, Queen of Spain, Silver-washed and Niobe Fritillaries, Cardinal, Purple-shot Copper and Sloe Hairstreak. Look here and on the rest of the route for other invertebrates such as the gracious Spoon-winged Lacewing and the impressively large Bronze Bush-cricket (among other grasshoppers).

**4** Once on the ridge, take a breath and admire the view down to Madzharovo. From here you can see that Madzharovo lies in a crater-like depression, surrounded by steep cliffs. Look for raptors too. Griffon and Egyptian Vulture and Golden Eagle are all regular.

Turn right and follow the (unmarked) trail that leads to Momina Skala.

**5** This much narrower trail has the advantage of staying more or less level. It leads through bushy and rocky country on the west slope and ends at a saddle from which you again have superb views. The cliffs are botanically very attractive, with Yellow Leek, Rock Pink* (*Dianthus petraeus*) and Jovibarba – all species that also grow at Kovan Kaya and makes that a designated Important Plant Area but are more easy to see here. The open views provide excellent opportunities for watching raptors. Blue Rock Thrush and Ortolan Buntings breed around the cliffs and you can search between the bushes for Europe's largest insect, the Anatolian Predatory Bush-cricket, which is fairly numerous here.

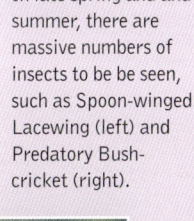

In late spring and and summer, there are massive numbers of insects to be be seen, such as Spoon-winged Lacewing (left) and Predatory Bush-cricket (right).

## ROUTE 3: MOMINA SKALA

Eastern Early-purple Orchid in the oak forests near the summit.

Return to the junction of point 3 and go straight, following the path underneath the peak (there are several parallel trails; they all arrive at the same point, and are way-marked). You arrive at a hairpin bend with several trails.

**6** The first goes left in the direction of a radio tower, again with a wonderful view over Madzharovo. A similar range of species can be seen from this tower – vultures and eagles in the sky, Ortolan and Cirl Buntings (plus Woodlark) singing from the trees and a chance of reptiles on the ground. The reptilian wildlife around Madzharovo is rather special, with many species that, in Bulgaria, only occur in this area, Byala Reka and Sakar, such as Sand Boa and Montpellier Snake, both of which we have seen on this walk. Caspian Whip Snake, Hermann's and Greek Tortoises are more widespread.

**7** Go back to the main track and continue. In the next bend to the left (you are on the ridge now) two unmarked paths branch off to the right, into the woods. This beautiful woodland has several attractive wildflowers including the Eastern Early-purple Orchid* (*Orchis pinetorum*), Lady and Bird's-nest Orchid.

Return and follow the track along the ridge. You now start your gradual descent back towards Madzharovo. Again, there are many parallel trails, but all follow the main ridge down. Follow the yellow flashes for the official trail.

**8** Look out for Roman Orchids, which grow alongside the trail and flower early in April. In the more open parts, notice the scrub and herbaceous species, like Prickly Juniper, Smoke-tree and Laxmann's Bugle* (*Ajuga laxmannii*). This is again a good reptile habitat.

The trail arrives at a broad track where you turn left. A bit further, the main track bends to the left. At this junction there are two left tracks. The first brings you to the guest house The Old Nest in the fields south of town; the sharp left brings you through the forest back into town and arrives right next to the post office on the main road.

# Route 4: Hisarya

**4 HOURS**
**4 KM ONE WAY, EASY**

*Easy walk through shady woods to a spectacular viewpoint. Great way to find orchids, reptiles, butterflies and birds on your own pace.*

**Habitats:** oak woodlands, flowery meadows, rocky outcrop
**Selected species:** Griffon Vulture, Middle Spotted Woodpecker, Roman Orchid, Balkan Lizard Orchid, Fire Salamander, Southern Festoon, Black Apollo

The shady track to Hisarya promises a relaxed walk, ideal for a warm day. There are a good number of orchids (peak time late April-mid May), some butterflies and you have a good chance of finding reptiles and amphibians. This is, as many walks in the Eastern Rhodopes, a linear walk and it finishes at a picnic spot with superb views over the plain and reservoir of Ivaylovgrad. This is a quiet walk throughout the year except on the 24th of May when the village festival takes place at Hisarya.

**Starting point** The pass on road between Madzharovo and Senoklas. (GPS: 41.605853, 25.885961)

**Getting there** From the bridge over the Arda, head towards Madzharovo, but rather than going right into the town, go straight (Sinoklas is signposted) and at the Y-junction right to follow the road up to a pass, approximately 7.5 kms further. Park just before the pass and walk the track that turns left, into the forest.

**1** You are now in a rather young Oak-Oriental Hornbeam forest whose trees are tall enough to provide shade. Look and listen for

## ROUTE 4: HISARYA

Hawfinch and Middle Spotted Woodpecker, for both of which this is a perfect habitat. In April before the leaf buds have unfolded there are thousands of Roman Orchids scattered over the forest floor. On warm days, reptiles retreat in the forest to stay cool. Tortoises and lizards are most in evidence. Halfway in the woods there is a well on your right, which is worth checking for Fire Salamanders.

Roman orchids are common in the forest in early spring (top). Later in spring, Balkan Marbled White flies over the pastures (bottom).

**2** 1.8 kms from the starting point, the landscape becomes more open. After the track passes some power lines, it forks. Follow the righthand track, marked with a Thracian heritage sign.

**3** Different birds are present here. Look and listen for Cirl Bunting, Hoopoe and Eastern Subalpine Warbler and for raptors that pass overhead. In May, there are many orchids in this area, such as Pink Butterfly, Green-winged, Mammose and Long-lipped Tongue Orchids. Look for lizards and snakes and butterflies such as Black Apollo and Southern Festoon.

**4** The track ends at a park-like area with tall trees and picnic facilities. This is Hisarya, a scenic spot in an open woodland with fabulous views over the Arda river and reservoir in the back. In the morning, as the air over the cliffs warms up and starts to rise, look here for raptors. Griffon Vultures and Black Storks are the most usual species, but Honey Buzzard, Booted, Golden, Short-toed and even White-tailed Eagles are possible.

Hisarya is also archaeological site, but the remains are hard or impossible to explore. There is a chapel next to the viewpoint, the St. Cyril and St. Methodius chapel, that celebrates the two sainted brothers (the 'Apostles to the Slavs') who are credited with devising the alphabet on the Day of Slavonic Alphabet (24th May).

Return via the same way.

# Routes around Kardzhali and Momchilgrad

The lively town of Kardzhali stands on the Arda River west of Madzharovo. The town is easy to reach from Haskovo and forms a second gateway to the Eastern Rhodopes.
Compared to the region of Madzharovo, Kardzhali is attractive in its variation of habitats, that includes steppe-like pastures and wetlands that are rare in the area of Madzharovo. However, it lacks many of the Mediterranean species that make Madzharovo attractive (e.g. Sand Boa, Little Tiger Blue). Perhaps more eye-catching, though, is the cultural difference. The small city of Kardzhali is a lively hotchpotch of ethnic Bulgarians, Turks, Pomaks and Roma, and its surrounding villages are predominantly Muslim, as is evidenced by the minarets that feature prominently in most of these places. Furthermore, there are various famous Thracian ruins, such as the ancient towns of Perperikon and Tatul, both of which are considered archaeological sites of international importance. The topography is hilly, with basalt cliffs fringing the reservoirs. Typical of the region are the concentrations of the white, clayey

Overview of the Kardzhali-Momchilgrad region, with the position of the routes. The letters refer to the sites on page 181-184.

Studen Kladenets reservoir, seen from the hunting reserve (site A on page 181).

zeolite, which forms weird formations, some of which became geological attractions, such as 'stone mushrooms' (site B on page 184) and a twin rock known as the Stone Wedding (route 5).

Another difference with Madzharovo is that Kardzhali sees very few tourists, whether birdwatchers, naturalists or otherwise. This is surprising as this area really has a lot to offer, ranging from meadows with Susliks, wetlands with breeding Pygmy Cormorants, lakeshores with pelicans and streams with Common Gliders (one of the more attractive butterflies of the region).

South of Kardzhali are two other regions that are very much worth a visit. The first is the entire area south of the Studen Kladenets reservoir, which can be visited from the small village of Nanovitsa (route 10; sites A and D on pages 181 and 183). This is the main rewilding area of the Eastern Rhodopes (see page 63) and the place where you'll not only see many vultures, but also roaming herds of Konik horses, Red, Fallow and Roe Deer and European Bison. Wolf and Golden Jackal are both common here.

Further east flows the Krumovitsa river from the town Krumovgrad to the Arda. This is another splendid region. The valley is rather broad, with large shingle banks along the river, fields and rocky, exposed slopes – a gem for birdwatchers, with many vultures, Western Rock Nuthatch, Roller and many others.

Directly south from Kardzhali runs the main provincial road 5 to the Makaza border crossing with Greece. Just before this crossing, lies the village of Kirkovo, which forms the gateway to the Kazalach Valley. This is a higher region, where the meadows are greener and the forest denser. This is the location of the Gyumyurdzhinski Snezhnik old-growth forest (route 12), which can be visited on a splendid, but tough, walk.

Classic Eastern Rhodope habitat of pastures, scrub and forest near the Nanovitsa ridge (route 10).

ROUTE 5: AROUND KARDZHALI

# Route 5: Around Kardzhali

**20 KM**
**EASY**

Variety of surprising sites very close to the Eastern Rhodopes' main town. Bird-packed wetlands, cliffs with vultures and meadows. Great options for bird photography at Kardzhali's heronry.

**Habitats:** dry grasslands, marshes, cliffs
**Selected species:** Suslik, Griffon Vulture, White-tailed Eagle, Black Stork, Pygmy Cormorant, Dalmatian Pelican, White Pelican, Night Heron, Squacco Heron, Western Rock Nuthatch, Eastern Black-eared Wheatear, Rock Bunting

In and directly around the town of Khardzhali are a number of highly attractive sites, particularly for birdwatching, geology and the scenery in general. Simply superb is the heron colony in the town centre, but just a little outside the city, there are cliffs with vultures and Black Storks, grasslands with Susliks and marshes on the reservoir edge. This route combines them all. The

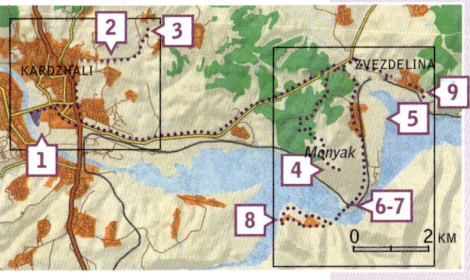

birdlife is the main focus, with classic Rhodope species like raptors, but, in addition, there are marshland birds like herons, Pygmy Cormorants and even pelicans.

**1** The heronry in Kardzhali is a phenomenon. In a small marsh right next to the River Arda (here canalised), hundreds of Little Egrets, Night Herons and Pygmy Cormorants nest. What's particularly attractive is that the trees in which they nest are very close to one of the main bridges in the town (the *Bulevard Bulair*). You can have a pleasant time just standing on the bridge (there's a wide pedestrian lane), watching the birds at eye level on the nest. The best light is in the evening, and since most birds fly directly towards you when they land, the photographic opportunities are simply excellent.

Besides the above species, there are small numbers of Squacco Herons and recently also Purple Herons and Glossy Ibis, the latter is not breeding

PRACTICAL PART

ROUTE 5: AROUND KARDZHALI

The river marshes in downtown Kardzhali (right) are home to an immense egretry with Night Herons (top) and Little Egrets (bottom).

(yet) but a few birds roost in the heronry. Kingfishers are relatively common, as are Great Reed Warblers.

Continue by car along the same Bulevard Bulair to the intersection with the Bulevar Belomorski, which is the main traffic artery of the town. Turn left and drive past the stadium (the Arena Arda). Some 600 metres beyond the stadium entrance look for a brown 'heritage' sign and turn right just past the hospital (a large building on the right just off the road but shrouded by trees). Look carefully, this turn is easy to miss. About 100 metres along this road a second sign will confirm you're on the right track and further signs will direct you to the Stone Wedding (Каменната сватба).

**2** Following this road you pass some fine, deep-soiled grasslands outside the town. Look here for Suslik, Isabelline Wheatear and Bee-eater. For the Susliks scan the mounds in the grass, which is where they prefer to create their burrows.

**3** Approximately 2.5 km after turning onto this road bear right at a fork and after 200m pull off onto a small parking spot with a sign for the stone wedding (GPS: 41.654785, 25.399301). Follow the trail uphill and then take the right branch to cross the stream and continue on the other side. The soft, white rock you see here is zeolite, a soft, very compact, clay-like material that formed when thick layers of volcanic ash were covered in seawater. The ash and the sea salts formed this material. Zeolite is able to absorb a lot of water, but when doing so, it gets soft and slowly erodes into the odd shapes you see here. The Stone Wedding is such an eroded form in which two zeolite columns next to each other resemble two lovers.

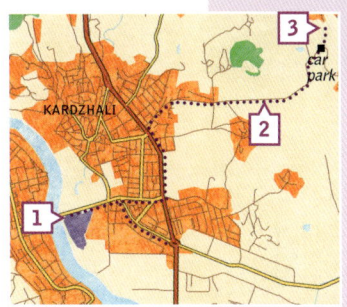

Return to Khardzali, turn left onto the main street for 1 km (passing the hospital and stadium again en route). Then go round the roundabout to follow the 507 towards Chiflik / Perperikon. After 7.5 kms turn right into what looks like a lay-by but turn very sharply right onto a road running almost parallel to the 507. A brown heritage sign for Monyak (sometimes written Monyek or Monek) castle is right next to this turning. Note – don't take the turning a 100m further on to Shiroko Pole which form a next element in this route.

Drive on for 2 kms and park at the small car park where a track branches off to the left and leads uphill. Follow this track to the mountain of Monyak.

**4** Monyak is a conspicuous, rocky hill at the shore of the Studen Kladenets reservoir, a little east from Kardzhali. Its sheer cliffs, the ruins of an ancient fortress and breath-taking views, in combination with its easy access, make it an attractive excursion.

Monyak has a spectacular birdlife and it is strange that this easy-to-access area attracts so few birdwatchers. From the cliffs you can see Griffon Vultures gliding by at eye level, and there are Blue Rock Thrush, Chukar, Raven, Black Stork, Black-eared Wheatear, Crag Martin, Alpine Swift, Rock Bunting, Blue Rock Thrush and in some years also Western Rock Nuthatch to be found here. Barred Warbler, Black-headed Bunting and Red-backed Shrike are found in the grasslands and scrub below.

On the cliff top there are numerous small trails through the scrubland. Explore them as you like – since you are on top of a table mountain, you can't get lost. The cliff edge to the south and east are the most attractive for birds, but be careful not to get too close.

While in Monyak, check the mouth of the river that flows into the reservoir to see where the birds are and if

there are pelicans present at the river banks. This area is the goal of point 8 of this route.

Return to the car and then back to the 507. Turn right and directly thereafter right again towards Shiroko Pole. In the village, turn left at the junction with the cafe, cross the railway and go straight on to the lakeshore.

**5** This stretch offers views of the cliffs with its raptors, and passes through dry grasslands and scrub where most of the aforementioned birds occur. Suslik and Marbled Polecat are listed for this site, although not seen recently. Of late, there have often been pelicans, both White and Dalmatian, on the lake here.

Dalmatian Pelicans often roost at the mouth of the Varbitsa River.

Return to the village, turn left at the crossroads and continue until you reach some woods where you park. Continue on foot on any of footpaths that eventually lead to the footbridge on the far side of the railway.

**6** The track leads through a dry scrubland of Christ's-thorn, in which the Purple Clematis winds up to the light. In spring, there are many Venus's Looking-glass flowering in the stony grasslands. Look too for Nose-horned Viper, European Glass Lizard and Little Tiger Blue.

**7** Crossing the footbridge over the wide reservoir is somewhat of an adventure in itself. It was built quite recently to connect Lisitsite village on the other side to the rest of the world. Before the reservoir was built, there was a road bridge over the Arda, but this is now flooded, leaving Lisitsite unconnected by roads or tracks.

**8** On the other side of the bridge, turn right and follow the shore of the reservoir to the mouth of the Varbitsa river. Depending on the water level, sandbanks of variable size are exposed here, but, there are often pelicans to be found here, sometimes waders, Black Storks and occasionally also Ruddy Shelduck and Goosander (both of which breed here, but are rather elusive). With a little luck, White-tailed Eagle, another breeding bird of the reservoir, comes by to hunt. Be aware that

**ROUTE 5: AROUND KARDZHALI**

View from Monyak over the reservoir and footbridge to the village of Lisitsite.

the pelicans are easily disturbed so keep a good distance from them. From the water's edge, you also have good views of the cliffs of Monyak and their breeding Griffons and Black Storks. From here you can clearly see that Monyak is an outcrop of columnar basalt. Most bird nests are found on top of the basalt pillars.
Return through the village, now inhabited by so few people that Hoopoes, Lesser Grey and Red-backed Shrikes probably outnumber them. Yellow-bellied Toads live in the village well.

Return to the 507. If you haven't seen Suslik yet or wish to see more cliff birds, go right and directly right again, to the village of Zvezdelina and the Sredna Arda protected site.

**9** The dry and grasslands on deep soils along the road up to the village should be a good place to find both Suslik and Isabelline Wheatear, which likes to breed in the Suslik holes.
In the village turn right and follow the road along the railroad track to the last house. From here you can walk along the railroad for some 300 metres (there are very few trains and they are slow, but nevertheless be careful) and you come to a good spot to scan the cliffs. Western Rock Nuthatch and Blue Rock Thrush may be present, but you need a telescope for good views.
This rocky outcrop is the western edge of Sredna Arda, which is in terms of rock-dwelling birds even more important than Monyak. However, the best bird cliffs are further away and cannot be visited, which is, perhaps, for the best as far as the birds are concerned.

**PRACTICAL PART**

ROUTE 6: THE BOROVITSA RIVER

# Route 6: The Borovitsa River

**36 KM**
**EASY**

*Scenic drive following the Borovitsa River.*

**Habitats:** River valley, steppe, stony grasslands, scrubland, cliffs, arable land
**Selected species:** Rock Thrush, Pygmy Cormorant, Black Stork, Golden Eagle, Isabelline Wheatear, Small Bath White, Yellow Banded Skipper, Rhodopean Toothwort, Suslik, Rhodopean Toothwort, Rock Thrush, Black Stork, Golden Eagle, Grey-headed Woodpecker, Goosander, Small Bath White, Yellow-banded Skipper, Common Glider

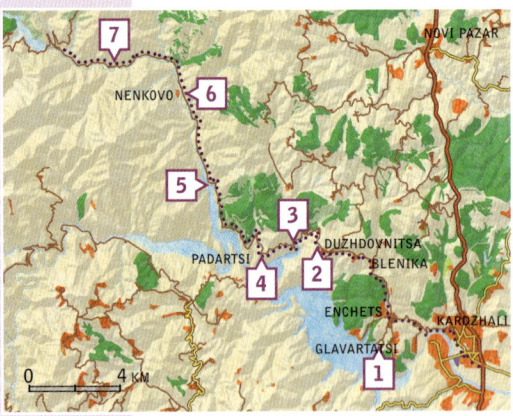

This scenic drive takes you from busy Kardzhali deep in the quiet and unspoilt Borovitsa river valley which forms the border between the Western and Eastern Rhodopes. The mountains are higher here and also very rocky, supporting many drought-adapted animals, alongside those typical of rivers. This route offers good bird and butterfly watching, opportunities against a very scenic backdrop of mountains and river valleys. The wild environment, with only tiny hamlets and patches of traditional agriculture, form a great contrast with the bustling provincial town of Kardzhali. The ancient five-arch bridge of Nenkovo is a beautiful historic monument.

**Starting point** Centre of Kardzhali, Stadium on the main road 5 through town (GPS: 41.641262, 25.376103).

From the stadium, go south and take the first major right turn (250m) onto the Bulevar Bulair. Before crossing the river, turn right (going straight on would bring you to the heronry, see point 1 of route 5). Follow the river

## ROUTE 6: THE BOROVITSA RIVER

road to the market (worth a visit), follow it as it turns right and at the roundabout, take the 4th exit. You're leaving town and climbing uphill along narrow minor roads to the village of Enchets (4.4 km). Two hundred metres after the shops in Enchets, take a left to Brosh and follow this road towards the reservoir (ignoring a left turn to Brosh after 500m).

**1** Khardzali reservoir is an upmarket area where the more well-off are building their villas. The reservoir is used to breed Sturgeon and other fish – according to the local fish breeders, it is the largest sturgeon rearing site in Europe. The floating fish restaurants are somewhat of a regional tourist attraction. The area between Enchets and the reservoir used to be a good area for steppe birds and susliks, but the unchecked building is taking its toll. We could not find the susliks where they were there before, but Isabelline Wheatear and Lesser Grey Shrike are still here.

Common Glider (top) and Rhodopean Toothwort (bottom) – two superb species to look for the river valley near Duzdovnitsa (point 2).

Return to the main road in Enchets and continue north to Blenika, Penyovo and Duzhdovnitsa. After approximately 2 km from the latter village in the direction of Padartsi, you pass some picnic benches on your way down to a valley. There are some beautiful cliffs in front of you.

**2** Park by the picnic benches from where you have good views of the cliffs. Scan them for Black Stork, Golden Eagle and Egyptian Vulture. Grey-headed Woodpecker breeds in the woodlands.
Further down the road, explore the valley where two streams come together. Near the waterfall on your right, there are a Rhodopian Toothwort and Pontic Fritillary plants. Follow a small trail downstream that leads to a side arm of the reservoir. Look here for Dipper and Grey Wagtail. The Common Glider, a spectacular and in spite of its name a rather rare butterfly, has a strong population along the river here.

**3** As the road climbs out of the valley, you gain increasingly wide views over the upper part of the Khardzali reservoir. Stop where you have good views and scan the water for Goosander.

ROUTE 6: THE BOROVITSA RIVER

This large, fish-eating species of duck is widespread in northern Europe and has an isolated population in the Balkans, considered a relict from the ice ages. Until recently, it was restricted to the larger lakes, such as the Ohrid-Prespa lakes on the border of Greece, North Macedonia and Albania. With the building of reservoirs, it has spread further into Bulgaria.

**4** A bit further (2.7km from the river valley; just before Padartsi village; GPS: 41.677155, 25.262936) you can park in a right bend and walk some 50 metres to a viewpoint (Yuren Kaya) over the reservoir. Another 7 km from there, the is a large countryside hotel-restaurant, again with more views over the reservoir.

**5** Continue and after another 2kms, you reach the top end of the reservoir, where the Borovitsa flows into it. Gone are the steep reservoir slopes – the Borovitsa river has a wide riverbed with large pebble banks. The point where the river flows into the reservoir can be attractive for birds – waders, herons, cormorants and Black Storks.
Continue for another 3.2kms and there is a car park on your left. Park here and walk further along the road for a kilometre or so to the old 5-arched bridge of Nenkovo.

The section of the Borovitsa River near Nenkovo is a beautiful spot with a conspicuous Byzanthine bridge (right). Among the many birds to be expected here is the Booted Eagle (top).

## ROUTE 6: THE BOROVITSA RIVER

**6** The area around Nenkovo bridge is one of those magical places for birdwatchers. There are cliffs, bushes, rocky grassland, and of course the river itself. In the immediate vicinity of the bridge, search for Barred Warbler, Eastern Black-eared Wheatear, Red-backed and Lesser Grey Shrikes. It is worth checking the wires near the road, which is a favourite singing post for Rock Thrush (a rare bird in the Eastern Rhodopes). Raptors breeding in the area include Booted Eagle, Egyptian Vulture and Long-legged Buzzard. Little Ringed Plover, Black Stork and Little Egret can be seen along the river. Insect enthusiasts should head for the river to search the stony riverbed, which is suitable habitat for the rare, local endemic Small Bath White. Then move on to the little side valley just 100 metres north of the bridge, on the right side of the road. This is a true butterfly hotspot, with Yellow-banded Skipper, Southern Small White, Grayling and Turquoise Blue flying near the stony scrublands and the flowery meadows. We also found Rock Bunting here.

**7** From Nenkovo bridge, continue along the river where you find many interesting places to stop to look for butterflies and birds. There are various 'rope' or suspension bridges that you can cross (on foot) to small villages on the other side.
A little further on, there are plenty of new reasons to stop and stroll. Tortoises and other reptiles may be found in the Christ's-thorn scrubland and Golden Eagles patrol the valley.

Return the way you came.

Look for Barred Warblers near the Nenkovo bridge.

**PRACTICAL PART**

# Route 7: Doirantsi

**FULL DAY**
**MODERATE-STRENUOUS**

Beautiful walk to a high basalt outcrop.
Superb views and chance on seeing Balkan Chamois at the easternmost edge of their range.

**Habitats:** gravelly river banks, oak scrub, pastures and farm, cliffs and rock slopes
**Selected species:** Reichenbach's Iris, Green-winged Orchid, Balkan Chamois, Red Deer, Golden Eagle, Nose-horned Viper, Chequered Blue

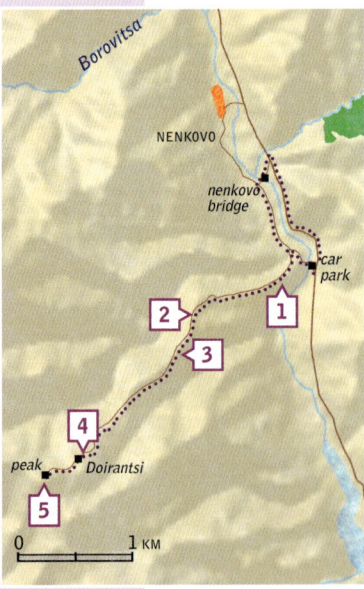

Doirantsi is a conspicuous basalt peak right on the border of the Eastern and Western Rhodopes. This is a wild walk in a little visited part of the region. In comparison to other parts of the eastern Rhodopes, the mountains are clearly taller and the views more dramatic, yet at the same time, the landscape retains its typically southern appearance due to the dry and rocky slopes.

Along the path, a wide array of wildlife is present and may reveal itself, but this walk is not for those looking for a high number of species with minimum of effort. However, if you want to submerse yourself in some stunning landscapes and enjoy being surprised by unexpected wildlife crossing your path, Doirantsi is your walk. Note that there is not much shade on this route and that it can be pretty windy around the peak.

This route starts on the road along the Borovitsa river, which is part of route 6. This walk can therefore be easily combined with the points on that route. The five-arched bridge of Nenkovo lies only 500 metres north of the starting point of this walk and it is a shame not to visit this beautiful spot (see point 5 of the previous route).

**Starting point** Car park near Nenkovo bridge (GPS: 41.726636, 25.224986)

## ROUTE 7: DOIRANTSI

The first section of the trail offers spendid views over the Borovitsa river.

Cross the river over the concrete weir. On the other side, the path forks. Turn right and at the next fork, go left.

**1** The trail follows a ridge that you climb up into the mountains. The first section leads through a dry and rather overgrazed area dominated by Oriental Hornbeam shrubs, mixed with Montpellier Maple. As you climb, you are treated on some beautiful views of the Borovitsa river that snakes through the gravel banks.
Note that here and further up, there are various paths that all run parallel to one another and all join each other again further on.

Look for Chequered Blue on the first rocky parts of the trail.

**2** Rather suddenly you arrive at a viewpoint that looks towards the mountains towards the west. You can see that you are on the boundary of the Eastern and Western Rhodopes as these mountains are higher and appear wilder than those further east.

**3** The next section of the trail leads through a landscape that consists of bare rock. In spring, there are two species of iris to be found here, the liver-purple *Iris reichenbachiana* and the somewhat taller *Iris suaveolens*. Among the butterflies the Chequered Blue is frequent, which has stonecrops as the larval food plant.

**PRACTICAL PART**

ROUTE 7: DOIRANTSI

**4** You round a cliff and continue through some woodlands to the hamlet of Doirantsi, which can only be reached via this track by foot, horse or mule. Thousands of Green-winged Orchids grace the meadows. Look carefully near the rocks and the ruins of the farm houses for the Nose-horned Viper. We found it basking on a rock.

At Doirantsi, the trail seems to end, but if you bear right from the houses and walk upwards, you'll pick up a new trail on the far side. The endpoint of this walk, the basalt peak of the Doirantsi mountain, is clearly visible from the hamlet. Head for it and you can't go wrong.

**5** On windy days, it is better not to climb the actual peak but to follow the trail that goes around it. On wind-free days, find a way up on the basalt outcrop from which you have magnificent views. The top is surprisingly flat and there are many 'hill-topping' butterflies – the behaviour in which butterflies fly up to the highest point to find a mate. Above, however, the views to the high mountains to the west are magnificent. Search the slopes here for Balkan Chamois and Red Deer. The latter rut on these slopes in September.

Return by the way you came. On your return, make sure to go right around the cliffs beneath Doirantsi (see map), otherwise, you end up walking away from the Borovitsa valley instead of towards it.

You have superb views from the basalt outcrop that is the Doirantsi peak (left). It is a good spot to look for Chamois (and Red Deer) on the slopes below (right).

# Route 8: The confluence of the Arda and Krumovitsa

**25 KM**
**EASY**

A not-to-miss route with a spectacular diversity of landscapes and wildlife.
Rocky canyons and strange-looking basalt cliffs.
Superb bird diversity, including many raptors.

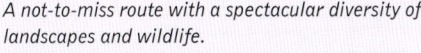 

**Habitats:** cliff, scrub, flowery grassland, rocky terrain
**Selected species:** Haberlea, Rhodopean Toothwort, Reichenbach's Iris*, Loose-flowered Orchid, Griffon Vulture, Black Vulture, Egyptian Vulture, Eleonora's Falcon, Levant Sparrowhawk, Masked Shrike, Lesser Grey Shrike, Roller, Pallid Swift, Worm Snake, Odalisque, Small Pincertail, Large Copper

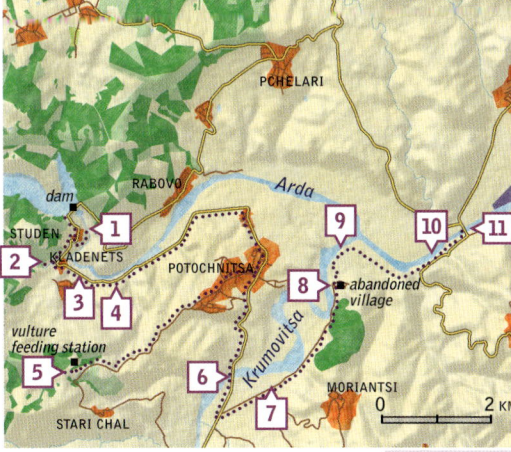

This route combines several very attractive sites at the eastern edge of the Studen Kladenets reservoir. This region has a special topography, where strange-looking, basalt rock formations combine with a flat fertile plain near the confluence of the Krumuvitsa and Arda rivers. The landscape is beautiful, although the dam and hydro-power station do affect the naturalness of part of this area. The combination of cliffs and river plains makes this a hotspot for wildlife.
This is more a collection of sites that are nearby than an actual route. It consists of a short walk near the confluence of both rivers and a number of nearby sites that you can visit by car. The village of Studen Kladenets and most stops are situated halfway along the road between Krumovgrad and Madzharovo and can be conveniently visited as a day trip from either of these places.

**Starting point** Village of Studen Kladenets

## ROUTE 8: THE CONFLUENCE OF THE ARDA AND KRUMOVITSA

The Devil's Canyon just a beneath the reservoir dam. Note the columnar basalt (top).
The Pontic Fritillary is a conspicuous spring flower in many open woodlands in the Eastern Rhodopes, including those near Studen Kladenets (bottom).

**1** There are various places to stop on the side of the main road in Studen Kladenets village.
The first is at a sign *Abrasive Wells*. Follow this track down to a stony gorge in the Arda river just beneath the dam, known as the Devil's Canyon. This odd rock formation is testimony to the shallow soils and great strength of the river in wet months. A common mineral to find here is turquoise coloured zeolite. It is formed at high temperatures and under high pressure out of layers of volcanic ash. The little pools close to the river host Yellow-bellied Toad, while the river itself is home to Otter. It is beautiful place to stroll around, and as you do this, scan the cliffs to the north-east (see map) where Blue Rock Thrush, Black Stork, Griffon Vulture and Egyptian Vulture may be seen. Pallid Swift breeds in the village.

Back on the road continue on foot along the road for about 500 metres past the hydroelectric station. Just before the bend to the left you cross a small valley. Follow it to the right for a 100 metres or so.

**2** A stream trickles over a small dam. This is a superb place to look for butterflies, which are often attracted to small wet patches. From mid-May onwards, this is a good place to look for the Odalisque, an attractive damselfly of the eastern Mediterranean.
The shady cliffs a little further on are a delight for botanists. They are carpeted with the endemic and rare Haberlea (see page 70). Closer examination will reveal Pontic Fritillary and Peacock Anemones.

## ROUTE 8: THE CONFLUENCE OF THE ARDA AND KRUMOVITSA

**3** Back on the road walk on for another 200 metres or so to a spot from which you can scan the Arda river. There is a large Cormorant / Grey Heron Colony here, it is a good spot for Kingfisher and other birds.
Pick up the car and drive along the road southbound until you pass some conspicuous basalt cliffs. Park here to watch them from the road.

**4** There are many beautiful outcrops of columnar basalt in the Eastern Rhodopes, but this is perhaps the most remarkable. These round cliffs consist entirely of folded, hexagonal rock columns, remnants of lava that cooled off rapidly and as the volume of the material shrunk with the dropping of the temperature, the lava cracked in these six-sided parts.
These cliffs form another good wildflower site, with again Haberlea, Sticky Catchfly, Bulbous Comfrey, Golden Alison and, high up, some Reichenbach's Iris. Check the river for birds, such as Bee-eater, Black Stork, Crag Martin, Red-rumped Swallow and, during migration, for any kind of oddity. Look here, and further along the route, for Eleonora's Falcon, for which this area is a favourite hunting area. Eleonora's Falcons breed on the Mediterranean islands in late summer, but some spend the late spring and early summer here on these river plains, before heading to their breeding sites.

Continue the road to the village of Potochnitsa. Next to the village's only tower block and some 200 metres before the mosque, turn right and follow the road to the feeding station, which is just before the hamlet of Stari Chal. Careful with the rather excessive speed bumps on this road in the village.

Spectacular columnar basalts along the road at point 4. Look for rare flowers here, including the endemic Haberlea (page 70).

PRACTICAL PART

## ROUTE 8: THE CONFLUENCE OF THE ARDA AND KRUMOVITSA

A meadow full of Loose-flowered Orchids.

**5** On your way, look for Woodchat and Red-backed Shrikes, which are numerous With a little Luck, Barred Warbler is present as well. Some four kms after turning right in Potochnitsa, you arrive at a track that leads to a hilltop. You can see the enclosure of the vulture feeding station on your right. Look here for the raptors. Egyptian Vulture, in particular, is regular here. This is probably the best place to observe them in the Eastern Rhodopes. Griffon Vulture is usually present and sometimes Black Vulture too. Black Kite, Buzzard and Long-legged Buzzard are all regularly seen here.

This spot is the also starting place for the walk to Boynik (see next route).

Return to Potochnitsa and turn right.

**6** Your next stop is the bridge over one of the Eastern Rhodopes' finest rivers: the Krumovitsa. Black Storks are frequent here. Check the area carefully for small birds of prey. Levant's Sparrowhawk breeds here, as does Hobby. Both Red-footed and Eleonora's Falcon frequently visit the site in spring. You can follow the river in southerly direction, searching for reptiles and insects.

750m after the bridge, turn left on a small road that turns into a rough track further on.

**7** If you are here between mid-May and mid-June, you are treated to a spectacular meadow full of Loose-flowered Orchids. It is washed purple by its blooms.

Continue (carefully) on this track to the abandoned village and park here to continue on foot.

**8** From the village you again have good views over the river. Look here for Black Storks feeding on the river shore, and for Bee-eaters that breed in the riverbank. Here and anywhere else on the following walk, keep a keen eye out of the smaller raptors: Hobby, Eleonora's Falcon and

## ROUTE 8: THE CONFLUENCE OF THE ARDA AND KRUMOVITSA

Levant Sparrowhawk are all present here in summer. This is also a good spot to look for Otter.

Follow the track further and go left through the fields to the riverbank, which you follow to the right until you reach the main track.

**9** Birdwatchers will find this is a hotspot. Hoopoes and Bee-eaters are very common, and three species of shrikes (Woodchat, Red-backed and Lesser Grey) breed here, while Rollers may be seen in the isolated poplars. Egyptian Vulture breeds nearby, and Short-toed Eagle and both stork species frequently soar over. Look for dragonflies like Small Pincertail and check the small pools for Dice and Grass Snakes.

The sandy plain near the confluence of the Krumovitsa and Arda rivers is a hotspot for birds like Rollers, Bee-eaters, all three shrikes, Levant Sparrowhawk and Eleonora's Falcon.

Go left on the main track, which is a potholed despite being tarmacked, leading to a bridge over the river.

**10** You walk through a patch of woodland with, as you're now slightly higher, occasional views over the river. Look here, for the attractive glossy-purple snail-eating beetle *Procerus scabrosus* – a big beast (for a beetle!) and fierce snail hunter. Early Spring visitors will have little trouble finding Primrose and the endemic Rhodopean Toothwort in flower.

**11** The route ends at the iron bridge over the Arda, again with good views over the river. The cliffs on the other side have many caverns which are, currently, one of the largest known Thracian cult complexes. Probably it was a burial site; the caverns being the location for urns of the deceased. You can see them well if you walk along the road on the other side of the river for a few hundred metres.

Return via the way you came.

**PRACTICAL PART**

# Route 9: To the abandoned village of Boynik

**FULL DAY
STRENUOUS**

Long walk through one of the wildest parts of the Eastern Rhodopes. Vultures, bisons and a whole lot more.

**Habitats:** dry grasslands, scrub, oak forest, beech forest (small patches), village
**Selected species:** Konik horses, Fallow Deer, European Bison, Wolf, Jackal, Egyptian Vulture, Griffon Vulture, Golden Eagle, Black Kite, Ortolan Bunting

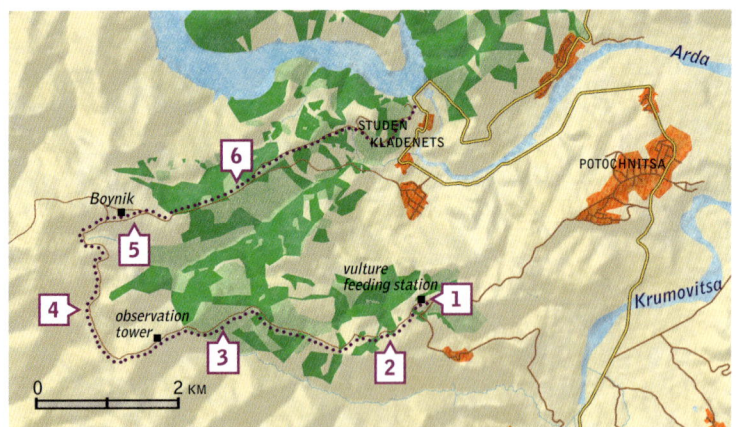

This is the longest walk in this book and requires careful preparation. It leads through the rewilding area and the edge of the hunting reserve and effectively circles around the wild river valley (and strict nature reserve) of Valchi Dol. Along this rather gentle walk over a rough and little visited track, you will be treated to raptors (mostly Griffon and Egyptian Vultures) and may see deer, Konik Horses and, if you are lucky, even

> **Walking preparations**
> Be aware that whilst this is perhaps not a difficult or particularly strenuous walk, it is long and for the larger part, there is not much shade. Take precautions (see page 259).

## ROUTE 9: TO THE ABANDONED VILLAGE OF BOYNIK

European Bison or Jackals. Even wolves are in the cards if you are very lucky. Closer by, there are numerous smaller birds and you have a good chance of finding tortoises, lizards and snakes.

The track is nowhere too steep or otherwise hard to navigate, but the length is something to consider, especially on warm days as approximately half of the route is without shade. Ideally, you organise two vehicles, one which you leave in the villages of Studen Kladenets (at GPS: 41.616724, 25.641693) and another at the starting point of the route, at the vulture feeding station. If this is not an option, then the walk to Boynik and back is already a long walk (18.5 kms back and forth). You may consider walking from Studen Kladenets up to Boynik and back instead (10 kms back and forth) and then driving to the Vulture feeding station and walking up to point 2 (3 kms back and forth).

**Starting point** Vulture feeding station of Potochnitsa (GPS: 41.593901, 25.644003; see point 5 of the previous route)

**Getting there** When approaching Potochnitsa from the south (Krumovgrad) you pass the village mosque on your right. Some 200 metres further on, turn left. Continue (mind the speed bumps here) for 4 kms until a broad track branches off to the right. Park here.

**1** From the parking spot you can already see the vulture feeding station, where you may find Egyptian and Griffon Vultures, Black Kites,

Although the walk to Boynik is long, it follws an easy track, offering you plenty of opportunities to look around for Bison, Wild Horses, birds and reptiles.

ROUTE 9: TO THE ABANDONED VILLAGE OF BOYNIK

168

Golden Eagles frequently hunt over the area.

Ravens and sometimes other raptors. This is the most reliable site in the Eastern Rhodopes for Egyptian Vulture, of which there are usually a few birds present in spring and summer.

Walk the rough track that rounds the hill to your left and then continues along a ridge further uphill.

**2** From the ridge you have great views over the hills to the south. This region is home to various herds of free-ranging Konik Horses and European Bisons. Search for them by scanning the open patches carefully. They were released in a joint project by Rewilding Nature and Ark Nature and now roam freely. The Rewilding Rhodopes and Rewilding Europe Foundations are pushing for the Konik Horse to be recognised as a wild species, which interestingly, is more of a political issue than a biological one.

The herds are steadily increasing ( by the early 2020s there were 80 animals in the area). This spot remains the main territory although they disperse further into the Rhodopes. Large predators such as Wolves keep the population in check. In 2013 this area was also the location where European Bison were introduced. At the time of writing, there were approximately 15 animals. Like the horse there is no fence that keeps them in a specific location, but, at least for now, they seem to be happy in these hills so the majority of the animals are found here.

**3** The next section of the walk leads through rather young and low oak scrub with many open patches, through which you have, every now and then, good views over the Krumovitsa river. Look for reptiles and butterflies along the path. Among the birds, the large numbers of Ortolan Bunting stand out.

**4** After 5 kms from the start, you arrive at a viewing tower and information panel. Beyond it the walk proceeds through increasingly tall woodland, which provides some welcome shade. You are walking on a north and east facing slope. The areas facing east are clad in a mature oak

**ROUTE 9: TO THE ABANDONED VILLAGE OF BOYNIK**

Sometimes you're lucky and find the antler of a Red Deer in the field.

and hornbeam forest, whilst those sections looking north are reserved for the beech. Beech trees need temperate conditions and are especially vulnerable to very dry and hot summers, hence in the Eastern Rhodopes they are only present on the higher northern slopes.
The birdlife is clearly temperate, with tits, Robins and Treecreepers. Higher up the beech forests have breeding Semi-collared Flycatcher and Grey-headed Woodpeckers, which may also be seen along the trail, so keep your eyes and ears open.

**5** After another 2.5 kms, the track bends to the east again and you reach the village of Boynik. The first things you see are two wells where Yellow-bellied Toads are common and reptiles and birds come to drink when it is hot.
Boynik is a scatter of ruins of abandoned houses so there are no streets or tracks. Look around and enjoy the large numbers of Ortolan, Cirl and Corn Bunting, the Eastern Orphean and Eastern Subalpine Warblers, Woodlarks, Red-backed Shrikes, Hoopoes and many more 'common birds' of the Eastern Rhodopes. Raptors should pass overhead frequently. On the upslope part of the abandoned village there are three conspicuous oaks (of two species) that can help you with your orientation. In the lower part there is a flag pole and a few houses which still have a roof. Standing at the flag, a track descends some 20 metres further on your left in the direction of Studen Kladenets.

**6** The walk down to Studen Kladenets will take another 1.5 hours and leads through similar habitat as that on the way up.

**PRACTICAL PART**

# Route 10: The ridge near Nanovitsa

**4-5 HOURS**
**MODERATE**

Walk through the habitats of the Eastern Rhodopes.
Chance of seeing the wild herds of Konik Horses and large numbers of raptors.

**Habitats:** scrubland, grassland, oak woodland, village
**Selected species:** Konik Horse, European Bison, Griffon Vulture, Golden Eagle, Eastern Orphean Warbler, Ortolan Bunting, Hermann's tortoise, Dahl's Whip Snake

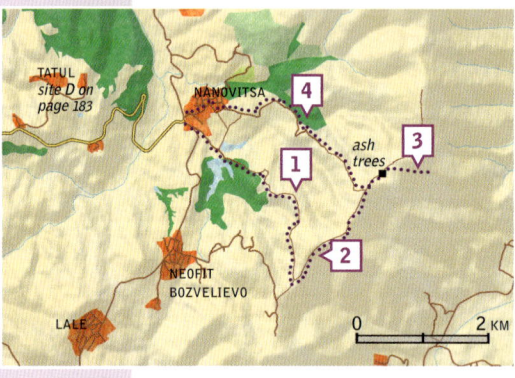

This fairly easy walk leads you uphill to the edge of the reserve where the Konik horses roam free. This route is within the home range of one of the wild Konik herds and on the edge of the core area for the European Bison. The chances of seeing the latter are not great, but the views are certainly wonderful and the 'classic' rich palette of Rhodopean birds, reptiles and butterflies can be found. Nanovitsa and the surrounding villages are original, Turkish villages with many Thracian remains. Note that over the larger part of this walk, there is little shade, so take precautions against the sun (see page 259).

**Starting point** Mosque in Nanovitsa (GPS: 41.548550, 25.565358)

Follow the road in southeasterly direction and after a few metres, in front of the school (a large yellow building) follow the narrow road to the left. Continue, past the village's reservoir and guest house and follow the now untarmacked track uphill through a dry pine forest which is in the process of turning into an oak forest.
Once out of the forest, you climb a hill (with nice views) to an abandoned village.

## ROUTE 10: THE RIDGE NEAR NANOVITSA

**1** Only a few houses are still in use and then only by shepherds in the summer months. Just after the first house, go right and follow the path along the stone wall. You pass a well here where Yellow-bellied Toads occur in the basins and should be easy to see.

The track brings you to a ridge where it forks. The righthand branch leads to another house; you follow the left branch uphill.

**2** The views on this part of the route are splendid. You overlook the valley of the Krumovitsa river near the village of Dolna Kula (route 11). Raptors cruise over the hills, with Griffon and Egyptian Vulture being the most numerous. Closer to the path, look for reptiles and butterflies on the dry grassland and in the Christ's-thorn bushes, which is the larval food plant of the pretty Little Tiger Blue.

The track passes along a rocky section before arriving at a saddle with some green meadows and several large ash trees. From these trees, leave the track and walk through the meadows to the right to the flank of the hill in front of you.

**3** About 300 metres from some ash trees you are in the territory of a herd of free-roaming Konik horses which were released in this area

A herd of Wild Konik Horses on the slopes of the Nanovitsa ridge (top).
Check the water basins in the villages for Yellow-bellied Toads. This specimen felt right at home underneath the trickle of water that fills the basin (bottom).

**PRACTICAL PART**

### ROUTE 10: THE RIDGE NEAR NANOVITSA

in 2011. These animals are part of the rewilding project in the Eastern Rhodopes and play an important role in the ecosystem. First and foremost, as grazing animals, they keep the mosaic landscape which is so rich in wildlife. Second, their excrement attracts many insects such as dung beetles, which in turn support the diversity of reptiles and birds. And finally, the horses are prey themselves; prey to wolves and, after their death, to carrion eaters like vultures and jackals. The Koniks are completely free-range and wild; their population is monitored, but otherwise they fend for themselves and go as they please. That being said, each of the herds are rather faithful to the area they know best and territorially defend against other herds. At present, this area is within the home range of a herd, which is why we can say that you have a fair chance of finding them here. Watch from a distance in order not to disturb them.

Besides horses, there are lots of birds in the area too. Eastern Orphean and Eastern Subalpine Warblers, Cirl and Ortolan Buntings and Red-backed Shrikes are all numerous.

Return via the same track and a little beyond the rocky section you passed on the way up, go right and follow a track that goes downhill.

*The conspicuous ash trees just before point three mark the spot where you leave the track and go right to look for the Konik Horses.*

**4** You pass a village that is still inhabited but seems to have no name – not in the field, nor on the map. This really is a place where time stood still. Water comes from the well, people tend the herds and chicken run around. Red-rumped and Barn Swallows nest under the eaves and an Ortolan Bunting sings from the trees on the edge of the village.

Continue further down the track until you reach Nanovitsa again.

### Nearby sites of interest

Near Nanovitsa lies the famous Thracian site of Tatul (see page 183). The access road to the hunting reserve on the shore of the Studen Kladenets reservoir starts in Nanovitsa village (see page 181).

# Route 11: Krumovitsa river near Dolna Kula

**4 HOURS, 15 KM
ONE WAY**

Great example of an intact river system with some small scale agriculture.
One of the best birdwatching routes of the Eastern Rhodopes.

**Habitats:** river, flowery grasslands, scrubs, oak woodland, cliffs, small scale agricultural land
**Selected species:** Hobby, Chukar, Lesser Grey Shrike, Roller, Western Rock Nuthatch, Olive-tree Warbler, Eastern Black-eared Wheatear, Sombre Tit, Black-headed Bunting, Grecian Copper, Eastern Copper, Anomalous Blue, White-letter Hairstreak, Little Tiger Blue, Eastern Festoon, Grass Snake

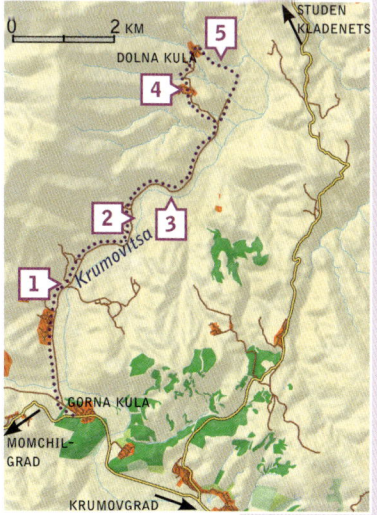

This short route lies a little away from the other ones, but it is well worth the detour, especially if you are a birdwatcher. This unspoilt river valley, with its arid fields, grasslands and sun-soaked cliffs are somewhat reminiscent of parts of Turkey. And with Western Rock Nuthatch, Sombre Tit, Olive-tree Warbler and some of the highest concentrations of Rollers in the area, so does the birdlife. Dolna Kula offers some of the best and easiest birdwatching in the entire region.

**Starting point** Gorna Kula, some 5 km west of Krumovgrad.

In Gorna Kula, turn left towards Dolna Kula. Park where a road branches off to the right to a big bridge over the Krumovitsa river.

**1** The attraction of this spot is the small, secluded river, which enters the bigger Krumovitsa, which you can overlook from the bridge. The small valley is home to Ascalaphids, Wolf Spiders, Grecian Copper and Knapweed Fritillary. Grass Snakes are common here in summer. You may well note your first Lesser Grey,

## ROUTE 11: KRUMOVITSA RIVER NEAR DOLNA KULA

The Krumovitsa river valley is excellent for birdwatching (top). The Western Rock Nuthatch is one of the key birds to look for here (bottom).

Woodchat and Red-backed Shrikes here, as well as Hobby, Roller, Golden Oriole and Short-toed Eagle. Look for Sombre Tit in scrubby areas.

Continue along the west bank (keep an eye out for Rollers, Lesser Grey Shrikes and Black-headed Buntings on the wires), and just when you see the cliffs on your left, take the dirt track on your right, down to the river.

**2** This track offers a closer view of the arable land along the river. Small fields are planted with corn and tobacco irrigated by water from the Krumovitsa. The fields are fenced the traditional way, with branches of Blackthorn and Christ's-thorn. Look for shrikes on the telephone wires overhead, warblers and Black-headed Bunting in the bushes, raptors in the sky, and Black Stork in the river. Grecian Copper and Knapweed Fritillary are frequent again.

Drive a little further and park, where you see cliffs on both sides of the road.

CROSSBILL GUIDES • RHODOPE MOUNTAINS

## ROUTE 11: KRUMOVITSA RIVER NEAR DOLNA KULA

**3** This is one of the best sites to see Western Rock Nuthatch in the region. Search the rocks for them carefully. We found them frequenting the mossy parts of the rocks where they search for insects. If you don't find them immediately, be patient as they fly from one rock face to another on a regular basis. Meanwhile, you may find Eastern Black-eared Wheatear or Chukar here as well. Pay attention to rocks themselves too, as the combination of metamorphic rock (composed of even-sized sediment particles) and conglomerate rock (with lots of pebbles mixed in) is so striking it could feature in a geology book.

Still no Western Rock Nuthatch? Stroll a little way down the road to the open patch where we found Little Tiger Blue and giant ant-lions (the latter in summer), while waiting for this illustrious bird.

Continue and turn left at the fork, to the village of Dolna Kula.

**4** Park close to the cemetery of the village. This is one of the most reliable spots to see Sombre Tit – a southeast European bird that, although widespread, is thinly distributed in the Eastern Rhodopes. Beyond the village, follow the track to the right that leads down to the river. When you reach the tarmac again, there is a small car park.

Lesser Fiery Copper in the river valley.

**5** Stroll around in this varied landscape of fields and hedgerows, along the (usually dry) stream bed down to the Krumovitsa. This is one of those odd spots in the Eastern Rhodopes, which appears rather non-descript, like just any other spot, but is, for some reason, a hotspot for birds and butterflies. In a 100 metre radius from the little car park, we found Eastern Olivaceous, Barred and Olive-tree Warblers, Red-backed Shrike, Roller and Black-headed and Corn Buntings. Butterfly watchers should search for Lesser Fiery Copper, White-letter Hairstreak, Anomalous Blue and Eastern Festoon.

Go straight to return to Gorna Kula.

**PRACTICAL PART**

# Route 12: The border trail – Gyumyurdzhinski Snezhnik

**FULL DAY, 21 KM**
**STRENUOUS**

Hike to an old-growth primeval mountain beech forest.
The green Iron Curtain.
Superb views into Greece and the Aegean sea.

**Habitats:** Beech forest, forest streams, rocky mountain grassland
**Selected species:** Rhodope Lily, Rhodopean Toothwort, Dog's-tooth Lily, Elder-flowered Orchid, Semi-collared Flycatcher, Lanner Falcon, White-backed Woodpecker, Fire Salamander, Slow Worm, Erhard's Wall Lizard, Dahl's Whip Snake, Balkan Goldenring

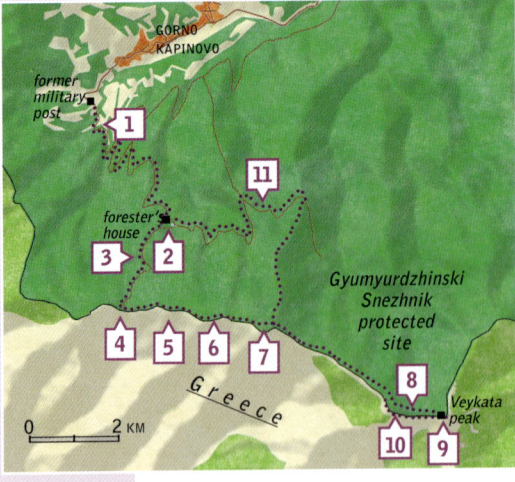

During the cold war, the border area between Greece and Bulgaria was off-limits. This helped to preserve the forest in a (near) natural state. The high, north-facing Bulgarian side, has an old-growth beech forest, part of the Gyumyurdzhinski Snezhnik protected site.
This route skirts the reserve, which is a refuge to rare and threatened wildlife and a spectacular flora of rocky grasslands. The latter is found on the high ridge which forms the border between Bulgaria and Greece. It was deliberately stripped of trees to prevent people from secretly crossing the border.
Gyumyurdzhinski Snezhnik is a rarely visited, wild area. There are few signs of human presence and this sense of desertedness is special. Choose a clear day, because then the views down to the Aegean coast are spectacular. The list of breeding birds is, with species like Lanner, Semi-collared Flycatcher, Grey-headed and White-backed Woodpeckers,

## ROUTE 12: THE BORDER TRAIL – GYUMYURDZHINSKI SNEZHNIK

quite spectacular, but the chance of actually encountering these birds is not very great and we wouldn't call this a route one for the dedicated birder. It is also quite a tough walk on which the greatest attractions are on the ridge and the area around the peak, which are furthest away. Expect to be walking a full day.

You can reduce the route by shortening the section on the ridge (see short-cut on map). The hotel in Gorno Kapinovo offers to drop you off at the forester's house (point 2). This is not cheap but takes 4 kms and 300 metres of climbing off the total. Contact the Hotel Lilium in Gorno Kapinovo (some of the staff speak English) to arrange this.

Orientation can be hard in the forest, so we advise you to install a route app on your (well charged!) mobile phone, which shows the trails accurately (see page 259).

**Starting point** Gorno Kapinovo

**Getting there** Drive up to the end of the village of Gorno Kapinovo and continue (carefully!) until you see an open area near some derelict buildings. This is an abandoned military station from the Cold War era that marked the border of the vast territory of communist countries. This was the 'Iron Curtain' and everything beyond this point was then off-limits to people. Park here and continue of foot. Follow the track for 4 km up the mountain to the refuge.

*An old piece of barbed wire in the beech wood reminds of the time that this was the iron curtain between the communist east and the capitalist west. This area was long off-limits for people, which is why these forests are in such a pristine state.*

**1** At the bend of the track you will find small wet meadows with dragonflies including Blue-eyed Hawker and Small Pincertail. On the rocky fields along this stretch, we found Dahl's Whip Snake, together with both tortoises, and the very common Wall and Green Lizards.

This part of the route already has a number of attractive wildflowers, which in May included Bird's-nest Orchid and in June and July Grecian and Green-flowered Foxgloves, Dotted Loosestrife (native here), Peach-leaved Bellflower and *Campanula lingulata*, endemic to the Balkans and southern Italy.

**2** A noticeboard with trails and a parking area marks the location of a refuge, which is a tall white building, hidden behind the trees.

ROUTE 12: THE BORDER TRAIL – GYUMYURDZHINSKI SNEZHNIK

Behind it is an artificial lake. In summer, butterflies are abundant on the flowering plants along the shore, while the undergrowth and scattered small puddles is good habitat for Grass Snake and Yellow-bellied Toad.

Follow the track further past the lake and take the next track right. It is marked with white-red-white flashes.

A massive old Beech tree along the border trail. This ecological feature of pristine mountain beech forest is clearly visible on this tree: it is old, gnarled and with lots of damaged branches.

**3** Much of the forest you're crossing now is not very old, probably cut and replanted about 50 years ago. This does not limit the very rich spring flora, including Hollow-root, Coralroot, Yellow Anemone, Wild Strawberry, Mezereon, Wild Liquorice and others. Look along the track for Slow Worm, Fire Salamander, Yellow-bellied Toad and Erhard's Wall Lizard. In the older sections keep your eyes open for Black and White-backed Woodpeckers and search the area for the Semi-collared Flycatcher for which it is promising habitat. During migration, other flycatcher species may well be found here too.

After 1.3 kms, the track ends in an overgrown section (GPS: 41.24742 25.24600). Here a small trail branches off to the left and climbs up steeply to the ridge, which is also the border with Greece.

**4** Take a moment to take in the views. The mountains in front of you appear almost completely deserted. Except for a few little-used tracks and an abandoned military post, there is no human presence. On clear days, you can see all the way to the Aegean coast. Test your geographic skills and find Vistonida Lake, Porto Lagos and the island of Thasos. Note just how wild and unpopulated the Greek section of the Rhodopes is.

The pasture is a haven for interesting wildflowers. Look for Dog's-tooth Lily, Wild Tulip, Drooping Star-of-Bethlehem, Reichenbach's Iris* (I*ris reichenbachii*) and Elder-flowered Orchid in spring. There are even a number of plants that we can consider northern species, like Bilberry and Burnet Rose. In late spring and summer, there are many

### ROUTE 12: THE BORDER TRAIL — GYUMYURDZHINSKI SNEZHNIK

butterflies, including Silver-studded Blue, Lesser Spotted Fritillary, Brown Argus, Baton Blue, Sloe Hairstreak and Purple-shot Copper.
Go left and climb the ridge following a rough track.

**5** The first section of this 'border trail' is quite steep and is dominated by tall herbs and rocky outcrops; great for wildflowers and butterflies. Also, check the sky at regular intervals; raptors are not common but Lanner Falcon and Griffon Vulture breed on the Greek side and Lesser Spotted Eagle and Black Vulture have also been seen here.

**6** After a rocky stretch the ridge suddenly becomes much gentler and grassier, with Bilberry, Juniper, Burnet Rose and the broom-like *Chamaecytisus albus*. For the short route, you can turn left here (look for the yellow signposts) to start your descent. Otherwise, continue.

The endemic Rhodope Lily is found in Beech forests of the Western and Eastern Rhodopes.

**7** Just before reaching the first peak the trail enters the forest and reappears on the other side of the peak. Just a little further a well signposted trail branches off to the left. This will be your return route. However, to reach the Veykata peak and the old-growth forest, continue further on the ridge.

**8** Further on, the trail leaves the open zone of the ridge and enters the old-growth forest that is the heart of the Gyumyurdzhinski Snezhnik protected site. It grows on the steepest and least accessible slopes of the mountain and was never logged – neither before WWII when it was too inaccessible, nor during the Cold War when it was the border zone between East and West and not directly thereafter, when it was declared a protected site. You'll see some spectacular old, gnarled Beech trees, many of which are multi-stemmed and damaged by lightning. The taller specimens are further down the slope. In principle you can walk down, deeper in the forest, but there are no trails and the terrain is very steep.

**9** You emerge from the forest just before the Veykata peak and for the last few hundred metres you'll walk again through an Alpine

## ROUTE 12: THE BORDER TRAIL — GYUMYURDZHINSKI SNEZHNIK

The border trail, with Bulgaria to the left and Greece to the right. The Bulgarian north slope is clad in old-growth beech forest.

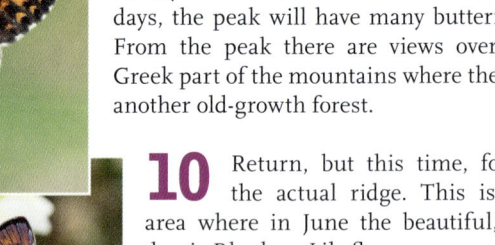

Two conspicuous butterflies along the border trail: Lesser Spotted Fritillary (top) and Purple-shot Copper (bottom).

meadow with grasses, Bilberry, and a variety of brooms and wildflowers. On calm days, the peak will have many butterflies. From the peak there are views over the Greek part of the mountains where there is another old-growth forest.

**10** Return, but this time, follow the actual ridge. This is the area where in June the beautiful, endemic Rhodope Lily flowers.

Find the trail that descends into the forest and follow it until you reach a broad track. Turning right would bring you, after 4 kms, to the central part of the old-growth forest, where it ends. Turn left to return to the foresters' house.

**11** The verges of this wide forest track are great for butterflies. In summer, the flowers are jam-packed with Silver-washed Fritillary, Common Blue and various coppers, leisurely fluttering around. Keep an eye out for White-letter Hairstreak on Dwarf Elder, and for the dragonflies Balkan Goldenring and Eastern Spectre in the shady patches.

## Additional sites in the Kardzhali-Krumovgrad region

### A– Studen Kladenets hunting reserve

When the reservoir of Studen Kladenets was created in the 1950s, the villages that originally sat on the bank of the River Arda were abandoned and the people relocated to the nearby towns. What remained was a large, uninhabited area that stretched out all the way to the valley of the Krumovits River. It was in this area that a hunting reserve was established that recently has become one of the key areas for rewilding with grazing animals.

In the reserve, the hunting rights are strictly regulated, which means that the poaching activities that are widespread elsewhere in the Eastern Rhodopes are (largely) absent here. This area is therefore a haven for Fallow and Red Deer, Free roaming Konik Horses and, more recently, European Bison (see page 63). Although the reserve is not fenced and the animals can roam as widely as they wish, the highest concentrations of them are found within the reserve area. The high grazing pressure is clearly shown by the vegetation, but in spite of this (or perhaps thanks to the high number of grazing animals) there is an enormous abundance of wildlife – Hoopoes, Rollers and shrikes (including Masked) can all be seen. Even more in evidence are the raptors – Griffon and Egyptian Vultures, Golden

The Studen Kladenets hunting reserve is the best place in the Eastern Rhodopes to watch large mammals. Fallow Deer are especially numerous.

ADDITIONAL SITES IN THE KARDZHALI-KRUMOVGRAD REGION

and White-tailed Eagles, Buzzards and Black Kites all occur; the vultures in particularly high numbers.
The hunting reserve is not so easy to visit. There is a potholed road that soon turns into a rough but drivable track that runs from the village of Nanovitsa to two hunting lodges on the shore of the reservoir. These lodges offer accommodation for all visitors (not just hunters) and even offer services of wildlife watching excursions into the reserve in 4x4 and photography hides for vultures and eagles. For birdwatchers, it is great to walk through the open woodlands on the lakeshore and search for White-tailed Eagle, Little Ringed Plover and Stone Curlew (try near the second lodge). There is also a population of Goosander, part of the curious, isolated non-migratory population that lives in the lakes in the border region of Greece, North Macedonia and Bulgaria. Black Storks can be seen all over the area. Look and listen too for Sombre Tit, which we found to be particularly numerous around the second lodge. Masked Shrike is regularly seen on the edges of riparian woodland that grows along the small streams that run into the reservoir. Rollers breed, mostly in nest boxes, along the river north of Nanovitsa.

## B – Stone Mushrooms near Beli Plast

Among the many strange geological features of the Eastern Rhodopes, the stone 'mushrooms' near Beli Plast are the most famous (see photo on page 12). These strange formations are the result of long volcanic underwater activity in the Paleocene, the period right after the Cretan period when most of the region was covered by a sea. After the sea withdrew, the sun, wind and rain sculpted the shapes you see now. Different colours appear on the largely white stone masses because of the presence of iron (red), manganese (green) and other oxides.
The protected mushroom site is just 3 ha, but the area where you can walk is much larger and stretches out on both sides of the road. There are waymarked trails, but you can go wherever it suits you.
Beside the rocks, the bushy vegetation of Holm and Hungarian Oaks attract many butterflies, such as Lesser Spotted Fritillary, Southern White Admiral, a good number of blues and hairstreaks, and despite their name, many Scarce Swallowtails.
In spring various kinds of orchids are present on the chalky slopes. To get to the 'Stone Mushrooms' take the Kardzhali – Haskovo road and (coming from the south) pass the village of Beli Plast. The site is on your left, close to the road. You can't miss it.

ADDITIONAL SITES IN THE KARDZHALI-KRUMOVGRAD REGION

## C – Perperikon

Perperikon is one of the major Ancient megalithic (dolmen) sites of Europe! It is still actively researched by archeologists. People were already present in the 6th millenium BC, when this was a place of worship. Later on, Perperikon became an important settlement. The prophecy that Alexander the Great would conquer the world was made here.

In terms of nature, Perperikon is an interesting spot as well. Western Rock Nuthatch, Long-legged Buzzard, Short-toed and Booted Eagles have been seen here, while in flowery patches, you might find the Amanda's, Meleager's and Chapman's Blues.

This is also a good site for reptiles. Instead of a Thracian king, Erhard's Wall Lizards now doze on the stone throne in the throne hall of Perperikon. There are many other reptiles here (e.g. Dice, Caspian Whip and Aesculapian Snakes and Spur-thighed and Hermann's Tortoises). Search for them between the rocks and stones of the archeological site, or even on the path heading up to the site.

Perperikon is open to the public between May and October. To get to the site, head from Kardzhali in the direction of Haskovo, and after Stremtsi, turn right signposted Perperikon. From then onwards the site is signposted. The entry is 6 leva (approx. €3) plus a small parking fee (2022 prices).

Be aware that the sun is relentless on the rocky hill slopes. You can buy water and souvenirs at the entrance. Allow at least 3 hours for a visit.

Laxman's Bugle* (*Ajuga laxmanni*) is a conspicuous wildflower in the open oak woods in spring.

## D – Tatul

The archeological site of Tatul, surrounded by a conspicuous 4th century stone wall, consists of a sanctuary and tomb of an influential Thracian leader who was deified after his death. This rare rite of burying leaders above the ground and on the top of a hill (as opposed to in a mound), dates back to 4000 BC. For a small fee, you can visit the ancient site of Tatul.

Although primarily a site of historic interest, Tatul will charm naturalists as well. Rock Brown and Southern White Admiral are frequent. Lizards (primarily Wall Lizard) are very common, while the pond near the site's car park was inhabited by a very obliging Grass Snake when we were

## ADDITIONAL SITES IN THE KARDZHALI-KRUMOVGRAD REGION

The archeological site of Tatul.

there. Broad Scarlet is plentiful.
To get to Tatul, leave Krumovgrad in the direction Ivaylovgrad and turn left onto the first tarmac road, following the signs Tatul. The ancient site is signposted.
On top of the hill of Tatul, you have a scenic view over a little valley, which is an interesting site to explore the surroundings. This valley can be reached by continuing the main road and turn right after the bridge. Follow the road for a few kilometres and park at the end of the village of Neofit Bozvelievo. Continue on foot along the dirt track that leads to the river. Cardinal, Marbled and Lesser Spotted Fritillaries are common, while Rhodope Toothwort flowers near the stream in early spring. Short-toed Eagle and Honey Buzzard are among the breeding birds here.

The Provence Orchid is an uncommon orchid that grows locally in the old oak forests.

### E – Traditional agriculture and forests near Kirkovo

 This site offers the chance of a fine stroll through a mature oak woodland (quite rare in the region) and some splendid traditional hay meadows with the highest concentration of Green-winged Orchids we have ever seen.
From the southern exit of Kirkovo turn left towards the east. Follow the road for approximately 2 km to the first spring on the right side and park here.
A gentle walk leads up from the spring into the forest and beyond into the flowery meadows, where all the Green-winged Orchids grow. Very typical here are the raised haystacks that protect the hay from the free-ranging herds of cattle. You can follow the track over the hill to a drinking trough, from where you turn left onto a track that leads back to the road where you parked.
Orchid enthusiasts should search the older oak woods and the damp meadows near the road. This is one of the places where the rare Provence Orchid grows (typical of open, old oak forests), in addition to the more widespread Pink Butterfly Orchids (in the woodland).

CROSSBILL GUIDES • RHODOPE MOUNTAINS

# Routes in the Ivaylovgrad region

Tucked away in the far south-east corner on the border with Greece, Ivaylovgrad and its surroundings are quite distinct from the rest of the Eastern Rhodopes. The landscape encompasses extensive areas of agricultural land, fields, meadows and scrubland in addition to more natural habitats, like dense forest, flower-rich semi-natural grasslands and untouched river systems. Typically, parts of the Ivaylovgrad region have a limestone bedrock with a more Mediterranean feel. As a result, the flora and fauna contains a striking mix of Mediterranean and Pontic species. Orchids and reptiles in particular are well represented. In fact, Ivaylovgrad is one of Bulgaria's richest regions for these groups. The region supports three famous protected nature sites: Dupkata (site B on page 193), Likana (site C on page 194) and the Byala Reka Meanders (route 14).

Overview of the Ivaylovgrad region, with the position of the routes. The letters refer to the sites on page 193-195.

Agricultural land in the Ivaylovgrad region. Some of the better wines of Bulgaria are from this region.

ROUTE 13: THE ARMIRA VALLEY

## Route 13: The Armira Valley

**5 HOURS, 3.2 KM ONE WAY**
**EASY**

*From dry steppes to a picturesque stream with a Byzantine bridge.
Rich birdlife of steppes, and plentiful reptiles and invertebrates.*

**Habitats:** river, oak woodland, flowery grasslands, steppe
**Selected species:** Grecian Foxglove, Pink Butterfly Orchid, Suslik, Lesser Spotted Eagle, Dice Snake, Grass Snake, Hermann's Tortoise, Blue Argus, Eastern Baton Blue, Freyer's Purple Emperor, Pearl-bordered Fritillary, Balkan Emerald, Turkish Goldenring, Bronze Bush-cricket.

The Armira valley is a lush surprise on the edge of the dusty plain of Ivaylovgrad. The pretty stream with a picturesque stone-arch bridge leaves one conflicted as to whether to lie down between the flowers to enjoy the quietude or to energetically track down the plentiful butterflies and look for the little Dice and Grass Snakes in the river.
The road over to the river valley leads through a splendid steppe grassland, which provides good birdwatching.

**Starting point** Ivaylovgrad (Ladzha)

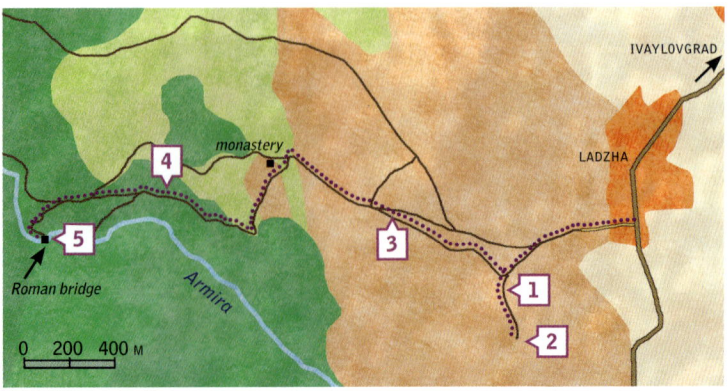

CROSSBILL GUIDES • RHODOPE MOUNTAINS

## ROUTE 13: THE ARMIRA VALLEY

Drive in southern direction to Ladzha and take the last street in the village right, signposted Lyutitsa. Beyond the houses, the tarmac ends in a track. Park at a bend and walk up the top of the hill on your left.

**1** The first attraction here are the birds. Look for Isabelline Wheatear, which is quite common in these parts, and for Black Stork, Lesser Spotted and Golden Eagles and Egyptian Vulture. Scan the steppes carefully for Suslik. This is one of the few places where good numbers of this now endangered little animal still occur. We found them on the slope facing towards Ivaylovgrad.

**2** Walk up in the direction of the hilltop. This is a great spot for wildflowers of steppes and fields like Hemp-leaved Mallow, Wild Clary, Felty Germander, Field Love-in-a-mist, Balkan Harebell\* (*Asineuma limonifolium*). In May you can see many Pink Butterfly Orchids flower a little further downhill. A good spot for butterflies is the hilltop on the north side of the track. Hilltopping butterflies include Swallowtail and Lesser Spotted Fritillary, which may congregate in large numbers on this hill.

**3** Walk the next 1 km to the Monastery. Along the way, scan the steppes for birds, and keep an eye out for Pink Butterfly Orchid and the butterflies Eastern Baton Blue and Oberthür's Grizzled Skipper. This patch of steppe is famous for its rare species of grasshoppers.

The trail over to the Armira river runs through steppe-like grassland and scrub (top).
Balkan Harebell\* (*Asyneuma limonifolia*) is one of the plants you can find here (bottom).

The monastery was founded in the 13th century but rebuilt in 1846. It is closed to the public, but do enjoy the impressive Oriental Plane tree. This is the tree species which has the biggest trunk in Europe – and that is not hard to believe when you look at this specimen.

PRACTICAL PART

**ROUTE 13: THE ARMIRA VALLEY**

Continue the track on foot, down the valley slope and look for the signs 'Roman bridge'. (alternatively, you can visit the Lyutitsa Castle ruin, which is another splendid site 3 km further on).

**4** This section leads through a well-developed oak woodland, a common forest type in the Eastern Rhodopes, but this one is distinguished by being rather old. Along the track look out for the butterfly Freyer's Grayling, tortoises and the plentiful Wall Lizards. Grecian Foxglove is also found here, together with a few Three-toothed Orchids.

**5** The Roman bridge over the Armira river lies a little further ahead. This bridge is reputed to date back to the Roman period, but the actual stonework from the 16th century. This picturesque and lush place is very good for naturalists, with Dice and Grass Snakes abundant in the river (at one fortunate moment we saw, as we surveyed the area from a rock in the river, three Dice Snakes in various spots). The location is superb for dragonflies as well, with Balkan Emerald, Turkish Goldenring and Odalisque. A little further away on the flowery swards, Blue Argus, Sandy Grizzled Skipper, Little Tiger and Anomalous Blues do their tours along the wildflowers (which include Pink Butterfly Orchid). The shady forests on the other side on the river have Black Woodpecker (rare in the area). All in all there is plenty to see here, but make sure you don't forget to sit down for a moment and simply soak up the beautiful, peaceful atmosphere!

The Armira river (top) is a great place to find wildlife. Look here for Dice Snakes in the water and along the banks (bottom).

# Route 14: To the Byala Reka Meanders

**FULL DAY, 5 KM ONE WAY**
**STRENUOUS**

Hike to the remote parts of the Byala Reka river valley. Unique oriental plane forest and rich flora and insect life.

**Habitats**: Habitats: rivers, oriental plane forest, oak forest, Mediterranean scrub, limestone grassland
**Selected species:** Balkan Lizard Orchid, Pink Butterfly Orchid, Long-lipped Tongue Orchid, Otter, Black Vulture, Dice snake, European Pond Terrapin, Balkan Terrapin, Bulgarian Emerald, Odalisque, Freyer's Purple Emperor

This trail takes you through damp forests, over sunny scrublands and across stony grasslands down to the breathtaking Byala Reka river close to the Greek border. The river valley is a protected site and supports one of the few Oriental Plane forests – an East-Mediterranean habitat type – in Bulgaria. The Byala Reka and surrounding hills support many orchids, an attractive butterfly fauna, and offers the chance to find the extremely rare and localised dragonfly, the Bulgarian Emerald.

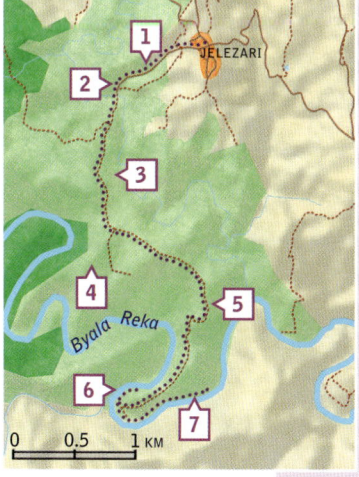

**Starting point** Jelezari

**Getting there** From Ivaylovgrad, head in the direction Krumovgrad and after 13 km turn left towards Plevun and continue to Jelezari. Park at the small square. Directly behind the bus stop, take the track to the right.

**1** The forest, dominated by mixed oaks and Oriental Hornbeam, is cool and damp, with water trickling over the track. Look carefully for European Pond Terrapin, which we found along the track. Keep an eye out for Grecian Foxglove at drier sections.

## ROUTE 14: TO THE BYALA REKA MEANDERS

The damp river forests of Oriental Plane and Black Alder form a corridor along the Byala Reka (top). Here, in places where the current is slow, fresh water crabs can be found (bottom).

**2** Just before the stream, explore the bramble bushes which are good for butterflies. Keep your eye out for Meleager's and Chapman's Blues, and Niobe Fritillary. On the wet track near the stream many butterflies, such as Silver-studded Blue and Blue Argus, congregate to drink. At the stream look for Grey Wagtail along the water's edge and Balkan Emerald Dragonfly which patrols low over the shady parts of the water.

Cross the stream by hopping from stone to stone or, for the less adventurous, by the small wooden bridge just to the right of the fork in the track.

**3** The forest on this stretch is a mix of large old trees, with a thick undergrowth of youngish trees. Woodland Grayling and Purple Hairstreak are common butterflies. Even though you might be more than a kilometre away from the main river, the trail is a used as a hunting ground for shade-loving dragonflies like Eastern Spectre and Balkan Goldenring. Turn right at the signpost (red arrow on a wooden surface, attached to a tree) onto a path.

**4** The cool and shady forests have made way for dry open woodland dominated by Christ's-thorn, Smoke-tree, Prickly Juniper and Bladder Senna. As the terrain opens up, you find yourself in limestone grassland, which is superb for wildflowers. Look for Purple Mullein, Wild Jasmine and Burning Bush. In April and May a number of orchids, including Long-lipped Tongue, Pink Butterfly, Mammose and Burnt Orchids can be found here. Visitors in June and July will be treated to the extraordinary flowers of the Balkan Lizard Orchid* (*Himantoglossum caprinum*). This place is not scrutinized as is the Dupkata or Likana protected sites (see pages 193-194) but seems to have the same potential, so explore! And while doing so, look out for both Hermann's and Spur-thighed Tortoises, and reptiles in general. Don't forget to scan the air for raptors and vultures either.

Return to the main track and turn right.

**5** Just after you start to descend to the Byala Reka, there are some excellent views over the valley. Note that the north-facing slopes are damp and densely wooded whereas south-facing slopes are typically hot, scrubby, with a decidedly Mediterranean feel to it. Here, along the track Pink Butterfly and Burnt Orchids are frequent in season. Scan the plateau for Wolves, they are regularly seen here.

The track ends at an extensive and impressive floodplain of the Byala Reka river which is hidden from view by a thick cloak of riverside forest. From this point you can explore the floodplain in two directions.

**6** Follow the lefthand trail to the stony river bank, where there is suitable habitat for the rare

The Long-lipped Tongue Orchid is a rare treat in the Eastern Rhodopes. The limestone grasslands around the Byala Reka Meanders is one of the places where this Mediterranean species can be found.

## ROUTE 14: TO THE BYALA REKA MEANDERS

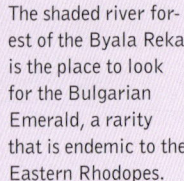

The shaded river forest of the Byala Reka is the place to look for the Bulgarian Emerald, a rarity that is endemic to the Eastern Rhodopes.

Small Bath White. Look around the willows for the flashy Freyer's Purple Emperor. The river's current here is slow, enabling you to look for fresh water crabs and the Balkan Terrapin. Grey Wagtails are everywhere and an early morning visit may even be rewarded with a sighting of one of the Otters that live along this river.

**7** Follow the righthand trail to an exposed floodplain with, depending on the water level, scattered ponds where large numbers of Dice Snake may be found. After about 200 metres turn right and enter the completely unscathed, damp river forest of Oriental Plane and Black Alder. Due to the strong 'Mediterranean' influence on the climate, this frost sensitive forest type reaches its northernmost distribution limit here. Note the evidence of the extreme fluctuations of the water level in the deposition of woody debris. The river itself is a good place to look for dragonflies, like the local endemic Bulgarian Emerald and the east Mediterranean Odalisque.

Take your time to explore this part of the Byala Reka. It is worth it!

Return to Zhelezari by the same track.

# Additional sites in the Ivaylovgrad region

## A – Steppe grasslands of Drabisna

This site consists of a rolling area of vineyards, partially abandoned fields and remnants of grazed forest steppes which offer superb options to explore. The birdlife is particularly rich, with Calandra Lark, Woodchat and Red-backed Shrike, Lesser Spotted Eagle, Booted Eagle, Tawny Pipit and Spanish Sparrow to name but few of the species we found here. The area also looks suitable for Long-legged Buzzard, Roller, Bee-eaters and Lesser Grey Shrike, but it is seriously under-watched so that the visitor has a rare opportunity to find out something new. The warmth-loving Snake-eyed Lizard and Balkan Wall Lizard may be present on the dry steppe grassland. There are several small ponds, from which Great Reed Warbler produce their loud scratchy songs and some shallow lakes which look very promising for Eastern Spadefoot. The site is superb for damselflies and dragonflies; we found Small and Common Spreadwings, Lesser Emperor, Spotted Darter and many more. Butterflies are plentiful, and include Eastern Pale Clouded Yellow, Lesser Fiery Copper and many Silver-studded Blues.

Leave Ivaylovgrad in the direction of Drabisna. After about 5km turn right before the village at the brick transformer unit. On this track you drive towards a small graveyard. Park here. Follow the track to the left.

## B – Dupkata protected site

This beautiful site is situated just 1,5 km from the centre of Ivaylovgrad. Dupkata is a limestone hill that overlooks the town. The shrubby grassland is home to many interesting plant species, including a good number of orchid species: Mammose, Horned Woodcock, Butterfly, Lady, Fragrant, Violet Bird's-nest and Balkan Lizard Orchids* (*Himantoglossum caprinum*), Lesser Butterfly-orchid and White Helleborine are

The steppe grasslands of Drabisna on a summer's evening.

ADDITIONAL SITES IN THE IVAYLOVGRAD REGION

The Turkish Helleborine is the great specialty of the Likana protected site.

all present. Wild Jasmin and Sintens Grass-leaved Iris* (*Iris sintenisii*) are abundant on the site, as are the summer species Lesser Yellow Asphodel, Immortelle, Balkan Harebell* (*Asyneuma limonifolium*), Field Cow-wheat and Broomleaf Toadflax. Keep an eye open for reptiles like tortoises, Erhard's Wall Lizard, Balkan Wall Lizard, Caspian Whip Snake and Montpellier Snake.

The south-facing exposed rocks on the edge of the town form the best parts of Dupkata. Unfortunately, the grassland is becoming increasingly overgrown, but the open parts remain nevertheless very rich. Note that this route is most interesting between late April and the beginning of June. To reach the site, drive to the tourism information centre in Ivaylovgrad, and turn left. Drive up the hill and park near a bend at the information panel.

### C – Likana protected site

The site is a botanical surprise on a limestone hill with grassland and steppe woodland. The most interesting orchid species to see here is the elegant Spurred Helleborine. Likana protected site is the only place in Bulgaria where this botanical treasure can be found. They are particularly frequent along the roadside. Look for its close relatives Narrow-leaved and White Helleborines further onto the shrubby grasslands. Besides these species, Green-winged, Lady, Bug, Pink Butterfly, Mammose, Horned Woodcock, Pyramidal and Balkan Lizard Orchids* (*Himantoglossum caprinum*) are reported from Likana (although we only found the latter two). Besides plants this is a good site for butterflies, with species like Marsh Fritillary, Amanda's and Chapman's Blues, Grecian Copper and Black-veined White. Further down along the road you will find shrubs of Dwarf Elder, which is great habitat for hairstreaks. Look for Southern White Admiral in the brambles. Likana is a protected area and plays a vital role in the conservation of many rare plant species and is a key location in Bulgaria. From Ivaylovgrad head south to the village of Svirachi. Stay on the main road and after 2 km beyond the village, park at the first hairpin bend.

**ADDITIONAL SITES IN THE IVAYLOVGRAD REGION**

## D – The Byala Reka at Medem Buk

Apart from the lengthy walk to the Byala Reka (route 10), there is another, much more accessible track towards this paradisical river via the village of Medem Buk. From this traditional village, a short, leisurely walk brings you via riverine forest and scrubland to a beautiful rocky section of the Byala Reka river. The recently discovered Bulgarian Emerald (see page 120) is one of several highlights of this trip. This endemic dragonfly is only known from a few rivers in this area.

To get here, drive south from Ivaylovgrad to Medem Buk where the road ends. Park at the small square with the bus stop. Walk in western direction and take the second track right towards the village and on to the river and cross the (provisory) bridge. Follow the track as it bends left, passes fields and woodlands and ends, less than 2 km further at a rocky section of the Byala Reka. Depending on the water level, you can continue through the river bed.

On the riverbank, the willows are host plant for the Freyer's Purple Emperor. Check the river where possible for dragonflies, such as Bulgarian Emerald, Beautiful Demoiselle and Common Clubtail. In the adjacent fields, the plants of arable land include Large Venus's-looking-glass and Hypecoum. The woodlands here have a distinct Mediterranean character, with Cretan Cistus and Wild Jasmine.

The rocky section of the river offers excellent habitat for European Pond and Balkan Terrapins, and Dice and Grass Snakes. From May to July, this is also a good spot for Odalisque, Common Clubtail, Small Pincertail, Bulgarian and Balkan Emeralds. There are freshwater crabs in the water.
On a hot day it is worth to bring your swimsuit for a cool dip in the refreshing water.

Two frequent orchids in the Dupkata protected site: the Horned Woodcock Orchid (top) and the Mammose Orchid (bottom).

**PRACTICAL PART**

ROUTES IN THE WESTERN RHODOPES

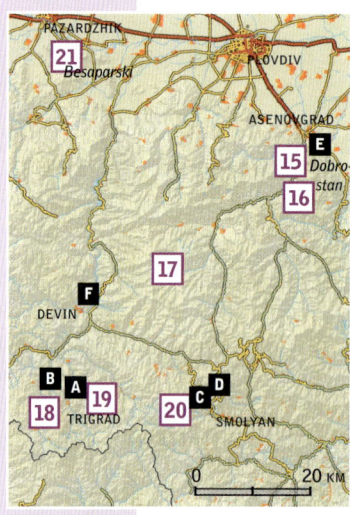

Overview of the Western Rhodopes with the position of the routes. The letters refer to the sites on page 224-227.

The karst plateau of Dobrostan (route 15 and 16).

# Routes in the Western Rhodopes

The Western Rhodopes rise up suddenly and steeply from the Thracian Plain. In the summer months driving into these mountains is like stepping into an air-conditioned house. The dusty, open plain gives way to verdant hills, pleasant shade and lower temperatures. In comparison to the Eastern Rhodopes, the western section of this range is much greener and much more like the mountains of continental Europe.

Even the mountains on the edge of the range are already quite high and green, and host many of the species that are so typical of these mountains, but are absent in the east – Balkan Chamois, Brown Bear, Capercaillie, Apollo, etc. At first glance, it seems to matter little where you base yourself in the Western Rhodopes. Nevertheless, there are subtle differences, which create some hotspots in the huge area. In this book, we concentrate on three areas.

To the north, close to Plovdiv, lies the small mountain range of Dobrostan (routes 15 and 16), which, being limestone, has a high biodiversity. It is officially listed as both a butterfly and a botanical hotspot and harbours species like the endemic Rhodopean Tulip, the Macedonian Marsh-orchid* (*Dactylorhiza kalopissii*) and Lady's-slipper (all of which though, are not easy to find). Among the butterflies, Russian Heath, Apollo and Balkan Copper are the specialties.

Dobrostan differs from the other two regions in having somewhat higher temperatures as it borders the warm Thracian Plain. The proximity of the plain also means it is easier to access than the other two sites. With the famous Bachkovski monastery, the nearby pretty Bachkovo village and Asen's Fortress, this region is also attractive from a cultural point of view.

## ROUTES IN THE WESTERN RHODOPES

Much further south and deeper into the mountains lies the region of Devin and Trigrad. This is amongst naturalists the most popular region, mainly because it is (usually) very easy to get good, up-close views of one of the most-wanted birds of the European continent, the Wallcreeper. But the region has much more to offer. This is a land of deep green gorges and open karstic plains with many wildflowers and butterflies. It is also the region where you can book excursions to see Bears, Capercaillies and other wildlife.

The third region is the largest and its sites are less concentrated and lies, roughly speaking, between the other two. This is the region where some of the highest mountains are situated near the small town of Smolyan. It is a bit further away from the main tourist routes, except in winter, when a small tourist industry revolves around skiing in the mountain of Snezhanka (1926 m). The main attractions for naturalists here are two areas of exceptional scenic beauty, both of which are in the middle of old, little visited forests, full of wildlife (e.g. Balkan Chamois, Brown Bear and Wolf). The first is the 'waterfall valley' of Smolyan (route 20), with its picturesque trail passing countless waterfalls in the only area covered in this book that isn't limestone. The second site is another natural phenomenon, namely that of the 'beautiful bridges'.

The rivers in the Western Rhodopes (here at Bachkovo; route 15) form a splendid habitat for a wide variety of wildlife (left).
Martagon Lily in its uncommon red form (top).

**PRACTICAL PART**

## Route 15: Dobrostan – some highlights

**FULL DAY, 70 KM**
**EASY**

*Easy car routes with short stops and trails.*
*Wildflowers, butterflies, but also cultural highlights.*

**Habitats:** river, riparian forest, gorge forest, limestone grasslands, wet meadows, Austrian Pine forest
**Selected species:** Golden Eagle, Yellowhammer, Dipper, Grey Wagtail, Apollo, Yellow Navelwort, Haberlea, *Dactylorhiza kalopisii*, Balkan Lizard Orchid

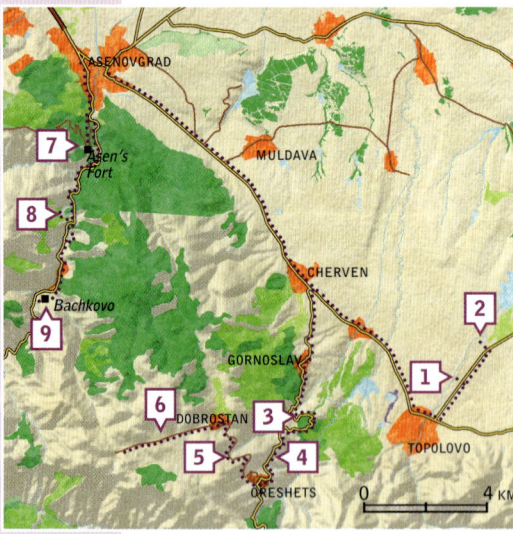

The limestone range of Dobrostan forms the northeastern end of the Western Rhodopes and is very easy to reach from the cities in the Thracian Plain. The mountain rises abruptly from the Thracian Plain to a height of 1517 metres (Staria Bunar) and is separated from the rest of the Rhodopes by the Susica and the Jugovska and Chepelare rivers that cut out steep canyons in the soft bedrock. Due to its strategic location on the edge of the plain, a large monastery and fortress were built, which are today's main tourist attractions. For naturalists, it is the limestone mountain itself that is the biggest draw, mainly because of the many rare plants and the good range of butterflies that are found here.

This short route combines the cultural sites with the more easy-to-reach wildflower and butterfly hotspots. The route has a western leg, with an emphasis on cultural sites and the river valley, and an eastern one, which climbs up the mountain and explores the dry grasslands. It is a pick-n-go route – just select those spots that sound most interesting.

## ROUTE 15: DOBROSTAN – SOME HIGHLIGHTS

The Chepelare River (left). In early summer, the Green-flowered Foxglove* (*Digitalis viridiflorus*) is common in the roadsides (bottom).

**Starting point** Asenovgrad

**Eastern route** Drive in an easterly direction to Topolovo. There, take the last turn left, towards Lenovo. After 1.5km, park at the beginning of a track on your left and walk to the forest.

**1** This is the first of two nearby stops in the nature reserve of Chinar Dere, which protects one of the few lowland Oriental Plane river forests. Whereas most river forests in Europe are dominated by willow, alder and ash trees, it is the Oriental Plane that takes over in Greece and in a few places in southern Bulgaria. This tree can grow to a magnificent size and there are some magnificent specimens here (although those at the monastery of point 7 of this route are much taller). Be warned that although the forest is very attractive, illegal fly tipping – a major environmental problem in Bulgaria – seriously degrade the scenery here.

Continue another 1.5km and just after a long bend to the right, turn left onto another track which you follow on foot.

ROUTE 15: DOBROSTAN – SOME HIGHLIGHTS

The Chinar Dere protected site protects a riparian forest of Oriental Plane trees.

**2** This is another part of the Chinar Dere reserve. There are fewer Plane Trees here, but there is usually more wildlife to see. There are a few oxbow lakes and some river grasslands. Look for Esculapian Snake, Southern Skimmer, Small Pincertail, Marbled Fritillary, Bee-eater and other wildlife here.

Return to Topolovo, turn right, pass through the village of Dolnoslav and just before Cherven, turn left to Gornoslav. 2km beyond this village, park next to a well (power lines cross the road here).

**3** Water trickles out of the mountain slope over a wider area, creating wet, alkaline meadows with a special flora. This is the location of a very rare species of marsh-orchid – *Dactylorhiza kalopisii*, known from just a few localities in central Greece and Bulgaria. It flowers between mid-May and late June and grows along the roadside, together with Giant Horsetail. If you climb a few metres upslope through the woodland, you arrive at an abandoned meadow full of Giant Horsetail, where you can find more of these orchids plus Marsh Helleborine.

**4** The following section of road climbs further up hill and passes some very attractive limestone grassland. Park at the open section 3.5 kms from the previous point and explore the roadside. Balkan Lizard Orchid grows here, together with a whole series of other plants, such as the widespread but beautiful Clary Sage and Grecian Foxglove.
You may well spot Apollo butterfly here.

Continue and at the junction, turn right to the village of Dobrostan.

## ROUTE 15: DOBROSTAN – SOME HIGHLIGHTS

**5** The winding road leads through more excellent limestone pastures, full of butterflies and wildflowers. Apollos are common here in June-July. Just before the village, you pass a small old-growth forest of Austrian Pines, with some magnificent trees growing right by the road.

**6** Dobrostan village lies on the edge of a large karst plateau. It is almost the end of the road, but not quite. You can drive a little further until you reach a small car park, which forms the starting point of the walks for the next route in this book. Along the way, look for Red-backed Shrike, Mistle Thrush, Yellowhammer, Ortolan Bunting and Tree Pipit. Golden Eagle breeds nearby and frequently flies over the plateau. This is also a good place to look and listen for Nightjars at dusk.

Stop and venture out onto the plateau, which is rich in butterflies and because the terrain is level, it is easy watching here. Pearl-bordered and Lesser Spotted Fritillaries, Chestnut Heath, Apollo, Woodland Ringlet and Chequered Skipper are among the species here.

Return via the way you came.

Red-backed Shrikes are common on the Dobrostan Plateau (top).
Chestnut Heath is one of the many species of butterflies to be seen at Dobrostan (bottom).

**Western route** From Asenovgrad, follow road 86 to Smoljan. At the edge of town, follow the road to the right, which leads to Asen's fort. Drive up to the car park next to the fort.

**7** The medieval Fortress of Asen lies, very scenically, on a rocky outcrop high over the Chepelare river. There was already a fortification in Thracian times, but the current fort was built in the 13th century by Tsar Asen II to protect the Bulgarian lands from the crusaders,

**PRACTICAL PART**

## ROUTE 15: DOBROSTAN – SOME HIGHLIGHTS

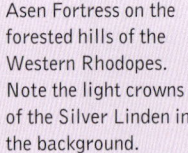

Asen Fortress on the forested hills of the Western Rhodopes. Note the light crowns of the Silver Linden in the background.

who occupied much of the former Byzantine Empire further south. Return to the main road and turn right. You now enter the beautiful gorge of the Chepelare river. Just after the tunnel, turn right onto a track and park. Continue on foot.

**8** The Chepelare river is lined with willows, poplars, alders and Oriental Plane trees. On your right look for butterflies and for Dippers and Grey Wagtails in the stream. The cliffs and steep, shaded slopes on your left are attractive for plants. On the cliffs, the pre-ice ages relict species *Haberlea rhodopensis* (see page 70) grows in large numbers. The Balkan endemic Green-flowered Foxglove, Martagon Lilly (which compared to the Martagon Lilies in the west-European mountains has small, deep-red flowers) and Yellow-flowered Navelwort can be found.

Continue and after 3 kms, you arrive at the monastery. Park and visit the site.

**9** The monastery of Bachkovo is Bulgaria's second largest and the most-visited. It is again beautifully situated next to the river, with massive Oriental Plane trees in front of it. It is worth visiting because of its beautiful buildings, frescos and fascinating history. The monastery dates back to the 11th century and was founded by Byzantine-Georgian Orthodox Christians. The monastery was partly destroyed during the Ottoman period but restored in the 15th century.

## Route 16: Two short walks in the Dobrostan mountains

**6 HOURS, 5/8.5 KM**
**MODERATE**

*Two walks with many butterflies and wildflowers.*

**Habitats:** Karst grasslands, Pine forest
**Selected species:** Chamois, Capercaillie, Golden Eagle, Crested Tit, Nightjar, Apollo, Geranium Blue, Chestnut Heath, Greater Butterfly Orchid, Violet Limodore, Eastern Spotted Orchid* (*Dactylorhiza saccifera*), Green-flowered Wintergreen

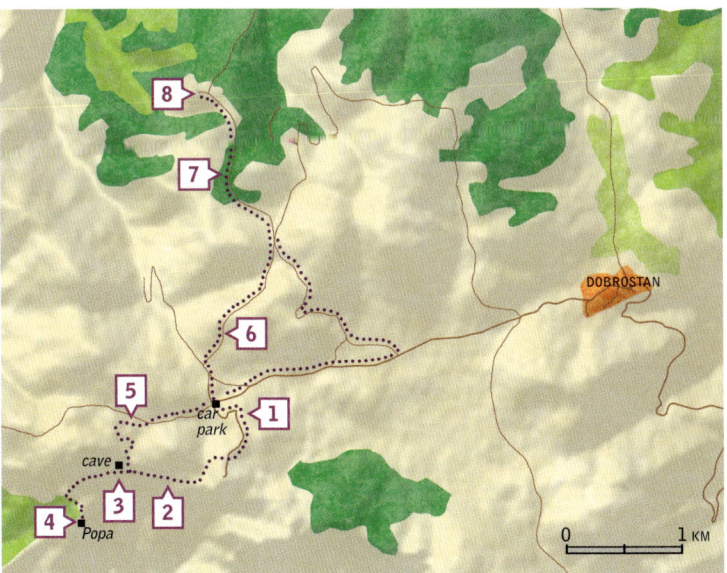

This route starts where the previous one ends at point 5 and consists of two fairly short and easy walks on the plateau of Dobrostan mountain. The limestone soil is particularly rich in wildflowers and butterflies in late spring and early summer. A bit earlier in the season (April-May), you stand the best chance of finding some of the birds and mammals of Dobrostan. Even though this mountain lies right at the edge of the Western Rhodopes,

## ROUTE 16: TWO SHORT WALKS IN THE DOBROSTAN MOUNTAINS

many of the species usually associated with the wild and untamed parts of the region are here, such as Brown Bear, Chamois and Capercaillie. Dobrostan is on the border of lowland and highland, of forest and dry grassland. As such, it has an impressive list of bird species of karst plains, rocky areas and scattered bushes. Most of these species are easier to find elsewhere, but even though this is not a birdwatching route per se, it is worth keeping your eyes open for species like Golden Eagle, Chukar, Capercaillie, both rock thrushes and Golden Eagle. Even Rock Nuthatches and Lesser Spotted Eagles have bred here in the past.

**Starting point** Village of Dobrostan
From the village continue, either by car or on foot, over the plateau to the end of the paved road. Here you can park and there is a gazebo and information panel.

**Walk 1** Follow the small road on your left (south).

**1** The road crosses an open forest of Austrian Pines. Look and listen for Coal and Crested Tits, Crossbill, Firecrest and Goldcrest. On the forest floor there are, in season, various orchids, including White Helleborine and Greater Butterfly Orchid.

Pass the barrier of the newly built hotel and then follow the trail to the right, indicated by white-red-white flashes. It leads to a trail up a slope. Turn right here.

The view over Mount Popa.

## ROUTE 16: TWO SHORT WALKS IN THE DOBROSTAN MOUNTAINS

**2** The slope faces south and was once grazed by sheep, but now it is covered with a dry forest of Hop Hornbeam. There are still lots of wildflowers and butterflies present – Pearl-bordered, Queen-of-Spain, Spotted and Duke of Burgundy Fritillaries, Apollo, Mazarine Blue, Woodland Ringlet, Pearly and Chestnut Heaths among the butterflies; St. Bernards Lily, the yellow yarrow *Achillea clypeolata*, White and Narrow-leaved Helleborine, Violet Bird's-nest Orchids, Yellow Woundwort, the goldendrop *Onosma rhodopea* and Clustered Bellflower among the plants.

**3** As a karstic area, Dobrostan abounds in caves. One of the finest is found on this trail and can be explored for an entrance fee of a few leva. The dry grassland around the cave entrance is especially rich in flowers and butterflies.

The second of the two walks of this route leads through an open pine-fir forest.

Continue further along the trail. Five hundred metres further at the edge of a meadow, the trail forks. Follow the unmarked lefthand trail.

**4** The trail soon reaches the edge of the plateau where there is a spectacular view of the mountains further south. Right in front of you lies a small peak, Mount Popa. Daredevils can search for the small trail down and then up to this peak. In all honesty, this is more for the sport of doing so than for anything else, although the views of Popa are beautiful. The descent and subsequent ascent are short but extremely steep and one shouldn't attempt this extension after rains.

Return to the cave and follow the broad trail that winds through the meadows to a forest with a hunting hide. Here, follow the righthand track to another track. Go right here to return to the starting point.

**5** This last section is again easy walking, with many butterflies and wildflowers. Look for Eastern Spotted Orchid\* (*Dactylorhiza saccifera*) and more butterflies.

**PRACTICAL PART**

ROUTE 16: TWO SHORT WALKS IN THE DOBROSTAN MOUNTAINS

**Walk 2** From the car park, walk along the metalled road northwards. It ends after 350 metres where three trails branch off to the right. Take the middle one, marked again with white-red-white flashes that goes to Chervenata stena (Червената стена; the Red Wall in Bulgarian).

**6** You walk through meadows and pine plantation that soon gives way to a more natural coniferous forest on the north slope. Austrian Pine is the dominant tree but there are also some tall Norway Spruce and Fir trees among them, typical for the damper and cooler north slopes of the mountain. There are again many butterflies in the opener sections here, such as Chequered Skipper, Chestnut Heath, Pearl-bordered and Heath Fritillary, Geranium Blue, and many more. Look here and in the other open parts of this walk for birds as well. Red-backed Shrike, Woodlark and Yellowhammer are quite common, Nightjar, Wryneck and Common Redstart are some of the rarer bird species in the region that also occur here.

Where the trail reaches a rough forest track, turn left.

**7** The next section leads uphill through an open Austrian Pine forest. Search here for Capercaillie – there's a lek (display ground) in this open forest in early spring which shouldn't be disturbed. Although the chances of seeing this impressive forest bird are not too great, you might as well get lucky. Both Roe Deer and Chamois are present in these forests.

**8** The trail ends at the cliffs known as the Red Wall, which gets its name from the reddish rock that lights up in the evening sun. You won't see this from where you are standing, but the views down to the valley and further right to the Thracian Plain are most attractive. On clear days, you can see all the way across the plain to the Central Balkan Mountains. The area up to the viewpoint is very rich in butterflies. Roughly similar species occur here as at point 2, but in higher numbers.

Return via the way you came, or, alternatively, stay on the track which leads you back to the village of Dobrostan where you turn right to get to the starting point. This latter loop offers easy walking over the karstic plateau with more opportunities for seeing the butterflies and birds of Dobrostan.

The Apollo is a highlight of the karst plateau of Dobrostan.

# Route 17: The wonderful bridges of Zabardo

**1 HOUR-FULL DAY**
**EASY-STRENUOUS**

Impressive karst phenomenon.
Dry limestone hills full of butterflies and wildflowers.
One of the best places to spot Chamois and other mammals.
Mature spruce forest with a rich birdlife.

**Habitats:** Karst grasslands, Subalpine meadows, coniferous forests, cliffs
**Selected species:** Brown Bear, Balkan Chamois, Red Deer, Three-toed Woodpecker, Black Woodpecker, Crossbill, Capercaillie, Golden Eagle, Rock Partridge, Apollo, Eastern Large Heath

The traditional village of Zabardo (pronounce *Zaburdo*) lies on the southern edge of a limestone mountain that has an exceptional karstic phenomenon known as 'the Wonderful Bridges'. A river sank into the fissures in the limestone pavement and formed a tunnel. Later, part of the ceiling of the tunnel collapsed leaving several tall arches standing which are the 'bridges' beneath which the river now flows. It is a peculiar and spectacular sight.

The Wonderful Bridges form, together with the limestone plateau, a superb and diverse destination, where you can easily spend a couple of days. There are mature spruce forests full of birds, a cliff where Golden Eagle breed and Chamois roam, and rocky slopes full of wildflowers and butterflies. The tricky thing about this area, though, are the trails. The Wonderful Bridges are easy to visit via the road, but the trails that cross the mountain to the village are not well signposted and some are partially overgrown. Moreover, many trails do not appear on the maps (apps) and some that do, don't actually exist in the field.

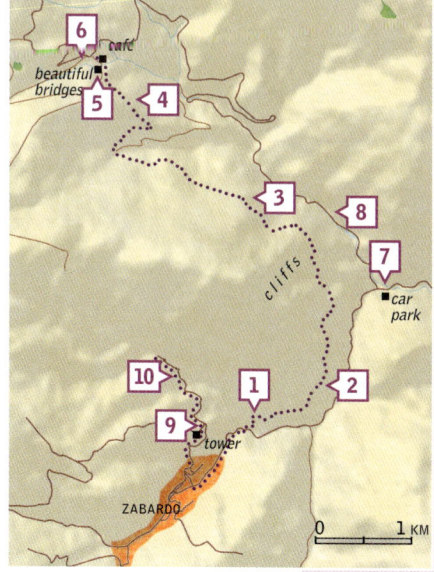

**PRACTICAL PART**

## ROUTE 17: THE WONDERFUL BRIDGES OF ZABARDO

There is one trail from Zabardo to the Wonderful Bridges that is well-marked and, save a few wet and slightly overgrown places, is easy to follow. From the arches, you either need to return by the way you came, or arrange a car to return you to the village. However, since the most attractive areas for wildlife are either close to Zabardo or to the Wonderful Bridges, you can also opt to only walk a little around those places and skip the full walk.

Here we'll first describe the walk, and then several separate points to explore near the road. Finally, there is a short walk from Zabardo (approx. 2 kms one way) that we'll describe at the end.

### Walk from Zabardo to the Wonderful Bridges

**Starting point** Zabardo (GPS: 41.785227, 24.592583)
Walk the main road in an easterly direction and a few curves beyond the peace monument outside the village, follow the trail that leads up the rocky hill, signposted Wonderful Bridges 2,5 hours (in Cyrilic).

**1** The path leads through a flowery 'rock garden', with thymes, sainfoins, milk-vetches, sages, Catmint, Yellow Woundwort, Clustered Bellflower, Balkan Harebells\*, Cross-leaf Gentian, the yellow-flowered flax *Linum capitatum* and many more. This is the kind of habitat where you'd expect orchids and there are some around (e.g. Pyramidal and Fragrant), but the forest further ahead is richer. There are many butterflies though, including Apollo, Spotted and Heath Fritillaries, Purple-shot Copper, Marbled White and Woodland Ringlet which are widespread.

**2** As the path rounds the cliffs, it leads through lusher meadows, with patches of woodland and coppiced Hazel (in places it is overgrown here, but it does continue). Twayblade, Eastern Spotted and Fragrant Orchids, Red and White Helleborines grace the trailside; Herb-Paris and Asarabacca grow in the shadiest parts. Scan the cliffs here for Golden Eagle and, particularly in the early and late hours, Chamois. In wet parts of the trail, here and further ahead, look for animal tracks. Roe Deer, Wild Boar and Red Deer slots can be found here, but the grand prize is the footprint of a Brown Bear. There is at least one bear that roams these hills and has been observed by members of the Rewilding Rhodopes team.

**3** As you climb higher, the open patches become fewer and a Spruce forest takes over. The path continues further as a forest track. This

## ROUTE 17: THE WONDERFUL BRIDGES OF ZABARDO

part is not very attractive, but it will get better further on.

After the righthand hairpin, a trail forks off to the left, signposted Wonderful Bridges.

**4** Following this trail, you soon enter older forest. There are clear signs of harvesting here, but in a way that maintains a forest with sufficient old trees. Look and listen here for forest birds – Firecrest and Goldcrest, Crossbill, Bullfinch, Crested, Marsh and Coal Tits and with luck even a Three-toed Woodpecker or Pygmy Owl. There are also some interesting wildflowers here, such as Green and One-sided Wintergreen – two species that are typical of the northern taiga and the subalpine forests of the central-European mountains.

Flowery grasslands at Zabardo (top). This is one of the best routes to watch Balkan Chamois in the Western Rhodopes (bottom).

**5** This trail ends at the Wonderful Bridges, where there is a bar/restaurant for refreshments. Follow the trail down into the valley and bear to the right to see the spectacular limestone arches. Follow the trail all the way down to the wooden bridge over the river to see how the river flows through a limestone tunnel with multiple 'windows' to the slopes above.

**6** Return to the café and walk up to the road. From here you can go left and follow the wide path (with green fencing) that leads over the arch you just saw from below. You can then look down into the valley. Note

PRACTICAL PART

## ROUTE 17: THE WONDERFUL BRIDGES OF ZABARDO

The spectacular 'Wonderful Bridges' are remnants of a tunnel cut out in the limestone by an underground river.

the immense spruces here, which must be over 50 metres tall. Continuing on leads back into another very old spruce forest, where the previously mentioned forest birds can also be found.

### The drive to the Wonderful Bridges

**7** The car route starts at the crossing where the road to the Wonderful Bridges turns off from the road to Zabardo. Stop at the crossing itself as the flowery grasslands have plenty of butterflies (e.g. Rock Grayling, Woodland Ringlet, Green-underside Blue). From the crossing you have unimpeded views over the cliffs to the west, which in the early morning and in the evening often have grazing Chamois. A telescope is needed to see them well. Golden Eagle, Eagle Owl and Peregrine also breed on this cliff, as does Alpine Swift and Crag Martin.

Drive along the road to the Wonderful Bridges.

**8** There are many orchids in the roadside. Wherever you can, park and walk parts of this road to look for Eastern Spotted, Fragrant, Greater Butterfly and Heart-flowered Marsh-orchids* (*Dactylorhiza cordigera*).

There is a car park at the Wonderful Bridges. From here, explore points 5 and 6 of the walking route above.

## ROUTE 17: THE WONDERFUL BRIDGES OF ZABARDO

### Short walk outside Zabardo

From the centre of Zabardo, walk up the south-facing slope and follow the track to the radio tower. Just beyond the tower, in a bend to the left, settle yourself on the rocks.

**9** Scan, preferably with a telescope, the slopes to the north-east, which gently rise to the cliffs you explored from the road at point 7 (but are not visible from here). In the evening, the open areas you have a near-guarantee of a sighting of Balkan Chamois. As in point 7 they are far away, but with good optics, you are front row seat for observing them as they graze in the fields. You may also see some raptors there and whatever else may appear. For example, both Brown Bear and Wolf occur nearby and there is an outside chance of seeing them. Your best chances are at dusk and dawn and night-vision optics with heat sensors greatly increase your chances.

**10** If you are here in the daytime, continue the track further ahead which turn into a trail that crosses a small river and gives access to the abandoned meadows and rocky grasslands of the lower part of the slope you've just observed. This is again a great area for butterflies and wildflowers. We've found Apollo, Eastern Large Heath, Spotted and Glanville Fritillaries, Balkan and Purple-shot Copper and a large collection of blues here. The birdlife includes Quail, Red-backed Shrike, Serin, Yellowhammer, Ortolan and Cirl Buntings. Higher up on the slopes, Rock Partridge breeds.

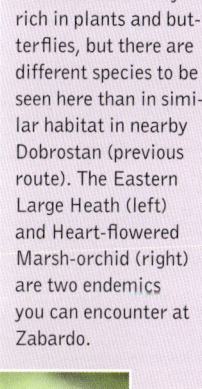

The karstic grasslands at Zabardo are very rich in plants and butterflies, but there are different species to be seen here than in similar habitat in nearby Dobrostan (previous route). The Eastern Large Heath (left) and Heart-flowered Marsh-orchid (right) are two endemics you can encounter at Zabardo.

## Route 18: The plateau between Trigrad and Yagodina

**19 KM ROUND WALK**
**FULL DAY, STRENUOUS**

*Pleasant walk through coniferous forests and limestone grasslands. A wealth of wildflowers and butterflies.*

**Habitats:** Subalpine meadows, karst grasslands, coniferous forests
**Selected species:** Balkan Chamois, Alpine Swift, Morina persica, Bug Orchid, Fragrant Orchid, Apollo, Black Apollo, Balkan Copper, Twin-spot Fritillary, Black Ringlet, Bright-eyed Ringlet

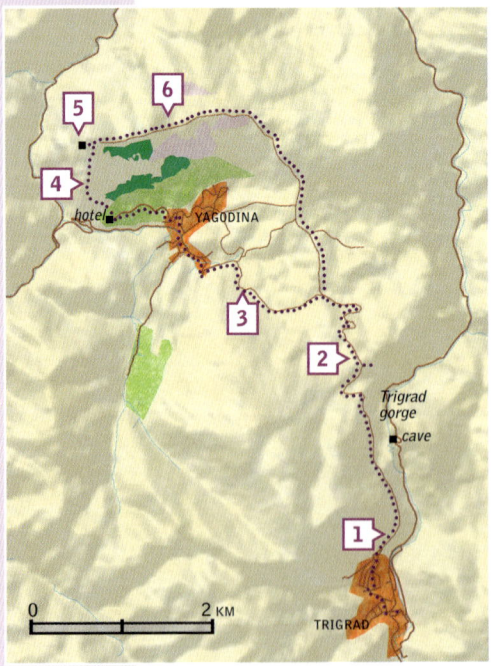

This beautiful walk connects Trigrad with Yagodina and continues further to the Devil's Rock viewpoint. It is a good way to explore the wildlife of the karst plateau, with its coniferous forests and rocky grasslands. This region is exceptionally rich in butterflies and is considered a hotspot for wildflowers in Bulgaria and you should be able to get a good taste of this on this walk. Here we start the description from Trigrad, but you may just as well start from Yagodina, if this is where you are based. Also, you can shorten the route by only walking the circuit above Yagodina to Devil's Rock – the area with the highest concentration of plants and butterflies.

**Starting point** post office in the village centre of Trigrad.

Walk the road up (in a southerly direction) and turn right before the hotel and directly thereafter right again. You pass the school and snake your way through the village. Continue where the tarmac ends and then where the road sharply bends left, go

## ROUTE 18: THE PLATEAU BETWEEN TRIGRAD AND YAGODINA

straight on. This point is not signposted but soon you'll pick up the first white-red-white markings of the trail.

**1** The first section leads along rocky grasslands, rich in butterflies. Apollo is in evidence here, just like Bright-eyed Ringlet. In summer, the thistle-like *Morina persica*, a large-flowered and conspicuous member of the mint family, is common. Look as well for Rock Bunting, Red-backed Shrike, Serin (near the village) and Alpine Swift.

You also pass some beehives – nothing special for in the mountains, you'd think. But note the intense protection with electric fence. This is a defence against the Brown Bears which are plentiful in these mountains.

**2** The route gradually leads through more wooded country. Just before you reach a meadow, there is a small, unofficial trail to the right to a cliff from which you have good views into the Trigrad gorge. It is worth spending some time both on the slopes here and in the meadows to look for butterflies. Both Balkan and Large Copper occur, Bright-eyed Ringlet is numerous and we found Heath and Twin-spot Fritillaries, Black Apollo and many more. There are also a few Burnt-tip Orchids here.

Look for Twin-spotted Fritillary (top) and Bug Orchid (bottom) in the meadows outside Yagodina.

The track continues through more woods until you arrive at the meadows surrounding the village of Yagodina. The track forks at a wooden shelter on the edge of the forest. Here follow the left track and keep left to walk down to Yagodina.

**3** Look for birds in the Yagodina meadows. Serin, Yellowhammer, Mistle Thrush and Red-backed Shrike should be present here. There are many Fragrant Orchid about and lower numbers of Bug Orchid (we found them mostly on the meadows near the village).
Walk into the centre of the village and follow the signs to a hotel (Hotel Mursal) and the Eagle Eye viewpoint.

**PRACTICAL PART**

## ROUTE 18: THE PLATEAU BETWEEN TRIGRAD AND YAGODINA

**4** Once outside the village you pass through some flowery meadows on your way to the beautifully situated hotel. From there you pick up a path that steeply zigzags up on the slope. This is a tough walk, but you are rewarded with increasingly beautiful views, plus a good range of wildflowers, butterflies and birds. Alpine Swift, Rock Partridge, Ortolan Bunting and Red-backed Shrike inhabit these slopes. In the early morning, there may be Balkan Chamois here as well.

**5** Just below the three 'phone masts on the hill's summit you'll find the Eagle Eye viewpoint which resembles a diving board hemmed in by railings. The need for caution becomes apparent once you realise that, instead of water rippling a few metres below you, there's a vertiginous void of several hundred metres that drops into the gorge below. Even with a safety rail it's not for the faint-hearted or sufferers from vertigo. The views are simply spectacular though, even from the edge and especially towards the sunset. Alpine Swifts fly by at eye level.

Continue to the masts and follow the broad track over the ridge.

**6** This section is unfortunately not so attractive anymore, as the grasslands have been largely destroyed by 4x4 vehicles driving tourists up to the Eagle Eye viewpoint. However, a bit further down, the cars follow a single track and the surrounding rocky grasslands are rich in wildlife again, roughly with similar species as those noted at point 4.

A little further down, on a ridge, you can turn right to walk down to Yagodina, or straight on to connect with the track that leads back to Trigrad.

The spectacular Eagle Eye viewpoint on a June evening. Besides the views, the constant passing of Alpine Swifts here is magnificent.

# Route 19: Walk to the Chairski lakes

**11.5 KM ONE WAY**
**FULL DAY, MODERATE**

*Beautiful, gentle and quiet walk.*
*Splendid old-growth forest and mires with a rare flora.*

**Habitats:** Mountain rivers, coniferous forests, Subalpine meadows
**Selected species:** Ghost Orchid, Fly Orchid, Broad-leaved Marsh-orchid, Bogbean, Geum rhodopaeum, Brown Bear, Dipper, Three-toed Woodpecker, Hazel Grouse, Poplar Admiral, Balkan Copper, Marsh Fritillary, Four-spotted Chaser

High up in the hills east of Trigrad lies a lovely area of meadows around the hamlet of Chairski where local farmers have their cattle in summer and a mountain hut welcomes guests with good coffee and a decent lunch. Dotted around these meadows are several lakes and marshes with an attractive flora. The Chairski Lakes are the goal of this walk but certainly not the only attraction. In order to get there, you have to walk through the beautiful Chair valley, which in places has the character of a gorge. The old-growth spruce-fir gorge forests are sublime. The flora of this route is particularly attractive and there is a good range of butterflies present. It is a fairly long route but the climb, following a rough track up through the valley, is quite gentle.

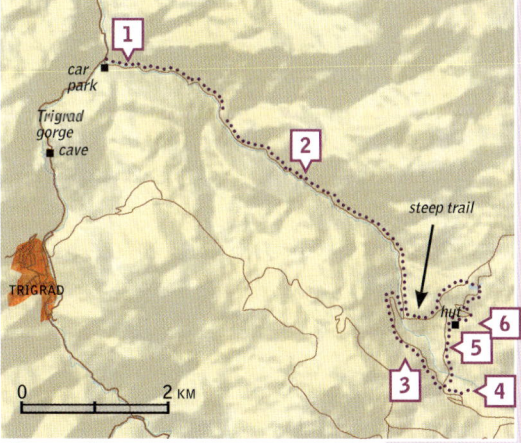

**Starting point** Road to Trigrad (GPS: 41.625105, 24.388646)

**Getting there** From Teshel, drive 7.5km in the direction of Trigrad to where River Chair river meets the River Trigrad. Park near the wooden shelter and follow the track up the Chair valley.

## ROUTE 19: WALK TO THE CHAIRSKI LAKES

The meadows around the mountain hut (point 6).

**1** Right from the very start, the route is beautiful. The steep slope on your right faces north and is covered with a tall, mature forest of Spruce, Fir, Beech, Sycamore, Hop Hornbeam and other trees. On the other side, it is mostly Austrian Pine that cover the slope. Closer to the river, willows, alders and poplars are common.

On sunny summer mornings, check the track and the verges of the vegetation for butterflies. Both White and Poplar Admirals can be found here in good numbers. The tall vegetation in the roadside, with Butterbur, Elecampane and Sticky Sage, indicate a nutrient-rich soil. Among these, there are some attractive wildflowers such as Fragrant and Eastern Spotted Orchid, Martagon Lily and the Balkan endemic Green-flowered Foxglove. In the river, Grey Wagtail is common and Dipper passes by from time to time.

**2** As you climb you'll see that the broad-leaved (deciduous) trees gradually disappear and the coniferous forest takes over. From the road the difference between spruce (cones hanging down from the branches) and fir (cones standing up from the branches) is very visible.

This is the habitat of Three-toed Woodpecker and Hazel Grouse. Both species occur here, although you'd be lucky to find either of them. Meanwhile, more interesting wildflowers present themselves – Red and Narrow-leaved Helleborines grow by the wayside, while Haberlea and the purple-flowered *Saxifraga sempervivum* grows on the cliffs.

The track crosses the river. Here you may choose to follow the very steep but short trail straight up the mountain to Chairski, but we advise to keep following the track, which is not only much easier, but also more attractive (albeit longer).

**3** The track winds up the slope into an increasingly dense and mossy spruce forest. If you are here in July, scan the forest floor carefully for the enigmatic Ghost Orchid, which grows here in annually varying numbers. In good years, there can be hundreds. Other plants can be added to the list – Green-flowered Wintergreen, Herb-paris, Rhodopean Toothwort, Yellow Bird's-nest, Bird's-nest Orchid. The latter three are, just like the Ghost Orchid, parasitic plants. In these shady conditions, getting enough nutrients is a challenge. Rather than producing it through photosynthesis, 'stealing' nutrients by tapping into tree roots or fungi is an effective survival strategy.

In the roadside where there is more light, look for the yellow-flowered flax *Linum capitatum*, Willow Gentian and Fly Orchid.

After a wooden shed, a track branches off to the left, which leads to the hamlet and the lakes (signposted *Chairski Ezera*). Before taking it, walk a little bit further and just before a glade, turn left on a path into the forest.

The larger part of the route follows a gentle track up through the gorge (left).
In early summer, look for Poplar Admiral that frequently rests on the path (top).

**PRACTICAL PART**

## ROUTE 19: WALK TO THE CHAIRSKI LAKES

In July, the mossy old-growth spruce forests of points 3 and 4 (bottom) harbour a large (but annually fluctuating) population of Ghost Orchid (top).

**4** This trail is maybe only 100 metres long but brings you into an old-growth coniferous forest. It is not completely free of human influence but gives you a good feel of the interior of such very old forests.

Return and follow the track to Chairski Ezera.

**5** You cross the river and proceed through old forest until you arrive at the first of the Chairski Lakes. Note that they are mires rather than lakes, with a special vegetation, with Marsh Cinquefoil, the orange-flowered avens *Geum rhodopaeum*, Bogbean, Heart-flowered Marsh-orchid and others. Look carefully from the edge of the marsh.

**6** Just beyond the lake you arrive at the hut where you can get refreshments in the summer months. In the meadows around the hut, there are more attractive plants and butterflies. We found Bug Orchid here and when you walk the track behind the hut to the right, there are some small marshes with Balkan Copper and Marsh Fritillary. Under the roof of the shed in front of the hut Crag Martin, Common Swift, Barn and Red-rumped Swallow breed.

Return by the way you came.

# Route 20: The waterfall walk near Smolyan

**7 KM (FROM CAR PARK)**
**5 HOURS, MODERATE**

Beautiful walk along a river with many waterfalls.
Splendid old-growth spruce forest.
Perhaps the best place to find the elusive Three-toed Woodpecker.

**Habitats:** Subalpine spruce forest, mountain meadows mountain streams
**Selected species:** Green-flowered Wintergreen, Rhodopean Lily, Three-toed Woodpecker, Black Woodpecker, Crested Tit, Fire Salamander

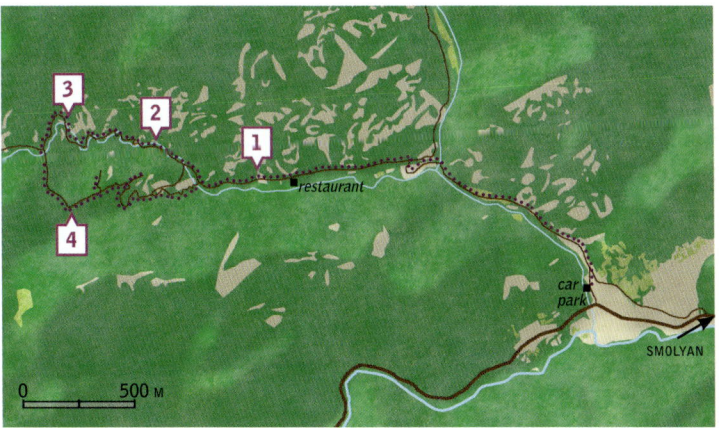

The waterfall valley in the Soskovtcheto nature reserve is a rather famous destination near the town of Smolyan. It lies a bit out of the way from the other locations in this book but is very much worth the effort to visit. This is the only west Rhodope walking route in this book that is not on limestone, but on hard, water-resistant volcanic bedrock. Rainwater doesn't sink away but flows down a steep valley in countless rapids and waterfalls. The gorge itself is so steep that commercial forestry is impossible. Massive spruces grow on the slopes and moss-covered trunks lie haphazardly over the river – the classic sight of an old-growth forest. Although the terrain is wild, the trail is reasonably easy, thanks to small flights of steps and no less than fifteen bridges that swing from one side of the river to

**ROUTE 20: THE WATERFALL WALK NEAR SMOLYAN**

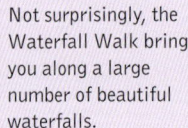

Not surprisingly, the Waterfall Walk brings you along a large number of beautiful waterfalls.

the other. The walk back leads over the mountain slope, where, still in old spruce forest but away from the roaring sound of the water, you have good chances of finding Three-toed Woodpeckers.

### Starting point Smolyan

Drive out of town in the direction of Mugla. Approximately 1km beyond the edge of town, just after a factory, turn right. The waterfalls and car park are signposted. The road is in a bad state, so it is best to use the car park some hundred metres along the road (or park near the turning and walk up).

Continue on foot and further on, ignore the turn to the right. You pass several stalls that offer off-road and horseback excursions. After 900m from the car park, you follow the bridge over the river, past an abandoned trout farm. At the crossing, go left to arrive at the visitors' centre / restaurant, which forms the official start of the trail.

**1** The route starts out as a broad track along the river. There are already some very tall and old spruce and fir trees in view here. Due to the acidic bedrock, the wildflower diversity is limited, but in (late) spring, you should be able to see the yellow-flowered Rhodopean Violet, Green-flowered Foxglove and various bellflowers. Look for Dipper and Grey Wagtail in the river.

## ROUTE 20: THE WATERFALL WALK NEAR SMOLYAN

**2** After the first bridge, go right to continue through the valley. The forest and river valley seems to get more attractive with each turn. The forest giants rise up all around you; others have tumbled down and cross the river, thickly covered in mosses and Rock Crane's-bill. Look for the tall, parasitic Rhodopean Toothwort and the bright, orange-flowered Rhodopean Avens here – both are endemic to these mountains.

**3** The trail zigzags over the river and reaches a small mountain hut. Just a little further on, you pass a large waterfall with some steep wet meadows. In June and early July, you can find a good number of the impressive Rhodope Lily here, next to the much more common Martagon Lily.

Upstream from the waterfall, the trail forks. Go left and cross the river one more time.

**4** The trail now leads uphill and away from the river. You cross a wonderful spruce forest, largely old-growth or closely resembling it. This is a good area to look for Three-toed Woodpecker, in addition to the more common spruce forest birds like both 'crests, Coal and Crested Tits.
The trail has two short side trails up to rocky outcrops from which you have a nice view down into the valley.

The trail descends to the first bridge, which you cross to return to the visitors' centre.

At the highest part of the walk (point 4) there are splendid views down into the valley you climbed up.

**PRACTICAL PART**

ADDITIONAL SITES IN THE WESTERN RHODOPES

## Additional sites in the Western Rhodopes

For the locations of the sites described below, see map on page 196.

### A – Wallcreepers and wildflowers in the Trigrad gorge

The impressive limestone gorge on the road just before Trigrad is a, perhaps even THE highlight of the Western Rhodopes, especially for birdwatchers. This is the location where Wallcreeper can be seen with relative ease. The best way to see it is by parking in the car park for the famous Dyavolsko Garlo Cave (GPS: 41.614171, 24.379489) and walk down through the short tunnel. Directly on the other side there is a small layby on your right. Sit there and scan the cliffs on either side for Wallcreeper. Most years it breeds on the cliff just to the right of the tunnel. While you are waiting for the Wallcreeper, watch the Alpine Swifts dash through the gorge. Occasionally, they are chased by a Peregrine that also breeds in the gorge.
Note that the gorge is dry at this point. The river that flows higher up near Trigrad has literally gone underground. When you walk further down the gorge, it will reappear.
It is worth walking down the gorge along the road for about 500 metres to enjoy the rock flora. The endemic Haberlea (see page 70) is very common here, as is Brittle Bladder and Limestone Ferns. Also look for the pink *Saxifraga sempervirens* and its white relative *Saxifraga paniculata*. Further down the rare thistle-like labiate *Morina persica* grows by the side of the road.

The Trigrad Gorge is one of the best places on the continent to watch Wallcreepers from up close.

### B – Yagodina gorge

The village of Yagodina lies on a plateau and can only be reached via a narrow road that passes through the spectacular Yagodina gorge. It is narrower and more spectacular than the Trigrad Gorge (see site A) and you have better up-close views of the old gorge forests. It lacks however, the good birdwatching locations of the Trigrad gorge.
About half way along the Yagodina gorge there is a small car park with

# ADDITIONAL SITES IN THE WESTERN RHODOPES

A narrow road winds through the Yagodina Gorge.

metal steps fixed to the rocks. This is the starting point of 'the Devil's Trail, one of the most spectacular trails in the Western Rhodopes. The Devil's Trail leads into a narrow side gorge, with bridges, ladders and other constructions that enables you to explore this otherwise inaccessible area. This trail comes with at least as many warnings as it does recommendations. It is not very strenuous, but difficult and potentially dangerous, because it is very steep and slippery, and the aids that are in place to help you are not always in a good state of repair and sometimes not very well placed either. We certainly advise against this trail during or several days after rain. At other times, go with extreme caution, don't walk it alone and bring a mobile phone in case you get in trouble (there is connection in most parts of the gorge).

## C – Smolyan lakes

 GPS: 41.607593, 24.666726. Still in the outskirts of Smolyan on the 866 north of the town, lies a pleasant hilly landscape with hay meadows, hedgerows, patches of woodlands and several lakes. It is quite a popular place for local tourists, so there are summer houses and B&B's scattered around, but not to the degree that it damages the scenery.

The reason for a stop here are the dragonflies that live in these small lakes. It is a good place to look for Yellow-winged Darter and Balkan Emerald. Spearhead Bluet, a northern damselfly species, is said to have a southern outpost in this area.

PRACTICAL PART

ADDITIONAL SITES IN THE WESTERN RHODOPES

## D – Pamporova

Pamporova is a ski region north of Smolyan, the highest mountain is just over 2000 metres and accessible by car, offering the easiest access to the high mountain zone. Although this is still too low for some of the Alpine bird species, the extensive coniferous forests and alpine heathlands are worth exploring for birds of the Subalpine forests, like Nutcracker and Ring Ouzel. The bedrock is acidic, so quite different from most of the routes and sites described in this guide. It creates a different kind of landscape, that is more akin to the classic Alpine mountainscapes, with (in summer) flowery meadows and majestic spruce forests. This bedrock limits the flora and butterfly fauna but has the advantage of finding different species. One common plant is the Heart-flowered Marsh-orchid, a Balkan endemic that grows in good numbers right along the 8641 road through the area. When traveling to Trigrad from Pamporova, you also pass through the village of Shiroka Laka, one of the more traditional and picturesque villages of the Western Rhodopes.

## E – Walk along the edge of Dobrostan

Just south of Asenovgrad, at the very edge of the Western Rhodopes, lies a rocky, limestone ridge with a splendid flora and butterfly fauna. It is an extension of the limestone plateau of Dobrostan (routes 15 and 16) and has a similar set of species. This mountain is famous for the occurrence of the Rhodopean Tulip, a crimson-red species endemic to Dobrostan and just a few limestone areas nearby. It flowers in late April and early May. You can walk up the ridge from Asenovgrad (difficulty: moderate) but it is easier to find your way from the monastery of Saint Petka, which lies halfway up the hill and can be reached by turning off the 58 road between Asenovgrad and Cherven (the same

The rare endemic Rhodopean Tulip grows on the northern edge of the Dobrostan plateau.

road you drive on for route 15). You turn off just east of the turn to the village of Muldava and continue past a quarry to the Monastery (GPS: 41.978131, 24.912613). From here, walk the trail uphill (on the southwest side of the monastery) to the small chapel of St Ilia (GPS: 41.980383, 24.897598). Here and beyond further along the ridge to Asenovgrad, look for butterflies and wildflowers, including the Rhodopean Tulip. The views down into the Thracian Plain are beautiful.

## F – Bear and Capercaillie watching excursions

Brown Bears, Chamois, Wolves, Capercaillies – the Western Rhodopes abounds in iconic wildlife that you stand little chance of finding by yourself. There is a small (budding) business revolving around watching and, with a little luck photographing these animals, run by people from the hunting association in Devin. The association runs a bear-watching hide (operational from mid-April – 1 Sept) and offers excursions to watch Capercaillie (1 April – early May). Less regularly, the association offers trips to watch Wolves, Chamois, Wallcreepers, Nutcrackers and other wildlife as well.

The bear watching takes place at dusk and the association estimates you have an 80% chance of actually seeing bears. You'll see them at dusk, making photography not easy but for roughly half of the visits, the bears show up when its sufficiently light to take decent photos. The Capercaillie excursions take place very early in the morning (from 3.30 to 7:00 am) and include a visit to the Wallcreeper site as well. Transportation is by 4x4 and the excursions typically do not involve extensive walking. The cost is €80 per excursion and takes up to four people. Note however that times, dates and prices may change, so ask the organisation for the details. Also, ask in advance for an English-speaking guide.

Brown Bears can be seen from the hide of the Devin Hunting Society.

# Routes in the Thracian Plain and Sakar mountains

The Thracian Plain is a large, wedge-shaped lowland that separates the massifs of the Central Balkan to the North and the Rhodopes to the south. It is at its highest and narrowest in the west and opens up towards the shores of the Black Sea. It is also the lowland through which you'll travel from Sofia to anywhere in the Rhodopes.

The Thracian plain is under-watched and underrated when it comes to wildlife. This is a great shame as its flora and fauna is not only rich but also complements that of the Rhodopes. The marshes and fertile agricultural land with its marsh birds is the great asset of the Thracian Plain for birders as it's precisely what the Rhodopes lacks. And since you'll drive through it anyway, why not enjoy some of its riches, such as Black Storks, Rollers, Collared Pratincoles, Levant Sparrowhawks, Masked Shrikes, Glossy Ibises and numerous herons and waders?

Most attractions of the Thracian Plain are somehow related to the Maritsa River. They are either the old floodplains or fishponds situated in the river plain or one of its tributaries (e.g. the sites on page 248-251) or it is the river and old meanders themselves (route 22).

The upside of the sites on the Maritsa is that they are all close to the main road from Sofia to the east. The downside is that they largely lack a tourism infrastructure. Apart from local fishermen, there are really very few people exploring these areas. The tracks to them are bumpy, sometimes up to the point that they are better suited for walking. There are no hides or waymarked trails, so you need to be a little adventurous to appreciate it.

Overview of the Thracian Plain and Sakar Mountains with the position of the routes. The letters refer to the sites on page 248-251.

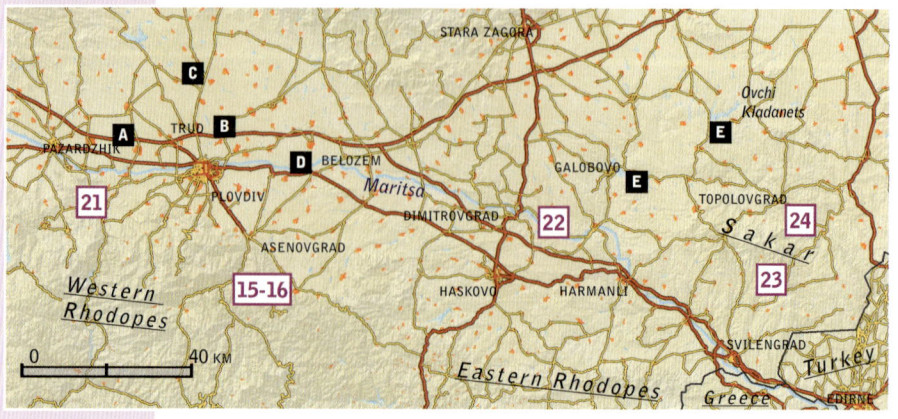

## ROUTES IN THE THRACIAN PLAIN AND SAKAR MOUNTAINS

At the far eastern end of our area, east of where the Maritsa turns south to the Aegean, lies the small mountain range of Sakar (routes 23 and 24). Few foreign visitors have visited this area and even for Bulgarian naturalists Sakar comes with a frisson of the excitement due to its potential for making new discoveries; a place where new locations of rare species are found every year. Above all, Sakar is the land of the Eastern Imperial Eagle – the vast majority of Bulgaria's breeding Imperial Eagles is found in Sakar.

At the far western end of our area lies another small range of limestone hills with a steppe-like character, the Besaparski Hills. Geologically they are part of the Thracian Plain and the hills lie close to the wetlands of Plovdiv (sites A to E). The landscape is very different though. Once again, the birds are the great attraction, with the Rose-coloured Starling, even though not annual, being the top species.

The Besaparski Hills (left; route 21) is, together with Sakar, the area with the largest expanses of steppe-like habitat. Interestingly, these are also the areas where, on a modest scale, lavander is grown.
The Long-legged Buzzard is among the many raptor species that can be seen here (top).

**PRACTICAL PART**

# Route 21: The Besaparski Hills

**4 HOURS, 21 KM**
**EASY**

Barren, steppe-like, limestone hills.
A unique flora and fauna.

**Habitats:** Stony pastures, deep-soil steppes, quarries
**Selected species:** Suslik, Long-legged Buzzard, Montagu's Harrier, Calandra and Short-toed Lark, Stone Curlew, Rose-coloured Starling (some years), Rock Sparrow, Great Spotted Cuckoo (rare), Short-toed Eagle, Bee-eater, Roller, Blue Rock Thrush, Black-eared Wheatear, Isabelline Wheatear

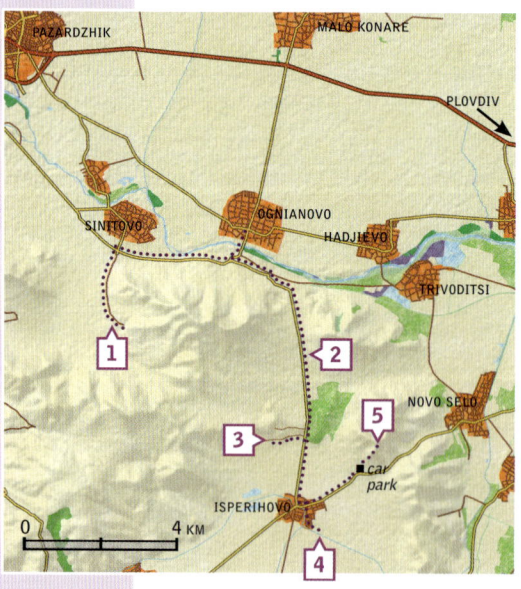

The Besaparski hills form an odd site between the green Western Rhodopes and the fertile Thracian plain. These hills are largely treeless and barren with just a scant growth of grasses and wildflowers over the thin limestone soils. They are an island of 'eastern' steppe-like habitats, more barren in comparison with Sakar and much further to the west. These areas are not entirely comparable, though – Besaparski is overall rockier and drier and supports different species. Testimony to this strange habitat and outlier position in comparison to the eastern steppes is Tekira's Gypsophila, which is endemic to Besaparski.

Most visitors will visit Besaparski for the birds though. Long-legged Buzzard, Stone Curlew and a variety of larks are present, as well as Rock Sparrow – a rarity in Bulgaria. The greatest attractions are Rose-coloured Starling and Great Spotted Cuckoo, which are not present annually but you nevertheless stand a fair chance of finding them.

## ROUTE 21: THE BESAPARSKI HILLS

**Starting point** Ognianovo, just southeast of the town of Pazardzhik. Follow the main road south out of town. You first cross the River Maritsa and then pass underneath the railway tracks. Go right and continue for 3.2 kms and turn left (the train station of Sinitovo is on your right).

**1** This little road passes through some good steppe habitat before ending at an abandoned quarry. This is one of the few reliable sites for Rosy Starlings in Bulgaria. These birds are highly nomadic and their breeding locations strongly depend on the weather when they arrive in the middle of May. If the weather is good (no rain), they stay to breed, otherwise, they continue north. So, their presence is erratic, but if they are there, they breed between the boulders in the quarry. Also, look for wheatears (all three species can be present) and Roller. Blue Rock Thrush is also sometimes found.

Return and just before the railway tracks, turn right. At the next crossing, stay on the south side of the tracks. The Besaparski area is heavily quarried, primarily for gravel, and you'll pass some gravel works en route. The road is covered with the fine dust of the quarrying.

Rose-coloured Starlings form one of the highlights of the Besaparski Hills. In some years, they are quite numerous, but in others, they are absent, so you need a little luck.

**2** The road bends to the right and passes through fine steppe habitat, past fields and nearby quarries. Scan here for Long-legged Buzzard, Short-toed Eagle, Montagu's Harrier and Raven (of which there are many).

**3** A good spot to park is just over the hill, where you look down on the road to Isperihovo, where there is a track that branches off to the right (GPS: 42.100847, 24.431241). Here you can pull off, park and walk further past the fields and into the grasslands.
Continue to Isperihovo, turn left at the junction and then the first right. Follow this road as it bears left and subsequently right until the pavement ends. Park and continue on foot.

## ROUTE 21: THE BESAPARSKI HILLS

Natural steppe habitat with deep soil (top) is the key habitat for the Suslik (bottom).

**4** After a few metres, the dirt road arrives at the river where it bends left and enters one of the few remaining unploughed grasslands on deep soil that is still grazed by sheep. It is a bit of a mess with rubble from the nearby village, but it is excellent for Susliks. The grassland is riddled with colonies of this adorable creature. Its faithful companion the Isabelline Wheatear, which breeds in abandoned Suslik holes, is also present, while Bee-eaters breed in the riverbank.

Take a moment to take in the landscape. Steppe grasslands on deep soil like these may not seem very exotic, but they rank high on the list of most threatened habitats on our continent because they are also suitable for crop farming. Sadly, this habitat is scarcely protected in Bulgaria or anywhere else.

Return to the main street in the village and turn right. After a straight section, the road bends left and then right. In this right turn, a concrete track branches off to the left. Park here.

**5** This is a convenient spot to explore the dry grasslands on foot. Just walk up the hill to the peak, from which you have excellent views all over the eastern section of the Besaparski Hills – a perfect spot to scan for raptors. Keep an eye out for Calandra and Short-toed Larks and, when you are here in the evening, look and listen for Stone Curlew.

# Route 22: Zlato Pole

**4 HOURS**
**EASY**

*Meander of the Maritsa river.*
*Rich birdlife, including Levant Sparrowhawk and Masked Shrike.*

**Habitats:** Riparian forest, marshes, dry grasslands, agricultural land
**Selected species:** Hypecoum, Birthwort, Golden Jackal, Levant Sparrowhawk, Black Kite, Masked Shrike, Lesser Grey Shrike, Golden Oriole, Kingfisher, Bee-eater, Roller, Black-headed Bunting, European Pond Terrapin, Blotched Snake, Syrian Spadefoot, Marsh Fritillary, Large Copper, Southern Festoon, Green Snaketail

Zlato Pole is a meander of the Maritsa but is now isolated from the nearby river. Its shallow waters, reedbeds and willow and poplar forest are protected as a Natura 2000 site. Together with the Maritsa which lies right next to it, this is a first-class birdwatching site. The two key birds here are undoubtedly the Levant Sparrowhawk and the Masked Shrike – two south-eastern rarities that occur here in relatively good numbers and usually show themselves on a spring visit. Additionally, there are very high numbers of Golden Oriole, Green Woodpecker, Bee-eater and Turtle Dove, plus a good population of Black Kite, Roller, Kingfisher, Night Heron, Little Bittern, Lesser Grey and Red-backed Shrikes and a lot more. The butterflies and dragonflies are also very interesting and Jackals roam the adjacent fields in the early morning and late evening.

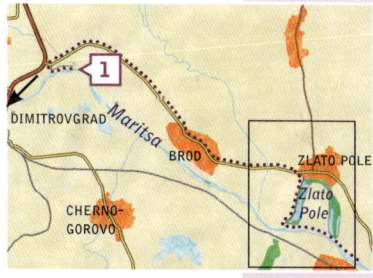

In this route, we describe three separate sites just a short drive from one another. The second and third are in the actual Zlato Pole protected site and the first lies on the shore of the Maritsa river.

**Starting point** Dimitrovgrad

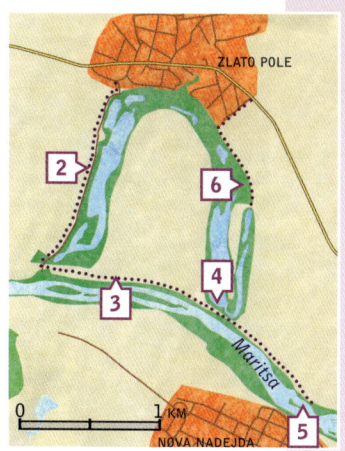

# ROUTE 22: ZLATO POLE

Take Road 5 in the direction of Raievo and Stara Zagora and after 2 km take the first right towards Zlato Pole protected site and Simeonovgrad. However, approximately 350 metres after this turn go right on the first option and follow the short track to the banks of the Maritsa.

**1** Explore this site on foot. This is probably the most reliable site to find Masked Shrike in the entire region. In spring, they frequently sing from the tops of the willow trees – listen for the rasping song, which somewhat reminiscent of Reed Warbler. Other birds to be found here are Little Bittern and Little Egret, Levant Sparrowhawk, Bee-eater, Golden Oriole, Kingfisher and Turtle Dove.

There are some small wetlands where European Pond Terrapin is numerous. Syrian Spadefoot also occurs but is hard to find except on warm, damp evenings or after rain.

Return to your car and continue towards Zlato Pole. As you enter the village, turn right (the reserve is signposted) and then right again down a track. Park at the small car park near the information panel and walk further along the track to the river.

**2** On your left is the old river arm of Zlato Pole, which is here converted to a series of fishing ponds. This is not yet the best section of the site, but when it is quiet you may well see Kingfisher, Little Bittern, Little Egret and Night Heron, while the poplars are home to an impressive population of Golden Orioles. If you are here in early spring (up to mid-May)

Zlato Pole is a former meander of of the Maritsa River and an important wetland for birds.

ROUTE 22: ZLATO POLE

the birds are active and you may well see them flying between the trees.
On your right are open fields where on quiet mornings or evenings, you should scan for Jackals.

Follow the track over the dam and turn left.

**3** You now follow the track between the marshes on the left (on the other side of the dam) and the Maritsa river which flows right behind the trees. This stretch of the walk can be magical, with Roller, Hoopoe, Bee-eater, Levant Sparrowhawk, Black Kite, Masked Shrike, Red-backed Shrike and Lesser Grey Shrike. There is even a Black Woodpecker territory – exceptional for this riparian habitat. Climb the dam at some point to scan the fields on the other side for birds.
The grassland between the dam and the river is also home to an interesting mix of butterflies, with Large Copper, Green-underside Blue, Marsh Fritillary and Southern Festoon. Note that the small yellow flowers here aren't buttercups, but the curious-looking Hypecoum, a small Mediterranean weed related to the poppies.

*The Levant Sparrowhawk is a quite numerous breeding bird of Zlato Pole and can be seen from mid-May onwards.*

**4** From the dam you overlook the eastern end of the Zlato Pole river arm, where a marshland with a rich vegetation is visible. Approach carefully (the birds are jumpy here) and scan the marshes. In early spring, there may be ducks (e.g. Garganey, Ferruginous Duck) and Black Storks. When the marshes start to dry up, fish congregate in the deepest part in the lefthand corner, where they form an easy meal for herons and storks. Local birdwatchers have seen over 40 Black Storks together here at such times.

**5** Continue on the bank of the Maritsa river. The bank overhangs the river and Bee-eaters, which have excavated their nests in the

PRACTICAL PART

ROUTE 22: ZLATO POLE

steeper parts, can be seen all around you in season. Scan the gravel banks for Little Ringed Plover and – unexpectedly – Oystercatcher. This latter bird has started to expand its breeding range along the river only recently which caused great excitement among Bulgarian birdwatchers. A little further on you can walk to the gravel banks to look for dragonflies.

It is not possible to walk along the dam at the southeastern end of the reserve, so you'd best return to the village, drive back to the main road, turn right and then at the eastern end of the village turn right again and drive to the marshes. Follow the dam on foot.

**6** This section of Zlato Pole is slightly different in having large areas of reed beds, where birds like Great Reed Warbler, Penduline Tit and, recently, also Cetti's Warbler may be found. There are two observation towers on this stretch but they are not well maintained and may be unstable, so we advise against climbing them.

Rollers breed in the river forest along the Maritsa, together with Bee-eater, Hoopoe, Kingfisher and Golden Oriole, completing the 'colourful quintet' of Zlato Pole.

### Additional remarks

Bird photographers may be interested in renting one of the photo hides in Zlato Pole, which have been placed here by one of Bulgaria's leading bird photographers. They are aimed at obtaining photos of Roller, Bee-eater and Levant Sparrowhawk. See www.bogdanboev.com.

# Route 23: Sakar round trip

**FULL DAY**
**160/175 KM**

Vast area of steppe-like pastures, open scrubland and scattered trees. Large populations of Suslik and birds of prey.

**Habitats:** pastures, steppe grasslands, villages, christ's-thorn scrub, oak forests
**Selected species:** Golden Jackal, Suslik, Marbled Polecat, Wildcat, Eastern Imperial Eagle, Lesser Spotted Eagle, Short-toed Eagle, Long-legged Buzzard, Lesser Kestrel, Isabelline Wheatear, Short-toed Lark, Calandra Lark, Woodchat Shrike, Masked Shrike, Olive-tree Warbler, Balkan Terrapin, European Glass Lizard, Aesculapian Snake, Grecian Copper, Anatolian Predatory Bush-cricket

This round trip over the backroads through Sakar is the best way to find the birds for which this area is famous: Eastern Imperial and Lesser Spotted Eagles, Lesser Kestrel and Olive-tree Warbler. Of the first, approximately 20 of Bulgaria's 25 pairs breed here, while the country's only population of (reintroduced) Lesser Kestrels are found in this region. Sakar also ranks as the top area in Bulgaria for the elusive Olive-tree Warbler.
This route passes several very attractive sites for other wildlife and some beautiful historic locations but we will focus mainly on the birds as the loop will otherwise take too long. Attractive locations for flora and other wildlife will be the topic of the next route.

**Word of warning**
Sakar lies on the periphery of Europe and is a little visited part of Bulgaria. It is perfectly safe to visit but be aware of the following.
- In places the roads are in a bad condition. The described route is driveable with a normal car unlike some of the roads shown by navigation apps. Some are not roads but (very rough) tracks, impossible to navigate without 4x4. When in doubt, turn back.
- You are close to the sensitive Turkish border. Bring your passport when you go into the field. You are permitted to explore all tracks and roads, but expect police checkpoints where you will be asked for your ID.
- Turn off roaming. Part of this route comes so close to the border that your phone may switch to a Turkish provider, in which case your phone bill may have an unwelcome surprise.

## ROUTE 23: SAKAR ROUND TRIP

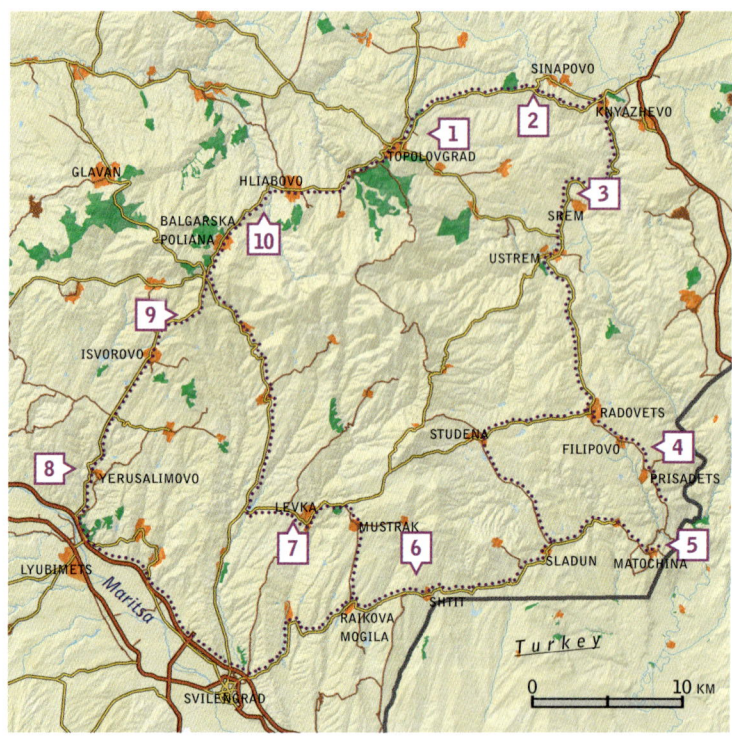

Note that the although the stops in the route below focus on birds, anything can turn up anywhere – not only birds. We have found Odalisques and Eastern Festoons, Golden Jackals and Wildcats, Aesculapean Snakes and European Glass Lizards (a legless lizard looking somewhat like a very thick eel). They are very slow and vulnerable when crossing road so take care and don't drive too fast. The sometimes very potholed roads are another reason to go slow.

**Starting point** Topolovgrad. Centre on Imperial Eagles (GPS: 42.087040, 26.342419).

Leave town towards Lesovo and Burgas. Just beyond the graveyard and the town exit sign, turn right onto a track that leads to a radio tower and church. Park here.

## ROUTE 23: SAKAR ROUND TRIP

**1** The surrounding area is perfect steppe habitat, with Suslik and Isabelline Wheatear, which breeds in the abandoned holes of the susliks. Look around for larks – Crested, Sky, Wood, Calandra and Short-toed Lark all occur here.

This is also one of the prime areas for watching raptors. When the temperatures rise in the morning, they fly up from the surrounding patches of woodlands and hunt over the pastures. It is especially a good area for Eastern Imperial Eagle, but Lesser Spotted, Short-toed and Booted Eagles are also frequent, as is Long-legged Buzzard. You can follow the track on foot further into the pastures. It goes on for several kilometres and eventually connects with the village of Oreshnik. In late spring and summer, explore the grasslands for insects. Besides the numerous owlflies, you may also find the Predatory Bush-cricket and the Bronze Bush-cricket, two superb beasts that never fail to impress (or scare the hell out of those who are afraid of big insects). Both insects are harmless though.

The area is attractive for butterflies as well. In this general area, we found Eastern Baton Blue and Eastern Knapweed, Spotted and Lesser Spotted Fritillaries.

Return to the road and turn right.

The country road between Isvorovo and Yerusalimovo, with the Eastern Rhodopes in the background (bottom). Isabelline Wheatears (top) breed in Suslik holes and often indicate the presence of this charming animal.

PRACTICAL PART

## ROUTE 23: SAKAR ROUND TRIP

**2** The only downside of this road is that it is the main road to Burgas, which means that there is some traffic and cars can be speeding. Otherwise, this road leads through prime habitat with a mixture of dry pastures, vineyards and patches of woodland and is prime habitat for raptors. Various pairs of Imperial Eagle breed in the region. There are some sidetracks where you can stop and scan, but be very careful pulling off and on the road.

One good stopping point is on the turn to the village of Sinapovo. Here it is easier to find a safe stopping point. Walking down this quiet road offers more opportunities of seeing raptors, plus Subalpine Warbler, Black-headed and Ortolan Buntings, Woodchat and Red-backed Shrikes, Golden Oriole, Hoopoe, Turtle Dove and Bee-eater – in short, the usual in this part of the world.

Continue along the Road 76 and in the village of Knyazhevo, turn right towards Radovets.

**3** Once outside the village the road follows the heavily wooded Thundza River which is a gem but one that is hard get a good look at. The Thundza springs from the central Balkan mountains and flows past Sakar (forming its eastern border) and then continues to Edirne in Turkey. Whilst the water flows south, Mediterranean wildlife travels up the valley in a northerly direction, making the Thundza (together with the Arda and Byala Reka in the Eastern Rhodopes and the Struma valley in southwestern Rhodopes) a main access point of Mediterranean species in Bulgaria (e.g. Balkan Terrapin, Kotschy's Gecko, Sand Boa). The finest stretch for wildlife is in the protected Thundza gorge on the border with Turkey, but that area is very hard to explore due to the lack of trails. On this stretch of road, it is a bit easier. For example, after 6 kms after Knyazhevo, in front of a hotel, there is the option to walk down to the river. There are better opportunities a bit further down, near the bridge to the village of Srem. Cross the bridge, park and walk the first road to the left. It soon becomes a track through the fields and, bearing left, reaches

Bukalon Fort.

the river. Among the masses of Banded Demoiselles, there are fair numbers of Odalisques, a beautiful and peculiar damselfly that reaches its northern limit in southern Bulgaria. There is also a large population of Eastern Festoon (a butterfly) here.

Continue the road to Ustrem and Radovets. This area is more wooded and although the raptors may be present here as well, it is generally less suitable. In Radovets, the main road turns sharp right. Don't follow it, but instead go left and directly right again, in the direction of Filipovo.

**4** The wide open fields before and beyond Filipovo attract many raptors. Look here also for Roller and Woodchat Shrike. On the left the land eventually drops down to the Tundzja River, which lies in a gorge and flows out to the Turkish lowlands further south. It is an important ecological corridor along which many southern species find their way into Bulgaria. One of them is the Balkan Terrapin, which may also be found in small tributary rivers and ponds. There are tracks from both Filipovo and Prisadets, the next village, to the Tundzja. The river is otherwise hard to visit.

At Prisadets the tarmac ends and you arrive at a fence that marks the border zone with Turkey. Return to Radovets and turn left, towards Studena. Turn left to Sladun and then left again to Varnik and Matochina.

**5** Matochina seems the end of the world and it certainly is the end of the EU. It is however also, unexpectedly, the most famous touristic site of Sakar, because of the conspicuous ruins of the Bukelon Fort, which is on the 'top-100' list of most remarkable Bulgarian sites. People from all over Bulgaria come over to see it (so it is perhaps best avoided on national holidays).

Lesser Spotted Eagles are fairly numerous in the Sakar mountains (top).
The woodlands near Shtit are the habitat of the of rare speedwell *Veronica multifida* (bottom).

ROUTE 23: SAKAR ROUND TRIP

Lesser Kestrels at Levka.

Bukelon played an important role in the protection of the Byzantine city of Adrianopolis, present-day Edirne.
From the hill next to the tower, you have great views over Turkey. On clear days you can see Edirne (with its giant mosque) and north to the south slopes of Sakar. Look for raptors, in particular Long-legged Buzzard which is numerous in this area. Closer by, the butterflies are of interest. The larger species like Scarce Swallowtail fly around the hilltop, while other species come to drink and soak up the sun on the south-facing slope with its many thyme plants. Also take note of the Fig Trees that grow in this general area. It is one of the few places in Bulgaria where this Mediterranean species occurs.

Return to Sladun and go straight in the direction of Shtit and further in the direction of Raikova Mogila.

**6** Just outside of Shtit lies an area of open grassland, with Suslik and Isabelline Wheatear. A little further on to your right, next to a green gazebo-like construction is a track with notice board that runs up into an open oak woodland. This is a reserve with a number of attractive wildflowers, including the very rare, spring-flowering *Veronica multifida*, which you'll find growing right along the trail. In the woodland there are many open patches and limestone grasslands, which are very promising sites for reptiles, butterflies and wildflowers.

Continue to Raikova Mogila. Here you have a choice – either to visit the Lesser Kestrel colony of Levka, or Bakarlia protected site. Both are very different and attractive sites that are not easily combined.
If you want to go to Levka, go right in Raikova Mogila to Mustrak just beyond which you turn left to Levka (beautiful viewpoint along the way). In Levka, follow the road all the way to the western end of the village where one of the last farmhouses on your left is the reintroduction site for the Lesser Kestrels. It lies a little away from the road but is easily

## ROUTE 23: SAKAR ROUND TRIP

recognisable by the many numbered nest boxes, and probably by the Lesser Kestrels on the wires.

**7** The Lesser Kestrel was reintroduced in Levka in a joint project of Green Balkans. The handsome, colonial falcon species is in decline due to habitat loss and disappearance of breeding sites. Sakar still offers a good environment for Lesser Kestrels and a special LIFE project is aimed at both improving the habitat and re-establishing a colony. There are 40 nest boxes at the project site in Levka and the birds can be easily seen here during the breeding season.

After Levka, continue and at the T-junction near the reservoir (Common Tern breeds here), turn right. After 3 km, the road turns into an airstrip from the communist times, when this area was at the border with the NATO-countries of Turkey and Greece. Pass the village of Mladinovo and Dripchevo and after another 4km, go under a bridge, then turn left and left again in the direction of Topolovgrad.

Your other option is to go straight from Raikova Mogila to Dimitrovche, after which the road bends to the left to Svilengrad, the last Bulgarian town on the main road between Sofia and Istanbul. Here, take the motorway towards Sofia but leave at the next exit, near Lyubimets.

The landscape near Yerusalimovo (left). Sakar is the best place in Bulgaria to look for Eastern Imperial Eagles (top).

PRACTICAL PART

ROUTE 23: SAKAR ROUND TRIP

Sakar is famous for its birds, but the insect life is just as impressive. The Bronze Bush-cricket (top) is quite common from late May onwards, as is the Eastern Owlfly* (*Libelloides macaronius*; bottom).

Then follow the signs to Yerusalimovo. After 5.5km you reach the only turn to this village (which lies a little off the road to the right). Park at this turn; there is a sign on your left about the nature reserve of Bakarlia.

**8** Walk down to the rocks that overlook the river valley. There is no clear path but you can't get lost here. The reddish, rounded rocks light up beautifully in the evening light. The great attraction here are the birds again. Masked Shrike may be found near the river, while Olive-tree Warbler is found in the scattered trees. Listen for its rasping song that somewhat reminds of Great Reed Warbler. This is also a good area for to search for reptiles. All the species of dry, rocky and shrubby grasslands could be expected.

**9** Continue along the road. The views become increasingly attractive as you climb up the hill. There are various places where you can stop. The pastures here are all part of the hunting territories of Eastern Imperial, Lesser Spotted and Short-toed Eagles, so it is worth scanning for these raptors again.

After 16 km from Yerusalimovo you reach the road crossing where the 'Levka branch' of this route (point 8) rejoins with this one. After another 6km you'll see a sign of the Thracian Rock Dolmen, with a small car park by the road.

**10** This dolmen, which lies a mere 100 metres from the road certainly isn't the only in the area but is one of the finer specimens and is very easy to reach. It is one of no less then 600 Thracian dolmens currently known from Sakar, making this region, together with Strandzja and the Eastern Rhodopes, a treasure trove of Thracian culture. Keep an eye out for raptors here as well. Lesser Spotted Eagle is a frequent sight in this area.

Continue to return to Topolovgrad.

CROSSBILL GUIDES • RHODOPE MOUNTAINS

# Route 24: Around Topolovgrad

**4-6 HOURS**
**EASY**

*A further exploration of woodlands and grasslands of Sakar. Short walks with focus on wildflowers and butterflies.*

**Habitats:** oak woodlands, steppes, christ-thorn scrub, quarry, limestone grasslands
**Selected species:** Mammose Orchid, Horned Woodcock Orchid, Suslik, Marbled Polecat, Eastern Imperial Eagle, Lesser Spotted Eagle, Isabelline Wheatear, Short-toed Lark, Calandra Lark, European Glass Lizard, Nose-horned Viper, Grecian Copper, Eastern Baton Blue, Bavius Blue, Odalisque, Bladetail, Anatolian Predatory Bush-cricket

The small town of Topolovgrad is the largest settlement in Sakar and has a large concentration of wildlife sites. Just towards the south of it, lies the highest peak of the mountain range (Vishegrad, 856 m) whose northern slopes are clad in woodland. The lower flanks have some excellent steppe grasslands.

This route focuses above all on the flora (including a good range of orchids), reptiles and butterflies of Sakar, although most of the region's birdlife could be found here as well. In contrast to the previous route, this route covers less ground by car and more on foot. It first explores the lowlands and then climbs up the mountain for two short walks in the forest.

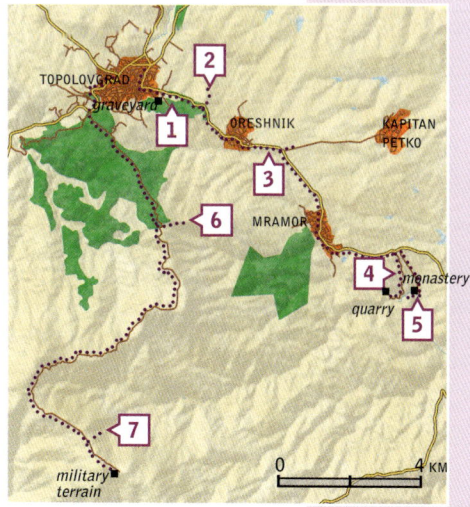

**Starting point** Topolovgrad.

Leave town towards Oreshnik. Just outside the town, you pass the village graveyard. Park on the track at the eastern end of it and explore the grasslands.

## ROUTE 24: AROUND TOPOLOVGRAD

*Jagged cliffs at point 6 of this route.*

**1** This part of Sakar consists of limestone grasslands, which are rich in orchids and butterflies. Explore the grasslands close to the track, where Mammose, Horned Woodcock, Bee and Monkey Orchids grow. There are more plants of interest though, such as the Drooping Sage, which is typical for the steppe grasslands of the east.

Continue for 1km (there are Balkan Lizard Orchids* (*Himantoglossum caprinum*) in the roadside) and just when you exit the pine plantation, where the road bends to your right, find a spot to park and walk the rough track that branches off to the north and enters the steppes.

**2** Walk towards the hill with the quarry, from which you have wonderful views over the steppe-like pastures east of Topolovgrad. These are some of the finest in the whole of Sakar and is an excellent spot to watch birds. In the morning, Eastern Imperial and Lesser Spotted Eagle may be seen, next to Long-legged Buzzard and Booted Eagle. There are Isabelline Wheatears and Susliks. No less than five species of lark can be found here (including Calandra and Short-toed).
You can wander freely over the grasslands, making this an excellent place to explore for its wildflowers, reptiles and insects, many of the latter are attracted to the thyme flowers (e.g. Sloe Hairstreak, Marbled White, Eastern Knapweed Fritillary and Eastern Baton Blue).

Return to the car and continue.

## ROUTE 24: AROUND TOPOLOVGRAD

**3** Just beyond the village of Oreshnik, you cross more open pastureland. This is worth scanning for the birds previously noted. You can drive down the track that branches off to the left approximately 1km from Oreshnik where it is easy to pull over.

Continue through the village of Mramor (Bulgarian for marble, which was quarried in the area). Some 1.5km beyond the village, there are two roughly parallel roads (c170 metres apart) that turn off to the right (the second is signposted for the Ustrem Monastery of the Holy Trinity). Both roads are worth exploring.

**4** The first road leads through a shrubby oak wood to a recently abandoned quarry. On the first stretch there are several limestone grasslands which are rich in orchids, as is the roadside itself. Mammose, Monkey and Lady Orchids, White Helleborine and Violet Limodore are found here, plus a good number of other attractive plants. One of them is the poisonous but beautiful Scarlet Peony.
The quarry itself is attractive for wildflowers and butterflies. The first place to stop is by a lefthand bend next to a rocky slope – you'll recognise it when you get there. The Burning Bush (also called Gas or Firework Plant) grows between the rocks in spring. Observe its spectacular flowers at a distance and don't touch this plant. Plant chemicals in combination with sunlight can cause severe blistering. In hot weather the Burning Bush produces inflammable esoteric oils.

Sakar has a great flora and many of its specialties can be seen on this route, such as the pasqueflower *Pulsatilla montana* (left) and the Balkan Lizard Orchid (right).

**PRACTICAL PART**

ROUTE 24: AROUND TOPOLOVGRAD

Later in the season, there is a wide variety of wildflowers. Towards the summer this place is very rich in butterflies. In addition to the many Marbled Whites, Spotted Fritillaries, Sloe Hairstreaks and other common butterflies, there is the very rare Bavius Blue – a species with just a limited number of colonies scattered over the Balkans. This is also an interesting spot for dragonflies, with the strange-looking Bladetail often resting on the ground and the Eastern Spectre in trees near the river.

Continue down into the quarry and explore the cliffs for Black-eared Wheatear and Rock Bunting. Both tortoises and European Glass Lizard occur and among the many snake species that are possible, the Nose-horned Viper has been found recently.

**5** The second road leads up to the Ustrem Monastery, a beautiful spot. Lavender fields flank the road up to the well-maintained monastery that sits next to a small stream (with picnic facilities) amidst the wooded hills – like the scene from the Provence. Sombre Tit and Eastern Bonelli's Warbler may be found in the woods. Butterfly lovers should look for the brightly coloured Grecian Coppers along the stream. Both Banded and Beautiful Demoiselles grace the river.

Burning Bush in the quarry near the monastery of Ustrem (point 4).

Return to Topolovgrad and leave the town to the west towards Svilengrad. Just out of town, in a long bend to the right, there is a very wide exit to the left that continues as a narrow but tarmacked road that leads up to the peak. There are two short, attractive walks to be made along this road, both through woodland to a rocky area.

**6** The first walk is 4km after the start of the road where at a righthand bend there is an open spot where you can park (GPS: 42.049861, 26.347330). A track with blue-white signs and a cyrillic text points you to a track to the left. It goes downhill through an oak-hornbeam forest to a rocky outcrop, 700 metres further on. This is volcanic rock and a very scenic site from which you have wonderful views over the plains to the north. The area around the rock has an attractive flora.

**7** The second site is botanically even more interesting. Drive on for another 10.5km until you reach a wooden gazebo on your left (GPS 41.997046, 26.324479); you are now about 1 km from the peak, which is a military land and cannot be accessed).
Walk the track downhill to your left and after a few metres, take the trail on the left, signposted with a red arrow. A short walk through the woods brings you to a glade with, further down again, a rocky outcrop. This is again both scenically and botanically attractive. In early spring, there are many pasque flowers, probably belonging to the species *Pulsatilla montana*, although the botanists are not in full agreement of the exact species. This area is special because it is rather high and on a north slope in an otherwise large dry and hot lowland, which makes this somewhat of an isolated 'island' for plant species. Other plants you can find here are Pontic Fritillary, Wild Tulip and Bulgarian Stork's-bill.

Return by the way you came.

Look for Bavius Blue in warm dry grasslands (top). The river next to the Ustrem Monastery is a scenic spot (bottom).

# Additional sites in the Thracian Plain and Sakar

For the locations of the sites described below, see map on page 226.

## A – Rice paddies west of Plovdiv

West of Plovdiv lies a low flat area of rice paddies and wet meadows. This was once a large wetland and although only scraps of it are left, the rice paddies and meadows attract a lot of birds. Black and White Storks are very common, as is Lapwing, which breeds here. Herons include Great White Egret (especially in winter and spring) and there are many waders on migration.

It is doubtful whether this area is worth a stop, but you cut right through it when you take the motorway from Sofia to Plovdiv. Since the deeper parts of the marshes are close to the motorway, you are likely to pick up the birds when driving along. Although local birdwatchers sometimes stop on the side of the highway here, this is illegal and potentially very dangerous, so we advise against it. If you want to explore the site, drive along the minor roads that connect Chernogorovo, Pazardzhik, Dobrovnitsa and Pishtogovo.

## B – Trud fishponds

East of village of Trud (just north of Plovdiv) lies a series of fishponds. It is part of a much larger area of fishponds and reservoirs which combined form an important wetland region for birds in south-central Bulgaria.

The Trud Fishponds

# ADDITIONAL SITES IN THE THRACIAN PLAIN AND SAKAR

The Trud ponds all have different owners and their attractiveness for birds differs from pond to pond. In the central part is a large heronry, with Little Egret, Grey, Night and Squacco Heron. Recently, Glossy Ibis has also been present, albeit (still) in low numbers. Additionally, there are Yellow-legged Gull, Great Crested and Little Grebe, Black-winged Stilt, ducks in winter and a variety of waders on migration (Wood Sandpiper being most numerous).

The surrounding fields are good for Lapwing, Crested Lark, Grey Partridge, Black-headed Wagtail, both storks, Montagu's Harrier and – perhaps the prime species for birders – Collared Pratincole.

The fishponds are not terribly attractive for wildflowers and other wildlife, but European Pond Terrapin and Grass Snakes are present and probably also Fire-bellied Toad and Syrian Spadefoot.

To get to the fishponds, head north along Trud's main street and turn right at the traffic lights (just short of a small park) and simply continue to the eastern edge of town. On the east side of the village, the road continues as a dirt track that is, depending on the weather, fairly good to extremely bad to drive. Consider carefully how far you want to drive, parking and continuing on foot as the conditions dictate. In any case, it's no more than 2km from the village to the ponds. Follow the dirt track along the ponds to the north, watching out for birds. There is a fisherman's hut which sells coffee and also has an observation tower (GPS: 42.237896, 24.760687). As you continue further north, you'll reach the heronry (see map). All tracks are open to the public, just don't disturb the fishermen.

A visit to the Trud Fishponds is easily combined with the Kaloyanovo reservoir (next site).

## C – Reservoir near Kaloyanovo

Just a little north of the Plovdiv fishponds lies a very different type of wetland. This is a shallow reservoir with broad marshy shores with sedges and reeds, surrounded by mostly unimproved wet meadows and dry loess pastures. These latter are excellent for Suslik and their predators, as well as for Lapwings and storks (both species). Grey Partridge is rather common here. In spring the thousands of Sand Martins and Swallows catch the eye, and there are often gulls and terns (e.g. black and white-winged)

among them. This site is also good for waders during migration. To get to the reservoir, follow Road 5 from Trud to the north and turn left after 11km towards Kalovanovo. 1.3km from this crossing, you pass a small river, directly after which you turn left. Park beyond the only house here, which is another 700m further (GPS: 42.334829, 24.742635) and walk the track to the right that will bring you to the lakeshore in approximately 1km.

## D – Fishpond of Belozem

This site is a little gem, consisting of only two fish ponds and a small wetland reserve with some reedy margins and willows. It would not be a remarkable site if it wasn't for the Little Bitterns. Little Bittern is quite common in Bulgaria, but the large population of around twenty pairs in such a small area is exceptional. Moreover, they show themselves very well and make excellent subjects for photography. Additionally, there are Great Reed Warbler, Kingfisher (some years) and other common birds like Bee-eater, Golden Oriole, Syrian Woodpecker, Spanish and Tree Sparrow and Turtle Dove, plus some very tame (introduced) Coypu. In the surrounding fields there are some excellent patches of dry pastures, with Suslik, raptors and Black Stork (before and after the breeding season). There is even a 'water hide' to photograph the birds from water level (wading suit required).

Little Bitterns are remarkably easy to spot at the small fishpond complex near Belozem.

To get to the site, take the exit from the motorway to Belozem, which lies some 25km east of Plovdiv. The road from the exit to the village leads through fine steppe-like habitat, which includes some saline steppes as well. Look for Susliks along this road. The village of Belozem is a stork village of sorts – all around the village are stork nests. The reservoir lies just west of the village. The route through the village is complicated to describe and it is best to enter the GPS location 42.190070, 25.029518 on your phone or GPS device and let it guide you to the reserve.

The reserve is private and the manager will ask for a small fee if you want to spend more than 30 minutes here. The site doubles as an unofficial and (very) low key camp site, where you can spend the night (mainly used by fishermen who are here for night fishing).

ADDITIONAL SITES IN THE THRACIAN PLAIN AND SAKAR

## E – Reservoirs of Galabovo and Ovchi Kladanets

There are two reservoirs between Zlato Pole and the Sakar mountains that are not particularly scenic but are great sites to watch pelicans up close. The most common one is Dalmatian Pelican, but in winter and on migration, White Pelican is also there. The White-tailed Eagle is present year round at Ovchi Kladenets, while low numbers of White-headed Duck are sometimes present in winter.

Like the famous Greek wetland of Kerkini, the pelicans at Galabovo are used to fishermen and are often very approachable, making the site excellent for photography. Very unlike the atmospheric Kerkini Lake, these Bulgarian sites are next to large power plants so the scenery is not particularly attractive. You can't have it all.

There is an upside to the power plant as the reservoirs were created to provide cooling water for the plant which means the lakes are several degrees warmer in winter. This favours some southern dragonflies and certainly Galabovo is a spectacular place to spot dragonflies. We've found Lesser Emperor, Violet Dropwing, Black Pennant and the superb Bladetail all in a single spot on the shore.

At Galabovo, first check the main road from the town to the power plant that skirts the northern edge of the reservoir. Then proceed eastwards and just turn right before crossing the railroad. On this parallel road, turn again right before crossing the tracks and follow it as it swings right and ends at the shore (GPS: 42.143132, 25.909820). This is the best place for both the dragonflies and the birds. At Ovchi Kladanets, follow road 55 northwards along the reservoir and just beyond the power plant, turn right and park (GPS: 42.255209, 26.142047). Walk the footbridge over the northern arm of the reservoir.

The Bladetail is one of the special dragonfly species to search for at the reservoir of Galabovo. This once localised Mediterranean species is expanding rapidly, probably a result of climate change.

# TOURIST INFORMATION & OBSERVATION TIPS

## Travelling to and in the Rhodopes

Three airports service the region: Sofia, Burgas and Plovdiv. Most people will arrive at Sofia International Airport because it is served by flights from most European airports. From Sofia, it is about 2.5 hours by car to Haskovo, the gateway to the Eastern Rhodopes. It is a similar distance from Burgas airport to Haskovo. Burgas lies on the Black Sea coast which happens to be an excellent wildlife destination that is often combined with a visit to the Rhodopes, making Burgas airport the better choice. The downside is that there are few flights in spring, as the Black Sea coast is above all a summer destination. Most flights to Burgas are from Poland, the Baltic States, UK, Ireland, Germany, the Scandinavian countries and Belgium. Plovdiv has the great advantage of actually being in the region. However, there are even fewer flights to Plovdiv – most of them are from London, Dublin and from a few places in Germany.

## Traffic

By far the easiest way to travel in the region is by car. The traffic is usually light and driving is generally safe. The roads have improved tremendously in the last decade and are mostly in good or even excellent condition. However, some driving along poor quality roads or tracks to reach all of the sites we mention is unavoidable so take care and always turn back if concerned.

There are plenty of car rental companies at the airports and all major towns. Also make sure you have a 'vignette' (road tax) for your time in Bulgaria. If you rent your car in Bulgaria, the vignette is arranged by the rental company. If you are travelling with your own car, buy a vignette at the border station, one of the large petrol stations on the motorway or at the post office.

## Public transport

To get to the areas covered in this book, the train is not of much use. There is only one line, which goes from Sofia to Istanbul and runs all along the Maritsa valley, via Plovdiv (with a branch to Asenovgrad) and further east to Simeonovgrad, Dimitrovgrad and, just before the border, Svilengrad.

The train is generally slower than the long-distance bus services from Sofia to Plovdiv, Asenovgrad, Kardzhali or Haskovo, from where you can continue via regional buses to almost all villages in the mountains. The two major companies are Union Ivkoni (**www.union-ivkoni.com**) and Ardatur (www.ardatur.bg). At the bus station in Sofia, you can explore the options from the many smaller bus companies.

## Planning your trip

### When to go

Spring is the ideal and most popular time to visit the region, but there are interesting things to be seen throughout the year. This is a quick seasonal overview of the highlights.

**December to early March** There is some great birdwatching to be had in winter. Most of the eagles and vultures are residents and can be seen throughout the year, with the winter being a good time for them. The Thracian Plain is full of wintering wildfowl and other birds. Most winter visitors to the region are birdwatchers and photographers who combine a visit to see raptors and mammals in the Eastern Rhodopes and Sakar, with geese and wildfowl watching on the Black Sea coast and/or pelican photography on Lake Kerkini across the border in Greece.

**March-April** Spring arrives in late March. Due to the continental climate, there isn't much flora present, but the woodpeckers and the grouse are active in the Western Rhodopes. April is a better month for them, and during this month, the spring flora appears as well. Roman Orchid, Lungwort and Rhodopean Toothworts start to bloom. In April, the first butterflies start to emerge, the reptiles enjoy the first rays of the sun and the migrant birds start to pour in. Towards the end of April, the Eastern Rhodopes are teeming with birds. Waders and terns start to pass through, Black Storks are everywhere, Bee-eaters flock in, etc. In the Western Rhodopes, the season for grouse and woodpeckers is in full swing.

**May** is even better. The later migrants are arriving (e.g. Black-headed Bunting, Olive-tree Warbler, Masked Shrike and Levant Sparrowhawk appear in the middle of May), which is also the peak time for most of the orchids and spring butterflies (e.g. the festoons, Marsh Fritillaries, Small Bath Whites and Clouded Apollos).

By **June**, the weather is starting to become hot. It is still an excellent time for birds and most dragonflies are on the wing. The spring flowers give way to the early summer species. It is still a good period for orchids, while the number of butterfly species is only increasing.

**Early July**, the birds have become quiet as all of them are either on their eggs or feeding their young, which requires keeping a low profile rather than shouting out one's presence from the treetops, as they do in spring. In the Eastern Rhodopes, the grass has turned yellow and the weather is hot. Some of the more spectacular insects can be found in this time. The Western Rhodopes is still green, with lots of wildflowers (including some rare and sought-after orchids). Mid-July is probably the best period for butterflies in the Western Rhodopes.

Come **August**, the summer slumber has kicked in. Most plants have finished blooming and butterflies are less evident. Tourists from the main towns flock in and enjoy themselves on the river. This is not the best period to go out for finding wildlife although there will be harbingers of the coming autumnal migration.

Between **September and early October**, the bird migration peaks along the river, while the rutting season starts in the mountains. In October the leaves start to turn, the weather is usually fair and the mountains quiet, making this again an excellent time to visit the mountains. Not so much for the species this time, but for the atmosphere. To fully experience the splendour of autumn colours, visit the beech forests of the Western Rhodopes, which flare up in blazing orange colours.

**The second half of November and early December** is, arguably, the least interesting period, but come Christmas, the first snow falls again and the first winter visitors arrive.

## Accommodation

There is plenty of accommodation in the Western Rhodopes and in the main cities in the Thracian Plain. The villages of Trigrad, Yagodina, Devin, Smolyan and Asenovgrad are quite popular with Bulgarian tourists who visit the mountains not only for the scenery and geological sights, but also because the folklore and traditions of the Western Rhodopes have a deep fascination for them. Additionally, there are some spa resorts, particularly in Devin. All the main cities along the Maritsa River have hotels. Be aware however, that this is the main traffic artery from Turkey into Europe and part of this accommodation caters for this passing trade and are not the cosy little bucolic hotel you might have in mind for your holiday. So, check the booking sites carefully. Campers should be aware that there are virtually no camp sites in the region. Camping in the wild is allowed in Bulgaria, but only outside the protected areas. The Eastern Rhodopes and Sakar still receive few travellers and hotels are relatively scarce. Here are some suggestions.

## Accommodation by region

**Madzharovo** comes closest to an ecotourism centre in the Eastern Rhodopes. Most visitors to this a beautiful region come for the scenery and the wildlife and guest houses are used to travelling naturalists from abroad. There are few places to stay in the town itself, but there are options in the countryside around it, as well as in the nearby village of Gorno Pole. The touristic heartland is without doubt the Vulture Centre, which is stunningly located next to the Arda River (E: **vulturecenter@bspb.org**;

P: +359 878 252 720) It has a small hotel-restaurant – pretty and wonderfully low key. The Old Nest (**www.theoldnest.com**) is a beautifully renovated traditional farmhouse within walking distance from Madzharovo and the Arda River. Both the Vulture Centre and the Old Nest are run by expert wildlife guides and will help you to book excursions, photo hides for wildlife or canoe trips on the river.

**Kardzhali** is a lively town with an eclectic feel stemming from its diverse population and mixed fortunes over the years. There are hotels in the city, which make this an excellent base to explore the region. Keep in mind that, in contrast to Madzharovo, Kardzhali is not a tranquil centre for ecotourism since, even though it's a small place, everyday city life is quite hectic. Nonetheless, there is a one compelling reason for naturalists to spend the evening in the centre of Karzhali: the heronry next to the main bridge (see also route 5) over the Arda. With the low evening light from the behind you and the herons and Pygmy Cormorants flying in towards you, this is a rare opportunity for bird photography or for anyone who enjoys watching these birds from up close.

Quiet accommodation can be found in Glavatartsi and other villages surrounding the Kardzhali reservoir. Some of it is quite luxurious Hotel Borovitsa (**www.hotel-borovitsa.com**).

**Momchilgrad – Kirkovo** In the southern part of the Eastern Rhodopes, the sites are further apart and require more travelling. You may consider exploring this part from Kardzhali, since the town is now linked by a direct fast road to Greece (see also page 262). There are several trucker hotels along this road now, which are conveniently located if not exactly picturesque. The small towns of Momchilgrad or Kirkovo have some suitable accommodation. At the entrance of the village Gorno Kapinovo there is a family-run guesthouse (no English spoken). This may offer a great starting point for the hike to the Gyumyurdzhinski Snezhnik ridge (route 12), and the hotel owner offers a taxi service to the starting point of the trail. We also recommend staying at the hunting reserve on the shores of the Studen Kladenets reservoir and close to the vulture hides so you have wildlife right at you doorstep (most easily contacted through facebook: **www.facebook.com/LovnoStopanstvoStudenKladenec**/; P: +359 88 927 9801).

**Ivaylovgrad** has several hotels and guesthouses that form an ideal base to explore the Armira and Byala Reka valleys (**www.hotelarmira.info** and **www.kaloyanovikashti.com**).

**Sakar** The little hotel-restaurant in the village of Oreshnik (in the heartland of Imperial Eagle country) is the only venue in the northern part of Sakar. Note that at weekends, the fine restaurant attracts visitors from nearby Topolovgrad and other villages so it may be a bit noisier. Alternatively, you can spend the night on the southern side of Sakar, where there is plenty of accommodation in Svilengrad.

# Convenient travel and safety issues

## Annoyances and hazards
Among West Europeans, Bulgaria still has a reputation of an unsafe and even corrupt country. This is, insofar as travelling to the Rhodope mountains is concerned, entirely unjustified. The Rhodopes are safe and people are generally friendly and happy to help. This being said, it is always wise to take valuable items with you, or lock them away and out of sight.
Furthermore, pay attention to the following:
**Stray dogs** You don't need to worry about Wolves or Jackals but be beware of stray dogs! In some places they form packs like Wolves and can be very intimidating. When approached by an unfriendly dog, do not turn and run (although this may seem counter-intuitive). Stay calm and don't make any sudden movements. Throwing stones at a dog that threatens you (not to hit it but to scare it off!) is often effective. Carry a stick as well.
**Money** Although payment with bank card is generally excepted, there are still many places in the rural areas as well as in small shops in towns where you need cash to pay for your groceries.
Fortunately, there are ATM's aplenty throughout the bigger villages and towns in the region.
**Dangerous animals** Only the bite of the Nose-horned Viper is dangerous. This snake is not uncommon in rocky terrain but it is shy and will disappear as soon as it senses you. There are also poisonous scolopendra, scorpions, wolf spiders and hornets, which' bites and stings are painful rather than harmful. Luckily, you won't find them unless you look for them actively.
**Border police** In Sakar, particularly near the Turkish border, the border patrol is active and you may be stopped and asked for identification when driving the back roads in this area. Make sure you have your passport with you.
**Costly phone networks** Another issue for Sakar specifically – switch off roaming when you travel in this area! Roaming in Bulgaria is free for EU-citizens, but at the border your phone may pick up a Turkish telecoms mast, which may become a costly affair when using the internet.

## Dining customs
Bulgaria has a greater tradition of eating out than most East European countries. In the region covered by this book, most restaurants are simple but decent and not very expensive. The food clearly has Turkish influences (with excellent stews!), which is not surprising in a region that was under Ottoman rule for so many centuries. In some places, often at bus stations or other communal locations, there are canteen-like restaurants with pre-cooked dishes that you can point out at the counter.

They are a remnant of the communist days and ridiculously cheap.

Two things are very different than they are in West, South and North Europe. The first is that all side dishes need to be ordered separately and are paid for separately. Not just the fries or the salad, but also the bread. Nor do you just order a portion of bread, but the exact number of slices. And if you want butter too, it's ordered separately.

Second, and this may take some getting used to, ordering together doesn't automatically mean dining together. It is the preparation time in the kitchen that dictates when a dish is ready. If your dish takes 15 minutes less to prepare than that of your companions, you'll be served 15 minutes earlier. So, ask explicitly for the food to be served all at once – no guarantees but it will increase the chance that you are dining together.

## Responsible tourism

'Take nothing but your photo, leave nothing but your footprint', is the well-known phrase that summarises the idea of responsible tourism. It goes without saying that, as a visitor to a nature reserve, you have a responsibility to leave your surroundings and everything in it undisturbed. Buying local products will give you the best flavour of the region and is a good way to support the local economy. Along roadsides you will often find a wide variety of products. Buying here can be a great way to make contact with local people. Stay in local hotels in the villages rather than in the big ones on the plain. Eating in local independent restaurants is usually more enjoyable and certainly more memorable than using restaurant chains. Furthermore, book a guide for a day or two in a photo hide – these are not only great experiences for you, but also support a green economy.

When you arrive make it clear as to why you are here. Don't hide your binoculars and scope – local people need to see how their natural treasures are promoting tourism, hence supporting local economy. This is what will help to protect these special places.

The fact that access is unrestricted brings with it a special obligation on our part to demonstrate responsible behaviour – putting the needs of the environment and its inhabitants before our own. Where there are restrictions on access, it is important for you to respect them. There are a few regrettable instances of visitors disturbing breeding birds, particularly in wetlands and on cliffs, both particularly vulnerable habitats. Accordingly, be extra careful in such habitats and don't stray off the main tracks and roads.

The road is a killing zone for wildlife. Reptiles especially are run over frequently, and this takes a heavy toll on their populations. So, when driving the back roads, do so with care and be aware of lizards and tortoises on the road. Should you encounter a tortoise on the road, pull over (if safe to do so) and move the animal to the side of the road. At night, be aware of wildlife too. Anything may appear, from Wild Boar and deer to Jackals and Wolves, so drive carefully.

## Walking in the Rhodopes

Bulgaria is among those fortunate countries where very little land is fenced off. You are free to ramble almost anywhere. The diverse landscape is superb for daytrips and you can choose from easy short rambles to long demanding hikes and anything in between.

So far so good. More challenging is the fact that the infrastructure for walking in the Eastern Rhodopes is, with a few exceptions, poor. The few marked trails have been created in the last decade or so, but many of them are not well maintained or peter out in some abandoned pastures. Many routes, including the majority of those described in this guidebook, follow, at least in part, dirt tracks. The situation in this respect is better in the Western Rhodopes, but even here, trails and tracks, even the way-marked ones, may end halfway up the slope.

We strongly advise to invest in a good GPS map, either on a separate GPS device, or on a mobile. Although reception is quite good in most places, don't rely on Google maps as your sole resource as it requires an internet connection. Although the mobile network is generally good, there are frequent gaps in reception. Therefore, it is better to get an app which has the maps installed on your mobile. Maps.me is a free option, but there are better ones for a modest fee (We used Topo GPS, but there are others). If you have a garmin device, check out the free garmin maps on the website of the company Bulgarian Mountains: www.bgmountains.org/en/maps/garmin-maps.

Most of these apps use OpenStreetMap (www.openstreetmap.org) as a base, which is adequate, but by no means flawless. Expect to find details on the walk that do not exist on your device and, vice versa, tracks or even roads on the map that may be no more than a goat's trail in reality. This is all part of the adventure.

Hiking in the Rhodopes is pleasurable, but not entirely risk-free. Take note of the warnings under the header 'Annoyances and hazards' (page 257) and come prepared. Minimal preparations are:

- Protection for sun, rain and wind (hat, sunglasses, sun lotion).
- Sufficient food and water (it can be very hot).
- Pack sufficient food and water as a precaution in case you get lost.
- Keep your GPS device and/or phone (see above) fully charged.
- Layered clothing, warm enough for the cold, sufficiently covering against the sun, and easy to 'peel off' when it gets hot.
- Stout walking shoes or boots with good soles (the underground can be sharp and rocky).
- Tell the owner of your accommodation where you are going to walk and when you expect to be back.

# Additional information

## Recommended reading
Besides the standard European field guides, the following books are recommended.
**Wildflowers:** There is no single book or resource that covers the wildflowers of the region properly. Your best starting point is a mix of Greek floras (for example *Flowers of Greece, vol I and II* by Lafranchis an Sfikas; Diatheo publishers ISBN: 978-2-9521620-2-9 and 978-2-9521620-3-6) and floras on central Europe (e.g. the *Flora Alpina*). Combine these with three useful web resources. The first is **www.bgflora.net**. This is a quirky private project that combines photos and short descriptions of a large number of Bulgarian plants (neatly summed up in English) with some completely unrelated ultra-orthodox religious propaganda. If you can stomach the latter, this is a fine starting point for naming plants as long as you already have an idea of the genus of the plant you're looking for. The second is the *Conspectus of the Bulgarian vascular flora*, which is a pdf that can be downloaded for free from **www.academia.edu** and contains distribution maps of all known vascular plants in Bulgaria. Thirdly, on the website **www.researchgate.com** (free signup) you can download the important plant areas of Bulgaria.
**Birds:** The BSPB has published the *Atlas of the Birds of Bulgaria* (2007), ISBN 978-9549142174.
**Reptiles and amphibians:** The German *Die Amphibien und Reptilien Bulgariens* by Stojanov, Tzankov and Naumov (ISBN 978-3-89973-464-5) is the book to buy if you want to know about Bulgarian reptiles and amphibians. Online, look for **www.lacerta.de** (this site is also in English) – it has photos and distribution maps of all European Lizards.
**Insects:** Besides the general field guides, there are two good pdf downloads about the butterflies of Bulgaria. The first is **www.nmnhs.com/butterfly_areas_bg/** with detailed information on the butterfly hotspots in Bulgaria, including the most important species present. A photographic field guide by Mario Langourov can be downloaded for free from **www.nmnhs.com/downloads/e-pubs/e-bbg.pdf**

## Websites, apps and organisations
**Rewilding Rhodopes** is the Bulgarian rewilding project that is (often with other partners) working on nature conservation and the reintroduction of wild animals in the Eastern Rhodopes. This book is made in close collaboration with Rewilding Rhodopes. **www.rewilding-rhodopes.com**
**Bulgarian society for the protection of birds (BSPB)** is the Bulgarian birdlife partner. Their website contains a lot of information on birds and bird protection in Bulgaria. **www.bspb.org**
**Observation.org** is a huge source of information, with recent sightings in all species groups. **www.observation.org**

**eBird** – for those interested in birds this also a great resource giving a wealth of information with alerts, bar charts, lists for 'hotspots'. **www.ebird.org**

**SmartBirds** The app SmartBirds and SmartBirds Pro are recently created to facilitate the filing of observations and carrying out surveys. There is only an android version and if you have this system it is well worth downloading it and registering as it has many Bulgarian users and will give you access to many more data than observation.org or ebird does. **www.smartbirds.org**

**The Habitat Foundation** is an organisation for grassroot nature conservation initiatives in Europe. Anyone wishing to help with nature conservation or seeking volunteers for a new project can ask for assistance. In the Bulgarian Rhodopes, The Habitat Foundation coordinates research into, amongst others, the Mouse-tailed Dormouse. **www.thehabitatfoundation.org**

**Xeno-canto** is another jewel of a bottom-up project made possible by the internet. It is a huge database of bird songs and calls of pretty much every bird, with the location of the recordings. **www.xeno-canto.org**

## Tourist information addresses

**Nature Conservation Centre Eastern Rhodopes**, Bulgaria, Madzharovo 6480
E: **vulturecenter@bspb.org**
**Tourist Information Centre Ivaylovgrad**: Orfey 1, 4001, Ivaylovgrad;
T: +359 3661 60 39; E: **tic_ivaylovgrad@abv.bg**
**Tourist Information Centre Kardzhali**, Park Prostor, Stadium Arena Arda,6600, Kardzhali. Tel: +359 36 122 719 **www.kardjali-tourism.info**, E: **info@kardjali-tourism.info**

## Nearby destinations worth a visit

Many birdwatchers combine a visit to the region with a stay on the Bulgarian Black Sea coast, which is only a little over 100 kms further east. Here the coastal marshes near Burgas and the coastal steppes support a brilliant birdlife – a mix of wetland and steppe species, some of which are not present in our region (e.g. Pied Wheatear). A little south of Burgas, towards the Turkish border, lie the forested low mountains of Strandzha, with a unique flora, rare reptiles (including Reddish Whip Snake; Platyceps collaris) and many birds (including large populations of White-backed Woodpecker and Semi-collared Flycatcher).

Central Balkan National Park is even closer to the Rhodopes. You only need to cross the Thracian Plain to the Stara Planina Mountains – 60 kms north of Plovdiv. This high range (highest mountain: Botev – 2376 m) is densely forested, with beautiful beech woods. It is a wonderful region for mountain flora, butterflies and birds, including Red-breasted and Semi-collared Flycatchers and White-backed Woodpecker. To the west and not far south of Sofia, lies Pirin and Rila Mountains – Bulgaria's highest peaks. The wildlife here is distinctly Alpine, with various rare butterflies

and orchids. Interestingly, not far from this twin range lies the Struma valley that runs directly down to Greece and is, next to Sakar and the Eastern Rhodopes, the hottest part of the country and another region where Mediterranean species reach into Bulgaria.
Then there is Greece, of course. Across the border with Bulgaria lies the Greek region of East Macedonia and Thrace, a tempting destination for wildlife enthusiasts. Just across the border at the Struma valley lies Kerkini Lake, famous for its wetland birds, pelicans in particular, which are easy to photograph.
Further east is Falakro, a beast of a limestone mountain of over 2200 m, but which you can drive nearly up to the summit. It has a fabulous flora and many butterflies. More important sites are further east towards the Turkish border. The lagoons and associated wetlands on the Aegean coast and the Delta of the Maritsa River (here called Evros) are packed with birds. A little further north lies the famous Dadia forest, with its many raptors and rich reptilian life. It is not unlike the Eastern Rhodopes, which is logical, as it is only 30 km from the Bulgarian border.
The Greek coastal region would make an obvious trip from the Eastern Rhodopes as it is only a half hour drive from the border (and a little over an hour from Kardzhali). The only hurdle is political – Bulgaria is not yet part of Schengen and the consequence is that most rental companies don't allow you to take your car across the border.

## Finding reptiles and amphibians

The big lizards, terrapins and tortoises will simply cross your path during your walk, and with a little luck, this is how you'll find some snakes as well. It is just a matter of being out in the field and enjoying a bit of luck.
However, some species are easier to find when you know where to look for them. The water snakes (Dice and Grass Snake) for example, are found by scanning the still pools on edges of rivers and, in particular, the smaller streams like Byala Reka and Armira. Finding Kotchy's Gecko is a matter of checking walls of old buildings in Madzharovo and the warmer towns and villages in the eastern lowlands. They often prefer a spot close to streetlights where they catch insects. Most snakes, Worm Lizard and European Glass Lizard are rather secretive. Look closely on the track ahead of you when walking. In the morning, especially, they tend to warm up in sunny patches. Walk 'lightly' when searching for them, since they pick up vibrations in the ground easily, and will flee.
Yellow-bellied Toads are most easily found in basins of wells and puddles on the track. The nymphs of Fire Salamander are often seen in streams in the hills. In rainy weather, the adults cross tracks in well-wooded places. Look for Syrian Spadefoots on damp, warm evenings in sandy areas along the Maritsa River.

## Photo hides and guided excursions

There is a small but thriving business in guided wildlife excursions and wildlife photography from hides in the region. There are several professional wildlife guides active in the region, who will take you out birdwatching or looking for other wildlife, or just accompany you on walks and explain about the landscape and history of the region.
The bird photography hides can be rented and most focus on vultures and eagles, but there is also a bear hide in the Western Rhodopes (site F on page 225). The hides offer a high chance of getting wildlife in front of the lens because carrion is laid out to attract the animals. You never know for sure what may come in front of the hide. Besides vultures, there may be kites, eagles or even Jackals and Wolves. In the lowlands, there are some hides for Rollers and other birds. They are all set up by professional photographers, taking in light, angle of view and general composition of the photo into account.
The following companies and people (some of which also have accommodation) offer excursions and / or photography hides.

## Companies

**Nature Madzharovo** is a company based in Madzharovo offering excursions, hides for wildlife photography and canoeing and cycling trips in the Eastern Rhodopes. The company has a broad focus but is an authority on watching and photographing wild birds and mammals and has great knowledge of geology and historical sites. It is run by the local naturalist Marin Kurtev, who also runs the vulture photo hides (see above). Contact: Tel: +359 887 94 16 98; **www.madzharovo.com**, E: **madzharovo@abv.bg**;
**Travcobg** is another local tour company offering private and group wildlife tours, active holidays, arrange rural accommodation and organise cultural trips in the Eastern Rhodopes and Bulgaria. Travcobg is run by Mihaela Kircheva who was involved in the production of the first edition of this guidebook. Travcobg has experienced guides in archaeology, culture, wildlife and birdwatching. **www.travcobg.com**, E: **info@travcobg.com** Tel: +359 887831026.
**Neophron Tours** is based in Varna (Black Sea Coast) but is one of the larger companies to offer birdwatching and bird photography tours in Bulgaria. They are very knowledgeable and experienced. Tel: +359 888 42 01 59, **www.neophron.com**, E: **inquiries@neophron.com**
**Devin's Association for Hunters and Fishermen** has a Bear hide and offers photo safaris of Capercaillie and other species of the Western Rhodopes in the vicinity of Devin. Be aware that, unlike some of the other companies and individual guides below, the wildlife watching and photography is not the main activity of the association and non-Bulgarian visitors are not their main target group. Make enquiries with Vladimir Peykov, who speaks English, and make sure the guide you are booking is also able to speak english. **www.lrdd.bg** (in bulgarian), E: **lrd_devin@abv.bg**.

## Individual guides

**Bogdan Boev** is a professional wildlife photographer who works both in the Rhodope region and in his other homeland, Scotland: **www.bogdanboev.com**, E: **info@bogdanboev.com**
Bogdan has several hides in the Thracian Plain and the Eastern Rhodopes, not only for the big raptors, but also for the smaller birds like Rollers. Several of the bird photos included in this book are Bogdan's and were taken from these hides.

**Tsvetomira Yotsova** is a guide based in the beautiful village of Gorno Pole (near Madzharovo) and also has a B&B. Tsvetomira is an experienced, English-speaking ornithologist and wildlife guide – see Happy Rhodopes on facebook, or mail **tsvetomira.yotsova@gmail.com**

## Birdwatching list

The numbers within brackets (...) refer to the routes from page 133 onwards. WR refers to the Western Rhodopes and ER to the Eastern. TP refers to the Thracian Plain.

**Partridges** Chukar is an uncommon but widespread resident of the ER (3, 6, 11), while its European counterpart the Rock Partridge occurs in open areas in the WR (16, 18). Ring-necked Pheasant, Quail and Grey Partridge occur in agricultural terrain in the lowlands (e.g. 23 and sites B and C on page 248-249).

**Grouse** Both Hazel Grouse and Capercaillie breed in the higher parts of the WR (16 (only Capercaillie), 17, 19). The best way to find them is on a guided trip (see page 227 and 262).

**Swans, Geese and Ducks** The Thracian Plain is of great importance for wintering ducks, but only few stay to breed. Sites B-E on pages 248-251 and the Ivaylovgrad reservoir (1) have wintering Wigeon, Gadwall, Teal, Pintail, Shoveler, Red-crested Pochard (rare), Pochard, Tufted Duck, Goldeneye (rare) and Smew (rare) in winter. White-headed Duck regularly winters near Galobovo and Ovchi Kladanets (site E on page 251). Mute Swan, Mallard, Ferruginous Duck, Common Pochard and Garganey are scarce breeding birds of the Trud Fishponds (site B on page 248). The reservoirs in the ER are breeding sites of Ruddy Shelduck and Goosander (6, 10).
Among the wintering Geese (sites A-E on page 248-251), White-fronted is most common, Greylag less so and in larger flocks, there are usually the odd specimen of Red-breasted Geese (which is a common winter bird near Burgas).

**Grebes** Great Crested and Little Grebes are fairly common breeding birds of well-vegetated lakes (e.g. B on page 248). Red-necked and Black-necked Grebes are rare winter visitors, although Red-necked recently bred as well.

**Pelicans, Flamingos and Ibises** Both Dalmatian and White Pelican roost in increasing numbers on reservoirs in the TP (site E on page 251) and Studen Kladanets reservoir (5). Dalmatian is most common and present for much of the year, Great

White is there during migration. Greater Flamingo sometimes roost at Studen Kladanets (5), mostly in summer and autumn. Glossy Ibis is scarce but increasing. At time of writing, a small colony just established at the Trud Fishponds (site B on page 248) and birds roosted at the Kardzhali heronry (5).

**Cormorants** Great Cormorant is a common resident at all larger waterbodies. Pygmy Cormorant occurs very locally – there is a colony in Kardzhali (5) and a large winter roost near Plovdiv.

**Bitterns, Herons and Egrets** Grey Heron is present in all larger water bodies. Little Egret is fairly widespread. There is a breeding colony, together with Night Heron and a few Squacco Heron in Kardzhali (5). Sites A, B and C are good for Night Heron, Squacco Heron, Little Bittern and Great White Egret, the latter being above all a winter visitor. Site D on page 250 is excellent for Little Bitterns. Great Bittern is a rare breeding bird of the TP. The same goes for Cattle Egret, whose first breeding attempt was in 2020 (and is likely to become more widespread soon). Purple Heron is seen on migration and may breed as well.

**Storks** White Storks are common breeding birds of towns and villages throughout the area. Black Stork is a common breeding bird of the ER (e.g. 1, 2, 5, 6, 8, 11 and site A on page 181). Just before and after the breeding season, Black storks congregate in the Maritsa valley (22, sites A-E on pages 248-251).

**Vultures** The ER and Sakar are among the best areas to watch raptors in Europe. There are Griffon Vulture colonies at 1 and 5 and these birds can be seen all over the Madzharovo-Kardzheli area. Egyptian Vulture breeds throughout the same region. Black Vultures sometimes wander in from their breeding sites just across the Greek border. In 2022 a reintroduction program started on an undisclosed location in the Madzharovo region, so it is expected that this bird will become more numerous here in the coming years. The best places to see lots of vultures (including Egyptians) are route 1, 8 (the vulture feeding station) and the hunting reserve (site A on page 181). For photography from a hide, see page 262.

**Eagles** Golden Eagle is widespread in both the ER and WR (best 1, 6, 8 9, 10, 15, 16 and 17). Most of Bulgaria's Eastern Imperial Eagles breed in Sakar, where you stand a good chance of seeing them (23, 24). Lesser Spotted Eagle is another bird of Sakar, but it roams a bit more widely (13, 23, 24). White-tailed Eagle breeds on the larger reservoirs (1, 5, site A on page 181). Booted and Short-tailed Eagle are widespread though not very numerous in the TP, Sakar and ER (e.g. 1, 5, 6, 11, 21, 22, 23, 24).

**Other birds of Prey** Marsh Harriers are fairly common in wetlands (1, 22, sites A-E on pages 248-251). Hen Harrier is a widespread winter visitor of the TP, Sakar and ER. Montagu's Harrier is a scarce breeding bird of the TP (21, 23) and Pallid Harrier a scarce migrant. Black Kite is fairly common, especially along the Maritsa and Arda rivers (best 1, 5, 8, 22, 23, site A on page 181). Levant Sparrowhawk is another river bird, best seen on 22, but also 8. Goshawk, Sparrowhawk and Honey Buzzard are widespread in the forested parts of the mountains. Common Buzzard is widespread throughout, while Long-legged Buzzard is largely a steppe and lowland bird (best 21, 23, 24). Bonelli's Eagle no longer breeds, but occasionally wanders into the Rhodopes from the south. Osprey passes through in spring and autumn and is seen mostly on the reservoirs of the Arda, the Maritsa River and Thracian Plain.

**Falcons** Kestrel is widespread. Lesser Kestrel breeds at Levka (23). Hobby is widespread along rivers. Eleonora's Falcon hunts over the Rhodopes in late spring and early summer (best 8). Red-footed Falcon passes through in low numbers in April and May in the TP, but they haven't bred in the area in the past years. Of the big falcons, Peregrine is most common. Saker is subject of a reintroduction program just outside our area but may turn up in the TP and Sakar. Lanner is a rare, possibly extinct, breeding bird of the ER (best chance on 12).

**Crakes, Rails and allies** Low numbers of Coots and Moorhen are present in the lowland marshes (1, 22, sites A-E on pages 248-251). Rails are uncommon or rare at the same sites.

**Waders** Black-winged Stilt breeds in some of the TP marshes (best A-C on pages 248-249). Collared Pratincole breeds in scattered colonies essentially in the same region. We found large numbers in the fields around the Trud Fishponds (B on page 248). Stone Curlew is a scarce breeding bird of the steppes and lowlands (21, 23, 24) but also of bare reservoir shores (e.g. site A on page 181). Lapwings are fairly common breeding birds and common in winter and on passage (best A on page 248). Oystercatcher is a surprising breeding bird of islands in the Maritsa (22). Little Ringed Plover (common), Green and Common Sandpiper (both scarce) breed along the major rivers.

**Gulls and terns** Yellow-legged is the 'default' gull on all major water bodies. Black-headed is scarce in the lowlands, where Little Gull is sometimes found on passage. Whiskered and possibly Black Tern breed locally (best C on page 249); Black and White-winged Terns migrate through the same area in good numbers. Common Tern breeds on the river and the larger reservoirs (1, 5, 22).

**Doves and Pigeons** Turtle Dove is a common species of open woodlands and agricultural land. Ring-necked Dove is common in towns and villages. Wood Pigeon is widespread in the forests and recently started to breed in the city parks, while Stock Dove breeds in fairly low numbers in the WR.

**Cuckoos** Cuckoo occurs throughout the wooded parts of the area. Great Spotted Cuckoos are rare and erratic. It is most frequently seen at Besaparski (21).

**Owls** The most common lowland owls are Barn, Scops and Little Owls (the latter is often seen sitting on a pole or barn roof). Scops Owl is astonishingly common in Madzharovo and often seen around the building blocks at dusk. Tawny and Long-eared Owls are the most common owls of woodlands, joined by Eagle Owl in large woodlands and rock ledges. Both Tengmalm's and Pygmy Owls are rather scarce but widespread in the coniferous forests of the WR.

**Swifts and Nightjar** Both Common and Pallid Swifts are present throughout the area (with Pallid more patchily in the WR) and form a nice puzzle for birdwatchers. There are large Alpine Swift colonies in the Rhodopes (1, 5, 18, site A on page 222) and the bird itself can be seen everywhere in the mountains. Nightjar is common in the karstic parts of the WR and all over the ER and Sakar.

**Hoopoe, Kingfisher, Bee-eater and Roller** Hoopoes are common throughout the TP and the warmer parts of the ER. Kingfisher (1, 5, 8, 22, 23, site B, D and E on page 248-251), Bee-eater (1, 8, 21, 23) and Roller (8, 22, 23) are most common in the river valleys of the Arda and Maritsa.

**Woodpeckers** Although almost all European woodpeckers breed in the region, many are hard to find. Great Spotted is, as in most places, the most numerous woodpecker. Syrian Woodpecker largely replaces it in the TP (21-24; sites A-E on page 248-251). Green Woodpecker is common along rivers and larger forests. Grey-headed is locally common in Beech forest and mature oak stands (6, 9, 12, 16). Black Woodpecker is widespread, occurring in all older forests. Middle-spotted Woodpecker is widespread in mature oak stands (e.g. 3, 17, 22). Lesser Spotted prefers the same sites, but needs softer wood, which it finds mostly near rivers. Wryneck is not as frequent as in the past but can still be found in and around bushy areas near villages, particularly in the Rhodopes. White-backed Woodpecker is rather rare, occurring in mature Beech forest (12). Three-toed Woodpecker is restricted to old(-)growth) spruce forests (17-20).

**Larks** Woodlark is common in half-open woodlands and occurs commonly from Sakar to the karstic areas of the WR. Skylark is more local, in meadow landscapes in the same region. Crested Lark is common along roadsides, ploughed land and dry grasslands from the lowlands up to the dry slopes of the ER. Calandra Lark and Short-toed Lark are steppe birds that occur rather locally, but sometimes in good numbers (e.g. 13, 21, 23, 24).

**Martins and Swallows** House Martin, Barn Swallow and Red-rumped Swallow are common throughout the region. Sand Martin is locally common in the lowlands (21, 22). Crag Martin is common in rocky places in the Rhodopes.

**Pipits and Wagtails** Tawny Pipit is a local breeding bird of dry agricultural areas and steppe (21, 23, 24). Tree Pipit is a common breeding bird of the half-open woodlands in the WR (15-18). Water Pipit may breed on the highest slopes of the WR, but is widespread in winter in the TP. White and Black-headed Wagtails are common, the latter mostly in agricultural land in the lowlands. Grey-headed Wagtail is frequent along the larger streams of the WR and locally in the ER (6, 15, 19, 20).

**Wren, Robin, Dipper and Accentors** Wren occurs mostly in the mountains in well-vegetated ravines and mountain forests. Robin is a more widespread forest bird. Dunnock and Alpine Accentor breed in the highest parts of the WR, but are fairly widespread winter visitors to the WR and ER. Dipper is fairly common along the streams of the WR (6, 15, 19, 20).

**Redstarts, nightingales, chats and wheatears** Black Redstart is locally common in karst landscapes and on cliffs, plus in villages in the WR. Redstart is surprisingly rare. Nightingale is common in any damp, dense vegetation. Stonechat is widespread but rather uncommon in the lowlands, while Whinchat breeds in mountain meadows (18, 19) and during migration (in May) can be seen throughout the region. Northern Wheatear has become rather scarce and is mainly found in open, rocky areas. Isabelline Wheatear is locally common in deep-soiled steppe (5, 13, 21, 22, 23). Eastern Black-eared Wheatear breeds on cliffs and in quarries (1, 5, 11, 21, 24).

**Thrushes** Rock Thrush and Blue Rock Thrush are both uncommon breeding birds of cliffs, with the former seeking out the cooler, higher sites (1, 5, 6, 8, 16), and the latter present on the hotter part of the mountains (1, 3, 5, 6, 8, 21), but there is a considerable overlap. Song and Mistle Thrush breed in forests in the ER and WR and Blackbird is common throughout. Ring Ouzel breeds in open Subalpine forests (17, 18, 19). In winter, Fieldfare, Song Thrush, Mistle Thrush and Redwing occur in the lowlands.

**Warblers** There is a large diversity of warblers of the genus *Sylvia/Curruca* present in the region. The familiar Blackcap, Whitethroat and Lesser Whitethroat are perhaps most common. The latter usually breed in scrubland, together with the more localised Barred Warbler, the latter always in the vicinity of Red-backed Shrikes (1, 8, 9, 23, 24). Eastern Orphean Warbler is associated with scattered bushes and trees in the ER and Sakar (e.g. 1, 6, 7, 9, 10, 23 and 24). Eastern Subalpine and Sardinian Warblers are much less numerous and prefer the denser scrublands near hot, rocky areas in the eastern ER (1, 2, 4; site C on page 194).

Of the three *Hippolais/Iduna* warblers present in the region, Eastern Olivaceous Warbler is the most common, occurring in any shrubby, or wooded terrain in lowlands, particularly near water courses and, interestingly, in city parks (e.g. 1, 2, 6, 8, 11, 14, 22, 23). Olive-tree Warbler is local and rather rare in the ER, but locally fairly common in Sakar (11, 23). Icterine Warbler is sometimes found on passage. Of the marshland warblers, Reed and Great Reed Warblers are both numerous in reedy terrain (5, 22, sites A-E on pages 248-251). Sedge Warbler seen occasionally during passage. Sightings of Moustached and Savi's Warblers are both exceptional. Cetti's Warbler is a recent addition to the birdlife of the region, now breeding in lowland river habitat (22, 23). Eastern Bonelli's Warbler is pretty much restricted to the ER and Sakar, where it is widespread but occurs on low numbers in the denser oak stands (e.g. 3, 4, 9, 14, 23, 24). Wood Warbler breeds very locally in Beech forests (12).

**Crests** Both Firecrest and Goldcrest are fairly numerous in the coniferous forests in the WR, with Goldcrest preferring the pines and Firecrest the spruces (16-20).

**Flycatchers** Flycatchers are surprisingly rare in the area. Pied, Semi-collared and Collared Flycatchers all pass through on migration, but in low numbers. Semi-collared Flycatcher breeds in the ER and also in the WR in old beech and oak stands

(9, 12) but in very low numbers and in hard-to-access places. Spotted Flycatcher breeds in the ER and edges of the WR (e.g. 15) but also in low numbers.

**Tits and allies** Long-tailed, Blue and Great Tits are widespread. Marsh, Willow, Coal, and Crested Tits occur in the coniferous forests of the WR (16-20). Sombre Tit is widespread in the ER and Sakar in mixed oak woods, orchards and scrubland. It can turn up anywhere in the ER – we found them to be numerous in the hunting reserve (site A on page 248). Penduline Tit breeds locally along the Maritsa (22).

**Nuthatches, Treecreepers and Wallcreeper** Nuthatch is frequent in mature oak and beech forest. Western Rock Nuthatch is a local bird of dry rocky terrain (best 11, but also 1, 5 and is possible elsewhere, including in the WR). Eurasian Treecreeper is widespread in the coniferous forests of the WR, while Short-toed Treecreeper is rather uncommon in oak woods in the ER. Wallcreeper is a scarce breeding bird of the WR. For many years now, the Trigrad Gorge (site A on page 222) has been one of the easiest places on the continent to get good views of this bird.

**Shrikes** Both Red-backed and Woodchat Shrikes are common throughout the area (the latter not in the WR). Lesser Grey Shrike is more restricted to steppes, agricultural land and river floodplains (1, 5, 8, 11, 13, 21, 22 and 23). Masked Shrike is the rarest of the shrikes, occurring in open woodland, with a preference, it seems, to rivers. It has been seen in many places, but is notoriously difficult. The best place (by far) to find it is route 22 and 23.

**Crows and allies** Magpie, Jay, Hooded Crow, Jackdaw and Raven are all common in suitable habitat. Nutcracker is frequent in mountain spruce forest (18, 19). Rook is a common winter visitor to the TP.

**Starlings and Golden Oriole** Common Starling is abundant. The nomadic Rosy Starling occurs in invasion years (once every 2-3 years) and can then reliably be seen in Besaparski (21). Golden Oriole is common throughout the lowlands and lower mountains (very numerous at 22).

**Sparrows** House and Spanish Sparrow is common throughout (often occurring together). Tree Sparrow locally common in the lowlands. Rock Sparrow is a rare breeding bird of quarries in the Besaparski hills (21).

**Finches** Chaffinch and Hawfinch are common breeding birds of the Rhodopes. Bullfinch breeds in the beech forests of the WR. Linnet, Goldfinch and Greenfinch occur throughout the lowlands, while Serin is found in rural parts of the WR. Siskin and Crossbill breed in the coniferous forests of the WR.

**Buntings** Corn and Black-headed Buntings are common in all agricultural plains (but the latter arrives late, in the beginning of May). Cirl and Ortolan Buntings are abundant in park-like landscapes, open woodland and scrubland of the ER (3, 4, 5, 6, 9, 10, 11). Rock Bunting is rather uncommon and found in rocky terrain of the WR and ER (1, 5, 6, 12, 15, 16, 17, 18). Reed Bunting is a rare breeding bird of large reedbeds, but quite common there in winter.

# ACKNOWLEDGEMENTS

Crossbill Guides are rarely made by a single person. This is the case with this book even more than with others. The first version of this guide came out in 2013 under the title 'Eastern Rhodopes' and also included a part of Greece. It was written by four authors (the ones you see in the back flap) and a large number of supporters, in particular of the ARK Foundation and the predecessor of Rewilding Rhodopes.

This new version covers a much larger area on the Bulgarian side and left out the Greek part (that is for another book that is yet to be made). All the work involved with this remake was carried out in close collaboration with Rewilding Rhodopes, in particular Stefan Avramov and Polihron Karapachov. The selection of routes and all the field visits were done together with them and if it wasn't for their support, their knowledge, their good humour and the excellent conversations we had, this book would never have turned out the way it did. Thank you guys, for these unforgettable trips to your beautiful and beloved Rhodopes! Additionally, I thank Stoycho Stoychev of the BSPB (Bulgarian Society for the Protection of Birds) for his invaluable information on birds, tips on best locations to find them and for reading through the bird section of the book. Likewise, my gratitude goes to botanist Rossen Vassilev who has helped with the flora chapter and has shown me numerous plant sites in Sakar and pointed out many more in the Rhodopes. Timohir Stefanov provided information on the dragonflies of the region and wildlife photographer Bogdan Boev showed us around Zlato Pole – to all a great thank you.

Within our own team, enormous thanks go out to Kim Lotterman and his keen botanical eye, to Albert Vliegenthart for his corrections of the dragonfly and butterfly chapters, to Gino Smeulders for so patiently answering all my geological questions, and of course to Horst Wolter, Alex Tabak and Oscar Lourens for the illustrations, maps and lay-out respectively. Last but certainly not least, John Cantelo and Brian Clews (the 'UK-crew') have been invaluable again in transforming the text from 'Dutch English' to the conventional British style. You've all helped in making this book – a real team effort.

Dirk Hilbers
February 2023

# PICTURE & ILLUSTRATION CREDITS

The following numbers refer to the pages in the book. The letters refer to the position on the page: t for top, c for centre, b for bottom, l for left and r for right.

Avramov, Stefan: cover, 22 (t), 37, 48, 64, 71 (t+b), 84, 85, 86, 87, 89, 95, 96, 105, 109, 111 (t), 116, 131 (t+b), 152, 160 (r), 164, 181, 184 (b), 191, 194, 209 (b), 218 (t), 222, 224, 229, 234, 240, 241 (l)
Boev, Bogdan: cover, 43, 88, 93, 104, 106, 168, 233, 239 (t)
Crossbill Guides / Dierickx, Herman: 12, 51
Crossbill Guides / Hilbers, Dirk: cover, 17, 21 (t+b), 22 (b), 23, 24, 25, 26, 27, 28, 30 (b), 31, 33 (t+b), 34, 35, 39, 41(t+b), 44, 46, 58, 61, 66 (st and 3rd from top), 69 (b), 70 (t+b), 72 (t+b), 74 (t+b), 75 (t+b), 76, 77 (t+b), 79 (t+b), 80, 81 (t+b), 83 (b), 90, 98 (r), 99, 103, 104, 113, 117 (t), 124 (t+b), 130, 132, 136, 137, 140 (t+b), 142, 143 (l+r), 144, 146 (t+b), 147, 148, 150 (all), 153, 155 (t+b), 156 (t), 157, 159 (t+b), 160 (l), 162 (t+b), 163, 165, 167, 169, 171 (t+b), 172, 174 (t), 179, 180 (all), 183, 188 (b), 195 (t+b), 196, 197 (l+b), 199 (t+b), 200, 201 (t+b), 202, 204, 205, 206, 209 (t), 210, 211 (r), 213 (t+b), 214, 216, 217 (t+b), 218 (b), 220, 221, 223, 227 (t+b), 230 (t+b), 232, 237 (t+b), 238, 239 (b), 241 (t), 242 (t+b), 244, 245 (l+r), 246, 247 (b), 248, 250
Crossbill Guides / Swinkels, Constant: 174 (b)
Crossbill Guides / Tabak, Alex: 30 (t), 57, 115 (r), 178, 187, 190 (t)
Crossbill Guides / Ten Cate, Bouke: 101 (t), 115 (l), 117 (b), 118, 177, 190 (b)
Crossbill Guides / Vliegenthart, Albert: 8, 10, 29, 32, 83 (t), 120, 121, 123, 125, 127, 128, 129, 135, 138, 175, 184 (t), 185, 188 (t), 192, 193, 211 (l), 247 (t), 251
Mager, Jörg: 66 (2nd and 4th from top), 101 (b)
Minozig / Wikimedia commons (CC BY-SA 4.0): 98 (l)
Peykov, Vlado: 225
Saxifraga / Skornik, Iztok: 111 (b)
Teunissen, Twan: 15, 69 (t), 156 (b)
Zanderink, Frank: 62, 252

All illustrations by Crossbill Guides / Horst Wolter

# SPECIES LIST & TRANSLATION

The following list comprises all species mentioned in this guidebook and gives their scientific, German and Dutch names. Some have an asterisk (*) behind them, indicating an unofficial name. See page 5 for more details.

## Plants

| English | Scientific | German | Dutch |
|---|---|---|---|
| Alder, Black | Alnus glutinosa | Schwarz-Erle | Zwarte els |
| Alexanders, Perfoliate | Smyrnium perfoliatum | Stängelumfassende Gelbdolde | Doorwaskervel |
| Alison, Golden | Aurinia saxatilis | Felsen-Steinkraut | Rotsschildzaad |
| Alkanet, Dyer's | Alkanna tinctoria | Schminkwurz | Alkanna |
| Anemone, Peacock | Anemone pavonina | Pfauen-Anemone | Pauwanemoon |
| Anemone, Wood | Anemone nemorosa | Busch-Windröschen | Bosanemoon |
| Anemone, Yellow | Anemone ranunculoides | Gelbes Windröschen | Gele anemoon |
| Ash, Manna | Fraxinus ornus | Manna-Esche | Pluim-es |
| Ash, Narrow-leaved | Fraxinus angustifolia | Schmalblättrige Esche | Smalbladige es |
| Aspen, Trembling | Populus tremula | Zitter-Pappel | Ratelpopulier |
| Asphodel, Lesser Yellow | Asphodeline liburnica | Liburnische Junkerlilie | Kleine gele affodil* |
| Asphodel, Yellow | Asphodeline lutea | Gelber Affodil | Gele affodil |
| Avens, Bulgarian | Geum bulgaricum | Bulgarischer Nelkenwurz* | Bulgaars nagelkruid* |
| Avens, Red | Geum coccineum | Rote Nelkenwurz | Rood nagelkruid |
| Avens, Rhodope | Geum rhodopeum | Rhodope Nelkenwurz* | Rhodopenagelkruid* |
| Beech | Fagus sylvatica | Rotbuche | Beuk |
| Beech, Balkan | Fagus moesiaca | Krim-Buche | Balkanbeuk* |
| Bellflower, Clustered | Campanula glomerata | Geknäuelte Glockenblume | Kluwenklokje |
| Bellflower, Lingulate | Campanula lingulata | Hals-Glockenblume* | Halsklokje* |
| Bellflower, Nettle-leaved | Campanula trachelium | Nesselblättrige Glockenblume | Ruig klokje |
| Bellflower, Peach-leaved | Campanula persicifolia | Pfirschblättrige Glockenblume | Prachtklokje |
| Bellflower, Spreading | Campanula patula | Wiesen-Glockenblume | Weideklokje |
| Bellflower, Velebit | Campanula velebitica | Velebit-Glockenblume* | Velebit klokje* |
| Betony | Stachys officinalis | Echter Ziest | Betonie |
| Bilberry | Vaccinium myrtillus | Blaubeere | Blauwe bosbes |
| Birch, Silver | Betula pendula | Hänge-Birke | Ruwe berk |
| Bird's-nest, Yellow | Monotropa hypopitys | Fichtenspargel | Stofzaad |
| Birthwort, Pale | Aristolochia pallida | Bleiche Osterluzei | Bleke pijpbloem |
| Bittercress, Coral-root | Cardamine bulbifera | Zwiebel-Zahnwurz | Bolletjeskers |
| Blackthorn | Prunus spinosa | Schlehe | Sleedoorn |
| Bladderpod | Alyssoides utriculata | Blasenschötchen | Blaasschildzaad* |
| Bogbean | Menyanthes trifoliata | Fieberklee | Waterdrieblad |
| Bugle, Laxmann's* | Ajuga laxmannii | Laxmann's Günsel | Laxmann's zenegroen* |
| Bush, Burning | Dictamnus albus | Diptam | Vuurwerkplant |
| Butterbur | Petasites hybridus | Gewöhnliche Pestwurz | Groot hoefblad |
| Catchfly, Sand | Silene conica | Kegel-Leimkraut | Kegelsilene |

| English | Latin | German | Dutch |
|---|---|---|---|
| Catchfly, Spanish | Silene otites | Ohrlöffel-Leimkraut | Oorsilene |
| Catchfly, Sticky | Silene viscaria | Gewöhnliche Pechnelke | Rode pekanjer |
| Catmint | Nepeta cataria | Echte Katzenminze | Wild kattenkruid |
| Chamomile, Wild | Matricaria recutita | Echte Kamille | Echte kamille |
| Christ's-thorn | Paliurus spina-christi | Christusdorn | Christusdoorn |
| Cinquefoil, Hoary | Potentilla argentea | Silber-Fingerkraut | Viltganzerik |
| Cinquefoil, Marsh | Comarum palustre | Sumpf-Blutauge | Wateraardbei |
| Cistus, Cretan | Cistus creticus | Kretische Zistrose | Kreta-zonneroosje* |
| Clary, Whorled | Salvia verticillata | Quirlblütiger Salbei | Kranssalie |
| Clary, Wild | Salvia verbenaca | Eisenkraut-Salbei | Kleinbloemige salie |
| Clematis, Purple | Clematis viticella | Italienische Waldrebe | Italiaanse clematis |
| Clover, Hare's-foot | Trifolium arvense | Hasen-Klee | Hazenpootje |
| Clover, Purple | Trifolium purpureum | Balkan Purperklee* | Balkan purperen klaver* |
| Cockle, Corn | Agrostemma githago | Kornrade | Bolderik |
| Comfrey, Bulbous | Symphytum bulbosum | Knollen-Beinwell | Bolsmeerwortel* |
| Coralroot | Cardamine bulbifera | Zwiebel-Zahnwurz | Bolletjeskers |
| Cornflower | Centaurea cyanus | Kornblume | Korenbloem |
| Cowslip | Primula veris | Wiesen-Schlüsselblume | Gulden sleutelbloem |
| Crabapple, Three-lobed | Eriolobus trilobatus | Dreilappiger Apfel | Esdoornbladige appel |
| Crane's-bill, Bloody | Geranium sanguineum | Blutroter Storchschnabel | Bloedooievaarsbek |
| Crane's-bill, Rock | Geranium macrorrhizum | Balkan-Storchschnabel | Rotsooievaarsbek |
| Dropwort | Filipendula vulgaris | Kleines Mädesüss | Knolspirea |
| Elder, Dwarf | Sambucus ebulus | Zwerg-Holunder/Attich | Kruidvlier |
| Elecampane | Inula helenium | Echter Alant | Griekse alant |
| Elm | Ulmus sp. | Ulme | Iep |
| Fern, Brittle Bladder | Cystopteris fragilis | Zerbrechlicher Blasenfarn | Blaasvaren |
| Fern, Limestone | Gymnocarpium robertianum | Ruprechtsfarn | Rechte driehoeksvaren |
| Fir, Bulgarian | Abies borisii-regis | Bulgarische Tanne | Bulgaarse zilverspar |
| Fir, Silver | Abies alba | Tanne | Zilverspar |
| Flax, Pale | Linum bienne | Zweijähriger Lein | Tweejarig vlas |
| Foxglove, Grecian | Digitalis lanata | Wolliger Fingerhut | Wollig vingerhoedskruid |
| Foxglove, Green-flowered* | Digitalis viridiflora | Grünblütiger Fingerhut | Groenbloemig vingerhoedskruid |
| Fritillary, Pontic | Fritillaria pontica | Balkan-Schachblume | Pontische kievitsbloem |
| Gentian, Cross-leaf | Gentiana cruciata | Kreuz-Enzian | Kruisbladgentiaan |
| Gentian, Willow | Gentiana asclepiadea | Schwalbenwurz-Enzian | Zijdeplantgentiaan |
| Germander, Felty | Teucrium polium | Polei-Gamander | Viltgamander* |
| Gladiole, Wild | Gladiolus communis | Gladiole | Gladiool |
| Grape-hyacinth, Common | Muscari neglectum | Weinbergs-Traubenhyazinthe | Troshyacint |
| Greenweed, Winged | Genista sagittalis | Flügelginster | Pijlbrem |
| Gromwell, Purple | Buglossoides purpurocaerulea | Blauer Steinsame | Blauw parelzaad |
| Gromwell, Yellow | Neatostema apulum | Gelber Steinsame | Geel parelzaad |
| Ground-pine | Ajuga chamaepytis | Gelber Günsel | Akkerzenegroen |
| Haberlea | Haberlea rhodopensis | Haberlea | Haberlea |
| Harebell, Balkan* | Asyneuma limonifolium | Balkan Stern-Glöckchen* | Balkan sterklokje* |
| Hazel | Corylus avellana | Haselnuss | Hazelaar |

**SPECIES LIST & TRANSLATION**

| English | Scientific | German | Dutch |
|---|---|---|---|
| Helleborine, Green False | Veratrum lobelianum | Grüner Germer | Groenbloemige nieswortel* |
| Helleborine, Marsh | Epipactis palustris | Echte Sumpfwurz | Moeraswespenorchis |
| Helleborine, Narrow-leaved | Cephalanthera longifolia | Schwertblättriges Waldvögelein | Wit bosvogeltje |
| Helleborine, Red | Cephalanthera rubra | Rotes Waldvögelein | Rood bosvogeltje |
| Helleborine, Spurred | Cephalanthera epipactoides | Gesporntes Waldvögelein | Stijf bosvogeltje |
| Helleborine, White | Cephalanthera damasonium | Weisses Waldvögelein | Bleek bosvogeltje |
| Hemp-agrimony | Eupatorium cannabinum | Wasserdost | Koninginnekruid |
| Herb-paris | Paris quadrifolia | Einbeere | Eenbes |
| Hollow-root | Corydalis cava | Hohler Lerchensporn | Holwortel |
| Holly, Common | Ilex aquifolium | Stechpalme | Hulst |
| Horehound, Eastern White | Marrubium peregrinum | Ungarischer Andorn | Hongaarse malrove* |
| Hornbeam | Carpinus betulus | Hainbuche | Haagbeuk |
| Hornbeam, Hop | Ostrya carpinifolia | Hopfenbuche | Hopbeuk |
| Hornbeam, Oriental | Carpinus orientalis | Orientalische Hainbuche | Oosterse haagbeuk |
| Horsetail, Giant | Equisetum telmateia | Riesen-Schachtelhalm | Reuzenpaardenstaart |
| House-leek | Sempervivum sp. | Hauswurz | Huislook |
| Hyacinth, Tassle | Muscari comosum | Schopfige Traubenhyazinthe | Kuifhyacint |
| Hypecoum | Hypecoum imberbe / H. procumbens | Gelbäugelchen | Hypecoum |
| Immortelle | Xeranthemum annuum | Papierblume | Papierbloem |
| Iris, Dwarf | Iris pumila/attica | Zwerg-Schwertlilie | Dwerglis |
| Iris, Grass-leaved | Iris graminea | Grasblättrige Schwertlilie | Graslis |
| Iris, Oriental | Iris orientalis | Orientalische Schwertlilie | Oosterse lis* |
| Iris, Reichenbach's* | Iris reichenbachii | Reichenbach-Schwertlilie | Reichenbachs dwerglis |
| Iris, Variegated | Iris variegata | Bunte Schwertlilie | Bonte lis |
| Ivy | Hedera helix | Efeu | Klimop |
| Jasmine, Wild | Jasminum fruticans | Strauch-Jasmin | Struikjasmijn |
| Jovibarba | Jovibarba heuffelii | Balkan-Fransenhauswurz | Balkan-huislook* |
| Juniper, Prickly | Juniperus oxycedrus | Stech-wacholder | Stekelige jeneverbes |
| Larkspur, Eastern | Consolida hispanica | Orientalischer Rittersporn | Oosterse ridderspoor |
| Larkspur, Southern* | Delphinium fissum | Schlitzblättriger Rittersporn | Slipbladige ridderspoor |
| Leek, Bulgarian* | Nectaroscordum siculum (ssp. bulgaricum) | Bulgarischer Honiglauch | Bulgaarse look |
| Leek, Yellow | Allium flavum | Gelber Lauch | Gele look |
| Lilac, Common | Syringa vulgaris | Gewöhnlicher Flieder | Gewone sering |
| Lily, Dog's-tooth | Erythronium dens-canis | Hundszahn | Hondstand |
| Lily, Martagon | Lilium martagon | Türkenbund-Lilie | Turkse lelie |
| Lily, Rhodope | Lilium rhodopaeum | Rhodopen-Lilie | Rhodope lelie* |
| Lily, St Bernard's | Anthericum liliago | Astlose Graslilie | Grote graslelie |
| Linden, Silver | Tilia tomentosa | Silber-Linde | Zilverlinde |
| Liquorice, Wild | Astragalus glycyphyllos | Bärenschote | Hokjespeul |
| Loosestrife, Dotted | Lysimachia punctata | Punktierter Gilbweiderich | Puntwederik |
| Lords-and-Ladies | Arum maculatum | Gefleckter Aronstab | Gevlekte aronskelk |
| Lousewort, Rhodopean | Pedicularis leucodon | Weisszähniges Läusekraut | Rhodope kartelblad* |
| Love-in-a-mist, Field | Nigella arvensis | Acker-Schwarzkümmel | Wilde nigelle |
| Lungwort, Common | Pulmonaria officinalis | Geflecktes Lungenkraut | Gevlekt longkruid |
| Lungwort, Red | Pulmonaria rubra | Ziegelrotes Lungenkraut | Rood longkruid |
| Mallow, Hemp-leaved | Althaea cannabina | Hanf-Eibisch | Hennepbladige heemst |

| | | | |
|---|---|---|---|
| Maple, Balkan | Acer hyrcanum | Balkan-Ahorn | Balkanesdoorn |
| Maple, Field | Acer campestre | Feld-Ahorn | Spaanse aak |
| Maple, Greek | Acer heldreichii | Griechischer Ahorn | Griekse esdoorn |
| Maple, Montpellier | Acer monspessulanum | Französischer Ahorn | Franse esdoorn |
| Maple, Norway | Acer platanoides | Spitz-Ahorn | Noordse esdoorn |
| Medick, Sickle | Medicago falcata | Sichelklee | Sikkelklaver |
| Mercury, Dog's | Mercurialis perennis | Wald-Bingelkraut | Bosbingelkruid |
| Mezereon | Daphne mezereum | Gewöhnlicher Seidelbast | Rood peperboompje |
| Milk-vetch, Sainfoin* | Astragalus onobrychis | Esparsetten-Tragant | Esparcette-tragant |
| Milk-vetch, Shrubby* | Astragalus angustifolius | Schmalblättriger Tragant | Struiktragant* |
| Milkwort, Anatolian | Polygala anatolica | Anatolisches Kreuzblümchen | Turkse Vleugeltjesbloem* |
| Mulberry | Morus sp. | Maulbeer | Moerbei |
| Mullein, Purple | Verbascum phoeniceum | Violette Königskerze | Paarse toorts |
| Navelwort, Golden | Umbilicus erectus | Aufrechter Venusnabel | Balkan muurnavel* |
| Nonea, Brown | Nonea pulla | Braunes Mönchskraut | Bruin monnikskruid |
| Oak, Downy | Quercus pubescens | Flaum-Eiche | Donzige eik |
| Oak, Hungarian | Quercus frainetto | Ungarische Eiche | Hongaarse eik |
| Oak, Italian | Quercus virgiliana | Italienische Eiche | Italiaanse eik |
| Oak, Sessile | Quercus petraea | Trauben-Eiche | Wintereik |
| Oak, Turkey | Quercus cerris | Zerr-Eiche | Moseik |
| Oak, Thracian | Quercus thracica | Thrakische Eiche | Thracische elk |
| Orchid, Balkan Lizard* | Himantoglossum caprinum | Ziegen-Riemenzunge | Geitenorchis |
| Orchid, Bee | Ophrys apifera | Bienen-Ragwurz | Bijenorchis |
| Orchid, Bird's-nest | Neottia nidus-avis | Nestwurz | Vogelnestje |
| Orchid, Bog | Hammarbya paludosa | Sumpf-Weichorchis | Veenmosorchis |
| Orchid, Bug | Anacamptis coriophora | Wanzen-Knabenkraut | Wantsenorchis |
| Orchid, Burnt | Neotinea ustulata | Brand-Knabenkraut | Aangebrande orchis |
| Orchid, Common Lizard | Himantoglossum hircinum | Bocksorchis | Bokkenorchis |
| Orchid, Common Spotted | Dactylorhiza fuchsii | Fuchs' Knabenkraut | Gevlekte orchis |
| Orchid, Early-purple | Orchis mascula | Mannliches Knabenkraut | Mannetjesorchis |
| Orchid, Eastern Early-purple* | Orchis pinetorum | Kiefernwald Knabenkraut | Dennen-mannetjesorchis |
| Orchid, Eastern Spotted | Dactylorhiza saccifera | Langähriges Knabenkraut | Oostelijke gevlekte orchis* |
| Orchid, Elder-flowered | Dactylorhiza sambucina | Holunder-Knabenkraut | Vlierorchis |
| Orchid, Fly | Ophrys insectifera | Fliegen-Ragwurz | Vliegenorchis |
| Orchid, Fragrant | Gymnadenia conopsea | Mücken-Händelwurz | Grote muggenorchis |
| Orchid, Ghost | Epipogium aphyllum | Blattloser Widerbart | Spookorchis |
| Orchid, Greater Butterfly | Platanthera chlorantha | Berg-Waldhyazinthe | Bergnachtorchis |
| Orchid, Green-winged | Anacamptis morio | Kleines Knabenkraut | Harlekijn |
| Orchid, Heart-flowered Marsh | Dactylorhiza cordigera | Herzblättriges Knabenkraut | Hartbladige Brede orchis |
| Orchid, Horned Woodcock | Ophrys (scopolax ssp.) cornuta | Kleine Gehörnte Ragwurz | Gehoornde orchis |
| Orchid, Lady | Orchis purpurea | Purpur-Knabenkraut | Purperorchis |
| Orchid, Lesser Butterfly | Platanthera bifolia | Weisse Waldhyazinthe | Welriekende nachtorchis |
| Orchid, Long-lipped Tongue | Serapias vomeracea | Pflugschar Zungenstendel | Lange tongorchis |
| Orchid, Loose-flowered | Anacamptis laxiflora | Lockerblütiges Knabenkraut | IJle moerasorchis |

**SPECIES LIST & TRANSLATION**

| English | Scientific | German | Dutch |
|---|---|---|---|
| Orchid, Macedonian Marsh* | *Dactylorhiza kalopissii* | Kalopissis' Fingerwurz | Macedonische orchis |
| Orchid, Mammose | *Ophrys mammosa* | Busen-Ragwurz | Vrouwtjesorchis |
| Orchid, Monkey | *Orchis simia* | Affen-Knabenkraut | Aapjesorchis |
| Orchid, Pink Butterfly | *Anacamptis papilionacea* | Schmetterlings-Knabenkraut | Vlinderorchis |
| Orchid, Provence | *Orchis provincialis* | Provence-Knabenkraut | Stippelorchis |
| Orchid, Pyramidal | *Anacamptis pyramidalis* | Hundswurz | Hondskruid |
| Orchid, Reinhold's | *Ophrys reinholdii* | Reinholds Ragwurz | Reinhold's orchis* |
| Orchid, Roman | *Dactylorhiza romana* | Römisches Knabenkraut | Romeinse orchis |
| Orchid, Three-toothed | *Neotinea tridentata* | Dreizähniges Knabenkraut | Drietandorchis |
| Orchid, Violet Bird's-nest | *Limodorum abortivum* | Violetter Dingel | Paarse aspergeorchis |
| Orchid, Woodcock | *Ophrys scolopax* | Schnepfen-Ragwurz | Snippenorchis |
| Orchid, Yellow Bee | *Ophrys lutea* | Gelbe Ragwurz | Gele orchis |
| Orlaya | *Orlaya grandiflora* | Grossblütiger Breitsame | Straalscherm |
| Pea, Spring | *Lathyrus vernus* | Frühlings-Platterbse | Voorjaarslathyrus |
| Pear, Almond-leaved | *Pyrus spinosa* | Mandelblättrige Birne | Amandelbladpeer |
| Pear, Wild | *Pyrus pyraster* | Wildbirne | Wilde peer |
| Peony, Scarlet | *Paeonia peregrina* | Fremdartige Pfingstrose | Vreemde pioenroos* |
| Pine, Austrian | *Pinus nigra* | Schwarzkiefer | Zwarte den |
| Pine, Scots | *Pinus sylvestris* | Waldkiefer | Grove den |
| Pine, Turkish | *Pinus brutia* | Kalabrische Kiefer | Turkse den |
| Pink, Proliferous | *Petrorhagia prolifera* | Sprossende Felsennelke | Slanke mantelanjer |
| Pink, Rock* | *Dianthus petraeus* | Geröll-Nelke | Witte rotsanjer* |
| Plane, Oriental | *Platanus orientalis* | Orientalische Platane | Oosterse plataan |
| Poplar, Black | *Populus nigra* | Schwarz-Pappel | Zwarte populier |
| Poplar, White | *Populus alba* | Silber-Pappel | Witte abeel |
| Poppy, Common | *Papaver rhoeas* | Klatsch-Mohn | Grote klaproos |
| Primrose | *Primula vulgaris* | Stengellose Schlüsselblume | Stengelloze sleutelbloem |
| Ramsons | *Allium ursinum* | Bärenlapp | Daslook |
| Rowan | *Sorbus aucuparia* | Eberesche | Wilde lijsterbes |
| Sage, Clary | *Salvia sclarea* | Muskatellersalbei | Scharlei |
| Sage, Mediterranean | *Salvia aethiopis* | Mohren-Salbei | Moorse salie |
| Sage, Red-topped | *Salvia viridis* | Buntschopf-Salbei | Bonte salie |
| Sage, Silver | *Salvia argentea* | Silber-Salbei | Zilversalie |
| Sage, Sticky | *Salvia glutinosa* | Klebriger Salbei | Kleverige salie |
| Sanicle | *Sanicula europaea* | Sanikel | Heelkruid |
| Scabious, Balkan Sheep's-bit* | *Jasione heldreichii* | Heldreichs Sandglöckchen | Balkanzandblauwtje* |
| Scabious, Rhodope* | *Scabiosa rhodopensis* | Rhodopen-Skabiose | Rhodope duifkruid* |
| Scabious, Silvery* | *Lomelosia argentea* | Silber-Skabiose | Zilver-duifkruid* |
| Scabious, Yellow | *Scabiosa ochroleuca* | Gelbe Skabiose | Geel duifkruid* |
| Senna, Bladder | *Colutea arborescens* | Blasenstrauch | Europese blazenstrui |
| Service-tree, Wild | *Sorbus torminalis* | Elsbeere | Elsbes |
| Slipper, Lady's | *Cypripedium calceolum* | Frauenschuh | Vrouwenschoentje |
| Smoke-tree | *Cotinus coggygria* | Perückenstrauch | Pruikenboom |
| Spiderflower, Bird | *Cleome ornithopodioides* | Vogel-Spinnenblume* | Vogelkattensnor* |
| Spleenwort, Black | *Asplenium adiantum-nigrum* | Schwarze Streifenfarn | Zwartsteel |
| Spruce, Norway | *Picea abies* | Gemeine Fichte | Fijnspar |

| English | Scientific | German | Dutch |
|---|---|---|---|
| St. John's-wort, Balkan* | Hypericum cerastoides | Rhodope Johanniskraut* | Rhodope hertshooi* |
| St. John's-wort, Large-flowered | Hypericum calycinum | Grossblütiges Johanniskraut | Grootbloemig hertshooi |
| St. John's-wort, Olympus | Hypericum olympicum | Olymp-Johanniskraut | Olympus hertshooi* |
| Star-of-Bethlehem, Drooping | Ornithogalum nutans | Nickender Milchstern | Knikkende vogelmelk |
| Stonecrop, Yellow | Sedum ochroleucum | Ockergelbe Fetthenne | Bleekgeel vetkruid |
| Strawberry, Wild | Fragaria vesca | Wald-Erdbeere | Bosaardbei |
| Sycamore | Acer pseudoplatanus | Bergahorn | Gewone esdoorn |
| Toadflax, Broomleaf | Linaria genistifolia | Ginster-Leinkraut | Bremleeuwenbek* |
| Toothwort, Rhodopean | Lathraea rhodopea | Rhodope Schuppenwurz* | Rhodope schubwortel* |
| Tree, Judas | Cercis siliquastrum | Gemeiner Judasbaum | Europese judasboom |
| Tree, Turpentine | Pistacia terebinthus | Terpentin-Pistazie | Terpentijnboom |
| Tulip, Rhodopean | Tulipa rhodopea | Rhodope Tulpe* | Rhodopentulp* |
| Tulip, Wild | Tulipa sylvestris (ssp. australis) | Südliche Tulpe | Zuidelijke tulp |
| Twayblade | Neottia ovata | Grosses Zweiblatt | Grote keverorchis |
| Venus's-looking-glass, Large | Legousia speculum-veneris | Echter Frauenspiegel | Groot spiegelklokje |
| Vetchling, Yellow | Lathyrus aphaca | Ranken-Platterbse | Naakte lathyrus |
| Violet, Rhodopean | Viola rhodopeia | Rhodope-Veilchen* | Rhodope viooltje* |
| Viper's-bugloss, Italian | Echium italicum | Italienischer Natternkopf | Italiaans slangekruid |
| Willow, Crack | Salix fragilis | Bruch-Weide | Kraakwilg |
| Willow, White | Salix alba | Silber-Weide | Schietwilg |
| Wintergreen, Green-flowered | Pyrola chlorantha | Grünblütiges Wintergrün | Groen wintergroen |
| Wintergreen, Serrated | Orthilia secunda | Nickendes Wintergrün | Eenzijdig wintergroen |
| Woundwort, Balkan* | Stachys plumosa | Balkan-Ziest | Balkan andoorn* |
| Woundwort, Downy | Stachys germanica | Deutscher Ziest | Duitse andoorn |
| Woundwort, Yellow | Stachys recta | Aufrechte Ziest | Bergandoorn |
| Yew, European | Taxus baccata | Eibe | Taxus |

## Mammals

| English | Scientific | German | Dutch |
|---|---|---|---|
| Badger | Meles meles | Dachs | Das |
| Bear, Brown | Ursus arctos | Braunbär | Bruine beer |
| Bison, European | Bison bonasus | Wisent | Wisent |
| Boar, Wild | Sus scrofa | Wildschwein | Wild zwijn |
| Cat, Wild | Felis silvestris | Wildkatze | Wilde kat |
| Chamois, Balkan | Rupicapra rupicapra | Gemse | Gems |
| Coypu | Myocaster coypus | Nutria | Beverrat |
| Deer, Fallow | Damus damus | Dammhirsch | Damhert |
| Deer, Red | Cervus elaphus | Rothirsch | Edelhert |
| Deer, Roe | Capreolus capreolus | Reh | Ree |
| Dormouse, Roach's Mouse-tailed | Myomimus roachi | Mausschläfer | Muisslaper |
| Hare | Lepus europaeus | Hase | Haas |
| Hedgehog, Northern White-breasted | Erinaceus roumanicus | Nördlicher Weissbrustigel | Oost-Europese egel |
| Jackal, Golden | Canis aureus | Goldschakal | Gewone jakhals |
| Marten, Beech | Martes foina | Steinmarder | Steenmarter |
| Marten, Pine | Martes martes | Baummarder | Boommarter |

| English | Scientific | German | Dutch |
|---|---|---|---|
| Mole-rat, Lesser | *Nannospalax leucodon* | Westblindmaus | Westelijke blindmuis |
| Otter | *Lutra lutra* | Fischotter | Otter |
| Polecat, Marbled | *Vormela peregusna* | Tigeriltis | Gevlekte bunzing |
| Stoat | *Mustela ermina* | Hermelin | Hermelijn |
| Suslik | *Citellus citellus* | Ziesel | Siesel |
| Weasel | *Mustela nivalis* | Mauswiesel | Wezel |
| Wolf | *Canis lupus* | Wolf | Wolf |

# Birds

| English | Scientific | German | Dutch |
|---|---|---|---|
| Bee-eater | *Merops apiaster* | Bienenfresser | Bijeneter |
| Bittern, Great | *Botaurus stellaris* | Rohrdommel | Roerdomp |
| Bittern, Little | *Ixobrychus minutus* | Zwergdommel | Woudaapje |
| Blackbird | *Turdus merula* | Amsel | Merel |
| Blackcap | *Sylvia atricapilla* | Mönchsgrasmücke | Zwartkop |
| Brambling | *Fringilla montifringilla* | Bergfink | Keep |
| Bullfinch | *Pyrrhula pyrrhula* | Gimpel | Goudvink |
| Bunting, Black-headed | *Emberiza melanocephala* | Kappenammer | Zwartkopgors |
| Bunting, Cirl | *Emberiza cirlus* | Zaunammer | Cirlgors |
| Bunting, Corn | *Miliaria calandra* | Grauammer | Grauwe gors |
| Bunting, Ortolan | *Emberiza hortulana* | Ortolan | Ortolaan |
| Bunting, Reed | *Emberiza schoeniclus* | Rohrammer | Rietgors |
| Bunting, Rock | *Emberiza cia* | Zippammer | Grijze gors |
| Buzzard, Common | *Buteo buteo* | Mäusebussard | Buizerd |
| Buzzard, Honey | *Pernis apivorus* | Wespenbussard | Wespendief |
| Buzzard, Long-legged | *Buteo rufinus* | Adlerbussard | Arendbuizerd |
| Capercaillie | *Tetrao urogallus* | Auerhuhn | Auerhoen |
| Chaffinch | *Fringilla coelebs* | Buchfink | Vink |
| Chiffchaff | *Phylloscopus collybita* | Zilpzalp | Tjiftjaf |
| Chukar | *Alectoris chukar* | Chukarhuhn | Aziatische steenpatrijs |
| Coot | *Fulica atra* | Blässhuhn | Meerkoet |
| Cormorant, Great | *Phalacrocorax carbo* | Kormoran | Aalscholver |
| Cormorant, Pygmy | *Microcarbo pygmeus* | Zwergscharbe | Dwergaalscholver |
| Crow, Hooded | *Corvus corone cornix* | Nebelkrähe | Bonte kraai |
| Cuckoo | *Cuculus canorus* | Kuckuck | Koekoek |
| Cuckoo, Great Spotted | *Clamator glandarius* | Häherkuckuck | Kuifkoekoek |
| Curlew | *Numenius arquata* | Grosser Brachvogel | Wulp |
| Dipper | *Cinclus cinclus* | Wasseramsel | Waterspreeuw |
| Dove, Collared | *Streptopelia decaocto* | Türkentaube | Turkse tortel |
| Dove, Stock | *Columba oenas* | Hohltaube | Holenduif |
| Dove, Turtle | *Streptopelia turtur* | Turteltaube | Tortelduif |
| Duck, Ferruginous | *Aythya nyroca* | Moorente | Witoogeend |
| Duck, Tufted | *Aythya fuligula* | Reiherente | Kuifeend |
| Duck, White-headed | *Oxyura leucocephala* | Weisskopfruderente | Witkopeend |
| Dunnock | *Prunella modularis* | Heckenbraunelle | Heggenmus |
| Eagle, (Greater) Spotted | *Aquila clanga* | Schelladler | Bastaardarend |
| Eagle, Bonelli's | *Hieraaetus fasciatus* | Habichtsadler | Havikarend |
| Eagle, Booted | *Hieraaetus pennatus* | Zwergadler | Dwergarend |
| Eagle, Eastern Imperial | *Aquila heliaca* | Kaiseradler | Keizerarend |
| Eagle, Golden | *Aquila chrysaetos* | Steinadler | Steenarend |

| English | Scientific | German | Dutch |
|---|---|---|---|
| Eagle, Lesser Spotted | *Aquila pomarina* | Schreiadler | Schreeuwarend |
| Eagle, Short-toed | *Circaetus gallicus* | Schlangenadler | Slangenarend |
| Eagle, White-tailed | *Haliaeetus albicilla* | Seeadler | Zeearend |
| Egret, Cattle | *Bubulcus ibis* | Kuhreiher | Koereiger |
| Egret, Great White | *Ardea alba* | Silberreiher | Grote zilverreiger |
| Egret, Little | *Egretta garzetta* | Seidenreiher | Kleine zilverreiger |
| Falcon, Eleonora's | *Falco eleonorae* | Eleonorenfalke | Eleonora's valk |
| Falcon, Red-footed | *Falco vespertinus* | Rotfussfalke | Roodpootvalk |
| Firecrest | *Regulus ignicapillus* | Sommergoldhähnchen | Vuurgoudhaantje |
| Flamingo, Greater | *Phoenicopterus roseus* | Flamingo | Europese flamingo |
| Flycatcher, Collared | *Ficedula albicollis* | Halsbandschnäpper | Withalsvliegenvanger |
| Flycatcher, Pied | *Ficedula hypoleuca* | Trauerschnäpper | Bonte vliegenvanger |
| Flycatcher, Red-breasted | *Ficedula parva* | Zwergschnäpper | Kleine vliegenvanger |
| Flycatcher, Semicollared | *Ficedula semitorquata* | Halbringschnäpper | Balkanvliegenvanger |
| Flycatcher, Spotted | *Muscicapa striata* | Grauschnäpper | Grauwe vliegenvanger |
| Garganey | *Anas querquedula* | Knäkente | Zomertaling |
| Goldcrest | *Regulus regulus* | Wintergoldhähnchen | Goudhaan |
| Goldeneye | *Bucephala clangula* | Schellente | Brilduiker |
| Goldfinch | *Carduelis carduelis* | Distelfink | Putter |
| Goosander | *Mergus merganser* | Gänsesäger | Grote zaagbek |
| Goose, Greylag | *Anser anser* | Graugans | Grauwe gans |
| Goose, Red-breasted | *Branta ruficollis* | Rothalsgans | Roodhalsgans |
| Goose, White-fronted | *Anser albifrons* | Blässgans | Kolgans |
| Goshawk | *Accipiter gentilis* | Habicht | Havik |
| Grebe, Black-necked | *Podiceps nigricollis* | Schwarzhalstaucher | Geoorde fuut |
| Grebe, Great Crested | *Podiceps cristatus* | Haubentaucher | Fuut |
| Grebe, Little | *Tachybaptus ruficollis* | Zwergtaucher | Dodaars |
| Grebe, Red-necked | *Podiceps grisegena* | Rothalstaucher | Roodhalsfuut |
| Greenfinch | *Carduelis chloris* | Grünling | Groenling |
| Grouse, Hazel | *Tetrastes bonasia* | Haselhuhn | Hazelhoen |
| Gull, Black-headed | *Chroicocephalus ridibundus* | Lachmöwe | Kokmeeuw |
| Gull, Little | *Hydrocoloeus minutus* | Zwergmöwe | Dwergmeeuw |
| Gull, Yellow-legged | *Larus michahellis* | Weisskopfmöve | Geelpootmeeuw |
| Harrier, Hen | *Circus cyaneus* | Kornweihe | Blauwe kiekendief |
| Harrier, Marsh | *Circus aeruginosus* | Rohrweihe | Bruine kiekendief |
| Harrier, Montagu's | *Circus pygargus* | Wiesenweihe | Grauwe kiekendief |
| Harrier, Pallid | *Circus macrourus* | Steppenweihe | Steppekiekendief |
| Hawfinch | *Coccothraustes coccothraustes* | Kernbeisser | Appelvink |
| Heron, Grey | *Ardea cinerea* | Graureiher | Blauwe reiger |
| Heron, Night | *Nycticorax nycticorax* | Nachtreiher | Kwak |
| Heron, Purple | *Ardea purpurea* | Purpurreiher | Purperreiger |
| Heron, Squacco | *Ardeola ralloides* | Rallenreiher | Ralreiger |
| Hobby | *Falco subbuteo* | Baumfalke | Boomvalk |
| Hoopoe | *Upupa epops* | Wiedehopf | Hop |
| Ibis, Glossy | *Plegadis falcinellus* | Braunsichler | Zwarte ibis |
| Jackdaw | *Corvus monedula* | Dohle | Kauw |
| Jay | *Garrulus glandarius* | Eichelhäher | Gaai |
| Kestrel, (Common) | *Falco tinnunculus* | Turmfalke | Torenvalk |
| Kestrel, Lesser | *Falco naumanni* | Rötelfalke | Kleine torenvalk |

**SPECIES LIST & TRANSLATION**

| | | | |
|---|---|---|---|
| Kingfisher | Alcedo atthis | Eisvogel | IJsvogel |
| Kite, Black | Milvus migrans | Schwarzmilan | Zwarte wouw |
| Lanner | Falco biarmicus | Lannerfalke | Lannervalk |
| Lapwing | Vanellus vanellus | Kiebitz | Kievit |
| Lark, Calandra | Melanocorypha calandra | Kalanderlerche | Kalanderleeuwerik |
| Lark, Crested | Galerida cristata | Haubenlerche | Kuifleeuwerik |
| Lark, Short-toed | Calandrella brachydactyla | Kurzzehenlerche | Kortteenleeuwerik |
| Linnet | Carduelis cannabina | Bluthänfling | Kneu |
| Magpie | Pica pica | Elster | Ekster |
| Mallard | Anas platyrhynchos | Stockente | Wilde eend |
| Martin, Crag | Ptyonoprogne rupestris | Felsenschwalbe | Rotszwaluw |
| Martin, House | Delichon urbicum | Mehlschwalbe | Huiszwaluw |
| Martin, Sand | Riparia riparia | Uferschwalbe | Oeverzwaluw |
| Moorhen | Gallinula chloropus | Teichhuhn | Waterhoen |
| Nightingale | Luscinia megarhynchos | Nachtigal | Nachtegaal |
| Nightjar | Caprimulgus europaeus | Ziegenmelker | Nachtzwaluw |
| Nuthatch | Sitta europaea | Kleiber | Boomklever |
| Nuthatch, Western Rock | Sitta neumayer | Felsenkleiber | Rotsklever |
| Oriole, Golden | Oriolus oriolus | Pirol | Wielewaal |
| Osprey | Pandion haliaetus | Fischadler | Visarend |
| Ouzel, Ring | Turdus torquatus | Ringdrossel | Beflijster |
| Owl, Barn | Tyto alba | Schleiereule | Kerkuil |
| Owl, Eagle | Bubo bubo | Uhu | Oehoe |
| Owl, Little | Athene noctua | Steinkauz | Steenuil |
| Owl, Long-eared | Asio otus | Waldohreule | Ransuil |
| Owl, Scops | Otus scops | Zwergohreule | Dwergooruil |
| Owl, Tawny | Strix aluco | Waldkauz | Bosuil |
| Oystercatcher | Haematopus ostralegus | Austernfischer | Scholekster |
| Partridge, Grey | Perdix perdix | Rebhuhn | Patrijs |
| Partridge, Rock | Alectoris graeca | Steinhuhn | Steenpatrijs |
| Pelican, Dalmatian | Pelecanus crispus | Krauskopfpelikan | Kroeskoppelikaan |
| Pelican, White | Pelecanus onocrotalus | Rosapelikan | Roze pelikaan |
| Peregrine | Falco peregrinus | Wanderfalke | Slechtvalk |
| Pheasant, Ring-necked | Phasianus colchicus | Fasan | Fazant |
| Pigeon, Wood | Columba palumbus | Ringeltaube | Houtduif |
| Pintail | Anas acuta | Spiessente | Pijlstaart |
| Pipit, Tawny | Anthus campestris | Brachpieper | Duinpieper |
| Pipit, Tree | Anthus trivialis | Baumpieper | Boompieper |
| Pipit, Water | Anthus spinoletta | Bergpieper | Waterpieper |
| Plover, Little Ringed | Charadrius dubius | Flussregenpfeifer | Kleine plevier |
| Pochard | Aythya ferina | Tafelente | Tafeleend |
| Pochard, Red-crested | Netta rufina | Kolbenente | Krooneend |
| Pratincole, Collared | Glareola pratincola | Rotflügel-Brachschwalbe | Vorkstaartplevier |
| Quail | Coturnix coturnix | Wachtel | Kwartel |
| Rail, Water | Rallus aquaticus | Wasserralle | Waterral |
| Raven | Corvus corax | Kolkrabe | Raaf |
| Redshank | Tringa totanus | Rotschenkel | Tureluur |
| Redstart, (Common) | Phoenicurus phoenicurus | Gartenrotschwanz | Gekraagde roodstaart |
| Redwing | Turdus iliacus | Rotdrossel | Koperwiek |
| Robin | Erithacus rubecula | Rotkehlchen | Roodborst |

| | | | |
|---|---|---|---|
| Roller | *Coracias garrulus* | Blauracke | Scharrelaar |
| Rook | *Corvus frugilegus* | Saatkrähe | Roek |
| Saker | *Falco cherrug* | Würgfalke | Sakervalk |
| Sandpiper, Common | *Actitis hypoleucos* | Flussuferläufer | Oeverloper |
| Sandpiper, Green | *Tringa ochropus* | Waldwasserläufer | Witgat |
| Sandpiper, Wood | *Tringa glareola* | Bruchwasserläufer | Bosruiter |
| Serin | *Serinus serinus* | Girlitz | Europese kanarie |
| Shelduck, Ruddy | *Tadorna ferruginea* | Rostgans | Casarca |
| Shoveler | *Anas clypeata* | Löffelente | Slobeend |
| Shrike, Lesser Grey | *Lanius minor* | Schwarzstirnwürger | Kleine klapekster |
| Shrike, Masked | *Lanius nubicus* | Maskenwüger | Maskerklauwier |
| Shrike, Red-backed | *Lanius collurio* | Neuntöter | Grauwe klauwier |
| Shrike, Woodchat | *Lanius senator* | Rotkopfwürger | Roodkopklauwier |
| Siskin | *Carduelis spinus* | Erlenzeisig | Sijs |
| Skylark | *Alauda arvensis* | Feldlerche | Veldleeuwerik |
| Smew | *Mergellus albellus* | Zwergsäger | Nonnetje |
| Sparrow, House | *Passer domesticus* | Haussperling | Huismus |
| Sparrow, Rock | *Petronia petronia* | Steinsperling | Rotsmus |
| Sparrow, Spanish | *Passer hispaniolensis* | Weidensperling | Spaanse mus |
| Sparrow, Tree | *Passer montanus* | Feldsperling | Ringmus |
| Sparrowhawk | *Accipiter nisus* | Sperber | Sperwer |
| Sparrowhawk, Levant | *Accipiter brevipes* | Kurzfangsperber | Balkansperwer |
| Starling | *Sturnus vulgaris* | Star | Spreeuw |
| Starling, Rosy | *Pastor roseus* | Rosenstar | Roze spreeuw |
| Stilt, Black-winged | *Himantopus himantopus* | Stelzenläufer | Steltkluut |
| Stonechat | *Saxicola torquata* | Schwarzkehlchen | Roodborsttapuit |
| Stork, Black | *Ciconia nigra* | Schwarzstorch | Zwarte ooievaar |
| Stork, White | *Ciconia ciconia* | Weissstorch | Ooievaar |
| Swallow, Barn | *Hirundo rustica* | Rauchschwalbe | Boerenzwaluw |
| Swallow, Red-rumped | *Cecropsis daurica* | Rötelschwalbe | Roodstuitzwaluw |
| Swan, Mute | *Cygnus olor* | Höckerschwan | Knobbelzwaan |
| Swift, Alpine | *Tachymarptis melba* | Alpensegler | Alpengierzwaluw |
| Swift, Common | *Apus apus* | Mauersegler | Gierzwaluw |
| Swift, Pallid | *Apus pallidus* | Fahlsegler | Vale gierzwaluw |
| Teal | *Anas crecca* | Krickente | Wintertaling |
| Tern, Black | *Chlidonias niger* | Trauerseeschwalbe | Zwarte stern |
| Tern, Common | *Sterna hirundo* | Fluss-Seeschwalbe | Visdief |
| Tern, Whiskered | *Chlidonias hybrida* | Weissbart-Seeschwalbe | Witwangstern |
| Tern, White-winged | *Chlidonias leucopterus* | Weissflügel-Seeschwalbe | Witvleugelstern |
| Thrush, Blue Rock | *Monticola solitarius* | Blaumerle | Blauwe rotslijster |
| Thrush, Mistle | *Turdus viscivorus* | Misteldrossel | Grote lijster |
| Thrush, Rock | *Monticola saxatilis* | Steinrötel | Rode rotslijster |
| Thrush, Song | *Turdus philomelos* | Singdrossel | Zanglijster |
| Tit, Blue | *Cyanistes caeruleus* | Blaumeise | Pimpelmees |
| Tit, Coal | *Periparus ater* | Tannenmeise | Zwarte mees |
| Tit, Crested | *Lophophanes cristatus* | Haubenmeise | Kuifmees |
| Tit, Great | *Parus major* | Kohlmeise | Koolmees |
| Tit, Long-tailed | *Aegithalos caudatus* | Schwanzmeise | Staartmees |
| Tit, Marsh | *Poecile palustris* | Sumpfmeise | Glanskop |
| Tit, Penduline | *Remiz pendulinus* | Beutelmeise | Buidelmees |

SPECIES LIST & TRANSLATION

| English | Scientific | German | Dutch |
|---|---|---|---|
| Tit, Sombre | *Poecile lugubris* | Trauermeise | Rouwmees |
| Tit, Willow | *Poecile montanus* | Weidenmeise | Matkop |
| Treecreeper, Eurasian | *Certhia familiaris* | Waldbaumläufer | Taigaboomkruiper |
| Treecreeper, Short-toed | *Certhia brachydactyla* | Gartenbaumläufer | Boomkruiper |
| Vulture, Black | *Aegypius monachus* | Mönchsgeier | Monniksgier |
| Vulture, Egyptian | *Neophron percnopterus* | Schmutzgeier | Aasgier |
| Vulture, Griffon | *Gyps fulvus* | Gänsegeier | Vale gier |
| Wagtail, Black-headed | *Motacilla (flava) feldegg* | Maskenschafstelze | Balkankwikstaart |
| Wagtail, Grey | *Motacilla cinerea* | Gebirgsstelze | Grote gele kwikstaart |
| Wagtail, White | *Motacilla alba* | Bachstelze | Witte kwikstaart |
| Wallcreeper | *Tichodroma muraria* | Mauerläufer | Rotskruiper |
| Warbler, Barred | *Sylvia nisoria* | Sperbergrasmücke | Sperwergrasmus |
| Warbler, Cetti's | *Cettia cetti* | Seidensänger | Cetti's zanger |
| Warbler, Eastern Bonelli's | *Phylloscopus orientalis* | Balkanlaubsänger | Balkanbergfluiter |
| Warbler, Eastern Olivaceous | *Iduna pallida* | Blassspötter | Oostelijke vale spotvogel |
| Warbler, Eastern Orphean | *Sylvia crassirostris* | Östliche Orpheusgrasmücke | Oostelijke orpheusgrasmus |
| Warbler, Eastern Subalpine | *Sylvia cantillans* | Weissbart-Grasmücke | Balkanbaardgrasmus |
| Warbler, Great Reed | *Acrocephalus arundinaceus* | Drosselrohrsänger | Grote karekiet |
| Warbler, Icterine | *Hippolais icterina* | Gelbspötter | Spotvogel |
| Warbler, Moustached | *Acrocephalus melanopogon* | Mariskensänger | Zwartkoprietzanger |
| Warbler, Olive-tree | *Hippolais olivetorum* | Olivenspötter | Griekse spotvogel |
| Warbler, Reed | *Acrocephalus scirpaceus* | Teichrohrsänger | Kleine karekiet |
| Warbler, Sardinian | *Sylvia melanocephala* | Samtkopf-Grasmücke | Kleine zwartkop |
| Warbler, Savi's | *Locustella luscinioides* | Rohrschwirl | Snor |
| Warbler, Sedge | *Acrocephalus schoenobaenus* | Schilfrohrsänger | Rietzanger |
| Warbler, Wood | *Phylloscopus sibilatrix* | Waldlaubsänger | Fluiter |
| Wheatear, Eastern Black-eared | *Oenanthe melonoleuca* | Balkansteinschmätzer | Oostelijke blonde tapuit |
| Wheatear, Isabelline | *Oenanthe isabellina* | Isabellsteinschmätzer | Izabeltapuit |
| Wheatear, Northern | *Oenanthe oenanthe* | Steinschmätzer | Tapuit |
| Wheatear, Pied | *Oenanthe pleschanka* | Nonnensteinschmätzer | Bonte Tapuit |
| Whinchat | *Saxicola rubetra* | Braunkehlchen | Paapje |
| Whitethroat | *Sylvia communis* | Dorngrasmücke | Grasmus |
| Whitethroat, Lesser | *Sylvia curruca* | Klappergrasmücke | Braamsluiper |
| Wigeon | *Anas penelope* | Pfeifente | Smient |
| Woodlark | *Lullula arborea* | Heidelerche | Boomleeuwerik |
| Woodpecker, Black | *Dryocopus martius* | Schwarzspecht | Zwarte specht |
| Woodpecker, Great Spotted | *Dendrocopos major* | Buntspecht | Grote bonte specht |
| Woodpecker, Green | *Picus viridis* | Grünspecht | Groene specht |
| Woodpecker, Grey-headed | *Picus canus* | Grauspecht | Grijskopspecht |
| Woodpecker, Lesser Spotted | *Dryobates minor* | Kleinspecht | Kleine bonte specht |
| Woodpecker, Middle Spotted | *Dendrocoptus medius* | Mittelspecht | Middelste bonte specht |
| Woodpecker, Syrian | *Dendrocopos syriacus* | Blutspecht | Syrische bonte specht |
| Woodpecker, White-backed | *Dendrocopos leucotos* | Weissrückenspecht | Witrugspecht |
| Wren | *Troglodytes troglodytes* | Zaunkönig | Winterkoning |
| Wryneck | *Jynx torquilla* | Wendehals | Draaihals |

# Reptiles, Amphibians and Fish

| English | Scientific | German | Dutch |
|---|---|---|---|
| Adder | Vipera berus | Kreuzotter | Adder |
| Boa, Sand | Eryx jaculus | Sandboa | Zandboa |
| Frog, Agile | Rana dalmatina | Springfrosch | Springkikker |
| Frog, Balkan | Pelophylax / Rana kurtmuelleri | Balkan-Wasserfrosch | Balkanmeerkikker |
| Frog, Grass | Rana temporaria | Grasfrosch | Bruine kikker |
| Frog, Greek Stream | Rana graeca | Griechischer Frosch | Griekse beekkikker |
| Frog, Marsh | Pelophylax ridibundus | Seefrosch | Meerkikker |
| Frog, Tree | Hyla arborea | Europäischer Laubfrosch | Boomkikker |
| Gecko, Kotschy's | Cyrtopodion kotschyi | Ägäische Nacktfinger | Europese naaktvingergekko |
| Gecko, Turkish | Hemidactylus turcicus | Europäischer Halbfinger | Europese tjiktjak |
| Lizard, (Common) Wall | Podarcis muralis | Mauereidechse | Muurhagedis |
| Lizard, Balkan Wall | Podarcis tauricus | Taurische Eidechse | Taurische hagedis |
| Lizard, Erhard's Wall | Podarcis erhardii | Ägäische Mauereidechse | Egeische muurhagedis |
| Lizard, European Glass | Pseudopus apodus | Scheltopusik | Scheltopusik |
| Lizard, Green | Lacerta viridis | Smaragdeidechse | Oostelijke smaragdhagedis |
| Lizard, Meadow | Darevskia praticola | Kaukasische Wieseneidechse | Weidehagedis |
| Lizard, Snake-eyed | Ophisops elegans | Europäisches Schlangenauge | Slangenooghagedis |
| Lizard, Three-lined | Lacerta trilineata | Riesen-Smaragdeidechse | Reuzensmaragdhagedis |
| Newt, Alpine | Ichthyosaura alpestris | Bergmolch | Alpenwatersalamander |
| Newt, Danube Crested | Triturus dobrogicus | Donau-Kammmolch | Donaukamsalamander |
| Newt, Smooth | Lissotriton vulgaris | Teichmolch | Kleine watersalamander |
| Newt, Southern Crested | Triturus karelinii | Balkan-Kammolch | Balkan kamsalamander |
| Salamander, Fire | Salamandra salamandra | Feuersalamander | Vuursalamander |
| Skink, Snake-eyed | Ablepharus kitaibelii | Johannisechse | Slangenoogskink |
| Snake, Aesculapian | Zamenis / Elaphe longissimus | Äskulapnatter | Esculaapslang |
| Snake, Blotched | Elaphe sauromates | Östliche Vierstreifennatter | Oostelijke vierstreepslang |
| Snake, Caspian Whip | Dolichophis caspius | Balkan-Springnatter | Kaspische toornslang |
| Snake, Cat | Telescopus fallax | Europäische Katzennatter | Katslang |
| Snake, Dahl's Whip | Platyceps najadum | Schlanknatter | Slanke toornslang |
| Snake, Dice | Natrix tessellata | Würfelnatter | Dobbelsteenslang |
| Snake, Grass | Natrix natrix | Ringelnatter | Ringslang |
| Snake, Montpellier | Malpolon monspessulanus | Eidechsennatter | Hagedisslang |
| Snake, Reddish Whip | Platyceps collaris | Rötliche Schlanknatter | Halsbandtoornslang |
| Snake, Smooth | Coronella austriaca | Schlingnatter | Gladde slang |
| Snake, Worm | Typhlops vermicularis | Blödauge | Slanke wormslang |
| Spadefoot, Syrian | Pelobates syriacus | Syrische Schaufelkröte | Syrische knoflookpad |
| Sturgeon | Acipenser sturio | Stör | Steur |
| Terrapin, Balkan | Mauremys rivulata | Balkan-Bachschildkröte | Balkanbeekschildpad |
| Terrapin, European Pond | Emys orbicularis | Europäische Sumpfschildkröte | Europese moerasschildpad |
| Toad, Common | Bufo bufo | Erdkröte | Gewone pad |
| Toad, Fire-bellied | Bombina bombina | Rotbauchunke | Roodbuikvuurpad |
| Toad, Green | Pseudepidalea virides | Wechselkröte | Groene pad |
| Toad, Yellow-bellied | Bombina variegata | Gelbbauchunke | Geelbuikvuurpad |

**SPECIES LIST & TRANSLATION**

| English | Scientific | German | Dutch |
|---|---|---|---|
| Tortoise, Hermann's | Testudo hermanni | Griechische Landschildkröte | Griekse landschildpad |
| Tortoise, Spur-thighed | Testudo graeca | Maurische Landschildkröte | Moorse landschildpad |
| Viper, Nose-horned | Vipera ammodytes | Sandotter | Zandadder |
| Worm, Slow | Anguis fragilis | Blindschleiche | Hazelworm |

## Invertebrates

| English | Scientific | German | Dutch |
|---|---|---|---|
| Admiral, Poplar | Limenitis populi | Grosser Eisvogel | Grote ijsvogelvlinder |
| Admiral, Southern White | Limenitis reducta | Blauschwarzer Eisvogel | Blauwe ijsvogelvlinder |
| Admiral, White | Limenitis camilla | Kleiner Eisvogel | Kleine ijsvogelvlinder |
| Apollo | Parnassius apollo | Apollofalter | Apollovlinder |
| Apollo, Clouded | Parnassius mnemosyne | Schwarze Apollo | Zwarte apollovlinder |
| Argus, Blue | Aricia anteros | Balkan Sonnenröschen-Bläuling* | Balkan bruin blauwtje |
| Argus, Brown | Aricia agestis | Kleiner Sonnenröschen-Bläuling | Bruin blauwtje |
| Argus, Mountain | Aricia artaxerxes | Grosser Sonnenröschen-Bläuling | Vals bruin blauwtje |
| Argus, Scotch | Erebia aethiops | Graubindiger Mohrenfalter | Zomererebia |
| Ascalaphids | Ascalaphidae | Schmetterlingshafte | Vlinderhaften |
| Beauty, Camberwell | Nymphalis antiopa | Trauermantel | Rouwmantel |
| Bladetail | Lindenia tetraphylla | Seedrache | Vaandeldrager |
| Blue, Alcon | Maculinea alcon | Lungenenzian-Ameisen-Bläuling | Gentiaanblauwtje |
| Blue, Amanda's | Polyommatus amandus | Vogelwicken-Bläuling | Wikkeblauwtje |
| Blue, Anomalous | Polyommatus admetus | Östlicher Esparsettenbläuling | Oostelijk esparcetteblauwtje |
| Blue, Baton | Pseudophilotes baton | Graublauer Bläuling | Klein tijmblauwtje |
| Blue, Bavius | Pseudophilotes bavius | Salbei Bläuling* | Salieblauwtje |
| Blue, Chalk-hill | Polyommatus coridon | Silbergrüner Bläuling | Bleek blauwtje |
| Blue, Chapman's | Polyommatus thersites | Kleine Esparsetten-Bläuling | Esparcetteblauwtje |
| Blue, Chequered | Scolitantides orion | Fetthennen-Bläuling | Vetkruidblauwtje |
| Blue, Common | Polyommatus icarus | Hauhechel-Bläuling | Icarusblauwtje |
| Blue, Eastern Baton | Pseudophilotes vicrama | Östlicher Quendelbläuling | Oostelijk tijmblauwtje |
| Blue, Green-underside | Glaucopsyche alexis | Himmelblauer Steinkleebläuling | Bloemenblauwtje |
| Blue, Iolas | Iolana iolas | Blasenstrauch-Bläuling | Blazenstruikblauwtje |
| Blue, Lang's Short-tailed | Leptotes pirithous | Kleiner Wander-Bläuling | Klein tijgerblauwtje |
| Blue, Large | Maculinea arion | Schwarzgefleckten bläuling | Tijmblauwtje |
| Blue, Little | Cupido minimus | Zwerg-Bläuling | Dwergblauwtje |
| Blue, Little Tiger | Tarucus balkanicus | Balkan Tiger-Bläuling* | Klein christusdoornblauwtje |
| Blue, Long-tailed | Lampides boeticus | Grosser Wander-Bläuling | Tijgerblauwtje |
| Blue, Meleager's | Polyommatus daphnis | Zahnflügel-Bläuling | Getand blauwtje |
| Blue, Short-tailed | Cupido argiades | Kurzschwänziger Bläuling | Staartblauwtje |
| Blue, Silver-studded | Plebejus argus | Geissklee-Bläuling | Heideblauwtje |
| Blue, Turquoise | Polyommatus dorylas | Wundklee-Bläuling | Turkooisblauwtje |
| Blue, Zephyr | Plebejus pylaon | Spanischer Bläuling | Saffierblauwtje |
| Bluet, Azure | Coenagrion puella | Hufeisen-Azurjungfer | Azuurwaterjuffer |
| Bluet, Dainty | Coenagrion scitulum | Gabel-Azurjungfer | Gaffelwaterjuffer |

| English | Scientific | German | Dutch |
|---|---|---|---|
| Bluet, Spearhead | Coenagrion hastulatum | Speer-Azurjungfer | Speerwaterjuffer |
| Bluetail, Common | Ischnura elegans | Grosse Pechlibelle | Lantaarntje |
| Bluetail, Small | Ischnura pumilio | Kleine Pechlibelle | Tengere grasjuffer |
| Bronze, Geranium | Cacyreus marshalli | Pelargonien-Bläuling | Geraniumblauwtje |
| Brown, Large Wall | Lasiommata maera | Braunauge | Rotsvlinder |
| Brown, Lattice | Kirinia roxelana | Gelbbrauner Ringaugenfalter | Grote schaduwzandoog |
| Brown, Wall | Lasiommata megera | Mauerfuchs | Argusvlinder |
| Bush-cricket, Anatolian Predatory | Saga natoliae | Balkan Sägeschrecke | Anatolische roofsprinkhaan* |
| Bush-cricket, Bronze* | Bradyporus dasypus | Bronzene Sattelschrecke* | Bronzen sabelsprinkhaan* |
| Cardinal | Argynnis pandora | Kardinal | Kardinaalsmantel |
| Chaser, Blue | Libellula fulva | Spitzenfleck | Bruine korenbout |
| Chaser, Four-spotted | Libellula quadrimaculata | Vierfleck | Viervlek |
| Clubtail, Common | Gomphus vulgatissimus | Gemeine Keiljungfer | Beekrombout |
| Clubtail, River | Gomphus flavipes | Asiatische Keiljungfer | Rivierrombout |
| Copper, Balkan | Lycaena candens | Balkan Feuerfalter | Balkanvuurvlinder |
| Copper, Grecian | Lycaena ottomana | Griechischer Feuerfalter | Griekse vuurvlinder |
| Copper, Large | Lycaena dispar | Grosser Feuerfalter | Grote vuurvlinder |
| Copper, Lesser Fiery | Lycaena thersamon | Östlicher Feuerfalter* | Oostelijke vuurvlinder |
| Copper, Purple-Shot | Lycaena alciphron | Violetter Feuerfalter | Violette vuurvlinder |
| Damsel, Common Winter | Sympecma fusca | Gemeine Winterlibelle | Bruine winterjuffer |
| Darter, Red-veined | Sympetrum fonscolombii | Frühe Heidelibelle | Zwervende heidelibel |
| Darter, Yellow-winged | Sympetrum flaveolum | Gefleckte Heidelibelle | Geelvlekheidelibel |
| Demoiselle, Banded | Calopteryx splendens | Gebänderte Prachtlibelle | Weidebeekjuffer |
| Demoiselle, Beautiful | Calopteryx virgo | Blauflügel-Prachtlibelle | Bosbeekjuffer |
| Dropwing, Violet | Trithemis annulata | Rotviolette Segellibelle | Purperlibel |
| Duke of Burgundy | Hamearis lucina | Schlüsselblumen-Würfelfalter | Sleutelbloemvlinder |
| Emerald, Balkan | Somatochlora meridionalis | Balkan-Smaragdlibelle | Zuidelijke glanslibel |
| Emerald, Bulgarian | Somatochlora borisi | Rhodopen-Smaragdlibelle | Bulgaarse glanslibel |
| Emperor, Blue | Anax imperator | Grosse Königslibelle | Grote keizerlibel |
| Emperor, Freyer's Purple | Apatura metis | Donau-Schillerfalter | Oostelijke weerschijnvlinder |
| Emperor, Lesser | Anax parthenope | Kleine Königslibelle | Zuidelijke keizerlibel |
| Emperor, Lesser Purple | Apatura ilia | Kleiner Schillerfalter | Kleine weerschijnvlinder |
| Emperor, Purple | Apatura iris | Grosser Schillerfalter | Grote weerschijnvlinder |
| Emperor, Vagrant | Anax ephippiger | Schabrackenlibelle | Zadellibel |
| Festoon, Eastern | Zerynthia cerisy | Östlicher Osterluzeifalter | Oostelijke pijpbloemvlinder |
| Festoon, Southern | Zerynthia polyxena | Südlicher Osterluzeifalter | Zuidelijke pijpbloemvlinder |
| Fritillary, Dark-green | Argynnis aglaja | Grosser Perlmutterfalter | Grote parelmoervlinder |
| Fritillary, Eastern Knapweed | Melitaea ornata | Östlicher Flockenblumen-Scheckenfalter* | Oostelijke knoopkruid-parelmoervlinder* |
| Fritillary, Glanville | Melitaea cinxia | Wegerich-Scheckenfalter | Veldparelmoervlinder |
| Fritillary, Knapweed | Melitaea phoebe | Flockenblumen-Scheckenfalter | Knoopkruidparel-moervlinder |
| Fritillary, Lesser Spotted | Melitaea trivia | Bräunlicher Scheckenfalter | Toortsparelmoervlinder |

SPECIES LIST & TRANSLATION

| | | | |
|---|---|---|---|
| Fritillary, Marbled | *Brenthis daphne* | Brombeer-Perlmuttfalter | Braamparelmoervlinder |
| Fritillary, Marsh | *Euphydryas aurinia* | Skabiosen-Scheckenfalter | Moeras-parelmoervlinder |
| Fritillary, Niobe | *Argynnis niobe* | Stiefmütterchen-Perlmutterfalter | Duinparelmoervlinder |
| Fritillary, Pearl-bordered | *Boloria euphrosyne* | Frühlings-Perlmutterfalter | Zilvervlek |
| Fritillary, Queen of Spain | *Issoria lathonia* | Kleiner Perlmutterfalter | Kleine parelmoervlinder |
| Fritillary, Silver-washed | *Argynnis paphia* | Kaisermantel | Keizersmantel |
| Fritillary, Spotted | *Melitaea didyma* | Roter Scheckenfalter | Tweekleurige parelmoervlinder |
| Fritillary, Twin-spot | *Brenthis hecate* | Saumfleck-Perlmutterfalter | Dubbelstip parelmoervlinder |
| Fritillary, Weaver's | *Boloria dia* | Magerrasen-Perlmutterfalter | Akkerparelmoervlinder |
| Glider, Common | *Neptis sappho* | Schwarzbrauner Trauerfalter | Lathyruszwever |
| Glider, Hungarian | *Neptis rivularis* | Schwarzer Trauerfalter | Spireazwever |
| Goldenring, Balkan | *Cordulegaster heros* | Grosse Quelljungfer | Balkanbronlibel |
| Goldenring, Blue-eyed | *Cordulegaster insignis* | Türkische Quelljungfer | Blauwoogbronlibel |
| Goldenring, Sombre | *Cordulegaster bidentata* | Gestreifte Quelljungfer | Zuidelijke bronlibel |
| Goldenring, Turkish | *Cordulegaster picta* | Gezeichnete Quelljungfer | Turkse bronlibel |
| Grasshopper, Long-nosed | *Acrida ungarica* | Gewöhnliche Nasenschrecke | Gewone langneussprinkhaan* |
| Grayling, Delattin's | *Hipparchia volgensis* | Balkan Samtfalter* | Balkanheivlinder |
| Grayling, Eastern Rock | *Hipparchia syriaca* | Balkan-Waldportier | Balkanboswachter |
| Grayling, Freyer's | *Hipparchia fatua* | Freyers Samtfalter* | Donkere heivlinder |
| Grayling, Great Banded | *Brintesia circe* | Weisser Waldportier | Witbandzandoog |
| Grayling, Tree | *Hipparchia statilinus* | Eisenfarbiger Samtfalter | Kleine heivlinder |
| Grayling, Woodland | *Hipparchia fagi* | Grosser Waldportier | Grote boswachter |
| Hairstreak, Blue-spot | *Satyrium spini* | Kreuzdorn-Zipfelfalter | Wegedoornpage |
| Hairstreak, Brown | *Thecla betulae* | Nierenfleck-Zipfelfalter | Sleedoornpage |
| Hairstreak, Ilex | *Satyrium ilicis* | Brauner Eichen-Zipfelfalter | Bruine eikenpage |
| Hairstreak, Purple | *Favonius quercus* | Blauer Eichen-Zipfelfalter | Eikenpage |
| Hairstreak, Sloe | *Satyrium acaciae* | Kleiner Schlehen-Zipfelfalter | Kleine sleedoornpage |
| Hairstreak, White-letter | *Satyrium w-album* | Ulmen-Zipfelfalter | Iepenpage |
| Hawker, Blue-eyed | *Aeshna affinis* | Südliche Mosaikjungfer | Zuidelijke glazenmaker |
| Hawker, Green-eyed | *Aeshna isosceles* | Keilflecklibelle | Vroege glazenmaker |
| Hawk-moth, Eyed | *Smerinthus ocellatus* | Abendpfauenauge | Pauwoogpijlstaart |
| Hawk-moth, Small Elephant | *Deilephila porcellus* | Kleiner Weinschwärmer | Klein avondrood |
| Heath, Chestnut | *Coenonympha glycerion* | Rostbraunes Wiesenvögelchen | Roodstreephooibeestje |
| Heath, Eastern Large | *Coenonympha rhodopensis* | Balkan Wiesenvögelchen* | Balkanhooibeestje |
| Heath, Pearly | *Coenonympha arcania* | Weissbindiges Wiesenvögelchen | Tweekleurig hooibeestje |
| Heath, Russian | *Coenonympha leander* | Russisches Wiesenvögelchen* | Turks hooibeestje |
| Locust, Egyptian | *Anacridium aegyptium* | Agyptische Wanderheuschrecke | Egyptische |

| | | | |
|---|---|---|---|
| Longicorn, Rosalia | *Rosalia alpina* | Alpenbock | Alpenboktor |
| Mantis, Praying | *Mantis religiosa* | Gottesanbeterin | Bidsprinkhaan |
| Moth, Giant Peacock | *Saturnia pyri* | Wiener Nachtpfauenauge | Grote nachtpauwoog |
| Odalisque | *Epallage fatime* | Blaue Orientjungfer | Oriëntjuffer |
| Owlfly, Eastern* | *Libelloides macaronius* | Östlicher Schmetterlingshaft | Oostelijke vlinderhaft* |
| Owlfly, Milky* | *Libelloides lacteus* | Milchweisse Schmetterlingshaft* | Melkwitte vlinderhaft* |
| Pennant, Black | *Selysiothemis nigra* | Teufelchen | Zwarte korenbout |
| Pincertail, Small | *Onychogomphus forcipatus* | Kleine Zangenlibelle | Kleine tanglibel |
| Red-eye, Large | *Erythromma najas* | Grosses Granatauge | Grote roodoogjuffer |
| Ringlet, Black | *Erebia melas* | Schwarzer Mohrenfalter | Zwarte erebia |
| Ringlet, Bright-eyed | *Erebia oeme* | Doppelaugen-Mohrenfalter | Bontoogerebia |
| Ringlet, Woodland | *Erebia medusa* | Rundaugen-Mohrenfalter | Voorjaarserebia |
| Scarlet, Broad | *Crocothemis erythraea* | Feuerlibelle | Vuurlibel |
| Scolopendra | *Scolopendra sp.* | Riesenläufer / Gürtelskolopender | Reuzenduizendpoot |
| Skimmer, Black-tailed | *Orthetrum cancellatum* | Grosser Blaupfeil | Gewone oeverlibel |
| Skimmer, White-tailed | *Orthetrum albistylum* | Östliche Blaupfeil | Witpuntoeverlibel |
| Skipper, Chequered | *Carterocephalus palaemon* | Gelbwürfeliger Dickkopffalter | Bont dikkopje |
| Skipper, Oberthür's Grizzled | *Pyrgus armoricanus* | Zweibrütiger Würfel-Dickkopffalter | Bretons spikkeldikkopje |
| Skipper, Sandy Grizzled | *Pyrgus cinarae* | Balkan Würfel-Dickkopffalter* | Turks spikkeldikkopje |
| Skipper, Silver-spotted | *Hesperia comma* | Komma-Dickkopffalter | Kommavlinder |
| Skipper, Yellow-banded | *Pyrgus sidae* | Graubrauner Dickkopffalter | Geelbandspikkeldikkopje |
| Snaketail, Green | *Ophiogomphus cecilia* | Grüne Flussjungfer | Gaffellibel |
| Spectre, Eastern | *Caliaeschna microstigma* | Schattenlibelle | Schaduwlibel |
| Spider, Pontic Wolf | *Geolycosa vultuosa* | Balkan Tarantel* | Balkan-tarantula* |
| Spreadwing, Migrant | *Lestes barbarus* | Südliche Binsenjungfer | Zwervende pantserjuffer |
| Spreadwing, Small | *Lestes virens* | Kleine Binsenjungfer | Tengere pantserjuffer |
| Streamertail, Grecian | *Nemoptera coa* | Griechischer Fadenhaft | Griekse wimpelstaart |
| Swallowtail | *Papilio machaon* | Schwalbenschwanz | Koninginnenpage |
| Swallowtail, Scarce | *Iphiclides podalirius* | Segelfalter | Koningspage |
| Tiger, Cream-spot | *Arctia villica* | Schwarzer Bär | Roomvlek |
| Tortoiseshell, Scarce | *Nymphalis xanthomelas* | Östlicher Grosser Fuchs | Oostelijke vos |
| Tortoiseshell, Large | *Nymphalis polychloros* | Grosser Fuchs | Grote vos |
| White, Balkan Marbled | *Melanargia larissa* | Balkan Schachbrett | Oostelijk dambordje |
| White, Eastern Dappled | *Euchloe ausonia* | Östlicher Gesprenkelter Weissling | Oostelijk marmerwitje |
| White, Krueper's Small | *Pieris krueperi* | Krüpers Weissling | Schildzaadwitje |
| White, Marbled | *Melanargia galathea* | Schachbrett | Dambordje |
| White, Mountain Small | *Pieris ergane* | Steintäschel-Weissling* | Wedewitje |
| White, Small Bath | *Pontia chloridice* | Kleine Resedafalter | Klein resedawitje |
| White, Southern Small | *Pieris mannii* | Karstweissling | Scheefbloemwitje |
| White, Wood | *Leptidea sinapis* | Senfweissling | Boswitje |

**SPECIES LIST & TRANSLATION**

# CROSSBILL GUIDES
## IF YOU WANT TO SEE MORE

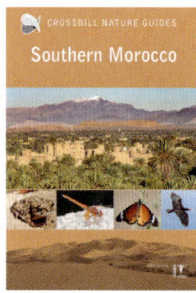
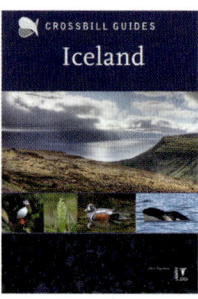
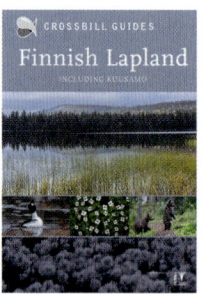
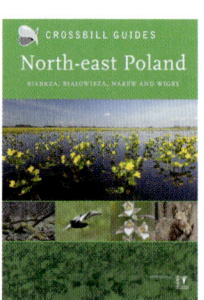
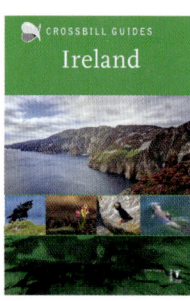
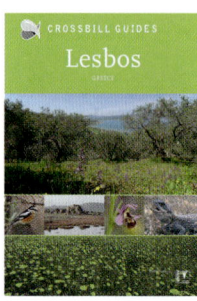
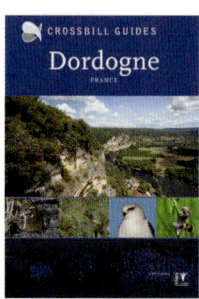
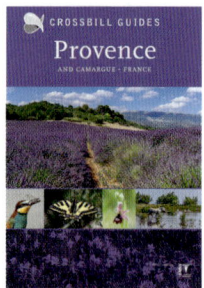
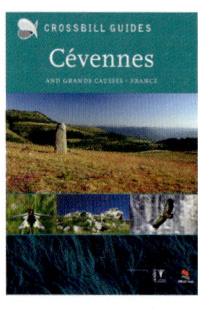
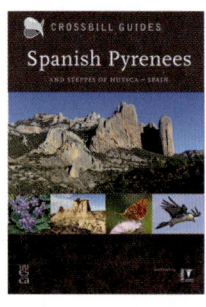
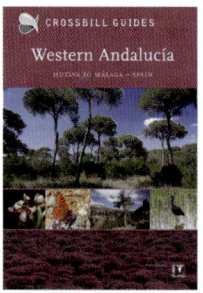
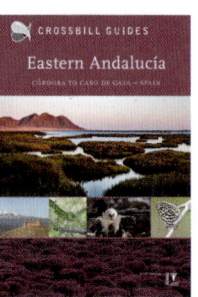
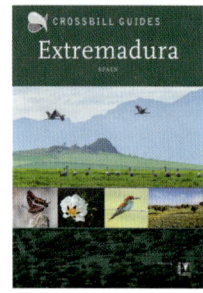
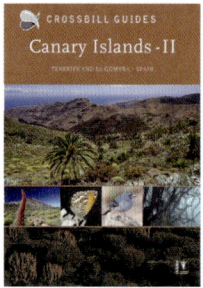

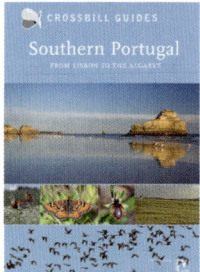

More titles are in preparation. Check our website for further details and updates.
**WWW.CROSSBILLGUIDES.ORG**